c.1

DATE			
JUL 1 3 1994			
APR 2 0 1995			
APR 2 0 1995			
MAY 1 5 1995			
APR 2 0 1998			

Eudora Welty's Chronicle

Eudora Welty's Chronicle c.1
A Story of Mississippi Life

By
Albert J. Devlin

UNIVERSITY PRESS OF MISSISSIPPI
Jackson

Library of Congress Cataloging in Publication Data
Devlin, Albert J.
  Eudora Welty's chronicle

  Includes bibliographical references and index.
  1. Welty, Eudora, 1909–   —Criticism and interpretation. 2. Mississippi in literature. I. Title
PS3545.E6Z64   1983   813'.52   82-19996
ISBN 0-87805-176-7

For my Parents
For Marlene, Eric, and Aaron

Contents

ACKNOWLEDGMENTS

Acknowledgment is made to Russell & Volkening, Inc., for generous permission to quote from the copyrighted works of Eudora Welty; to the *Mississippi Quarterly* for permission to reprint parts of chapter 2 which appeared in this journal; and to the Mississippi Department of Archives and History, Jackson, Mississippi, for permission to quote from the Welty Papers.

Most general acknowledgment is due to Welty critics and scholars who have made clear the range, diversity, and excellence of her work. Professors Kreyling, Prenshaw, and Vande Kieft are especially prominent in this regard and have no doubt saved the present author innumerable lapses in taste and judgment. The bibliographical effort of Professors W. U. McDonald and Noel Polk are no less warmly appreciated. Special thanks are due to colleagues who read the manuscript in various stages of preparation, especially Professors William Jones, William Peden, M. Gilbert Porter, Timothy Materer, Howard Hinkel, and Robert Sattelmeyer. The staffs of Ellis Library, University of Missouri-Columbia, and of the Mississippi Department of Archives and History, Jackson, Mississippi, were always prompt in meeting research needs, as was the UMC Research Council which provided funds for sabbatical leave, travel, and manuscript preparation. William Dawson, Kathy Overhulse, and Helga Meyer were generous in providing editorial assistance and in typing the manuscript.

Introduction

IN April 1935, Ford Madox Ford addressed the Southern Writers' Conference at Baton Rouge and reminded the participants that they enjoyed unique advantages. As the inheritors of "an undisturbed tradition," contemporary southern writers "possess the richest tract of soil that the earth holds on its surface."[1] Ford could not know that Eudora Welty, whose stories he would soon recommend to publishers of his wide acquaintance, was currently testing this regional hypothesis in her travels as a publicity director for the Works Progress Administration. Every writer who considers the importance of place in Welty's fiction dutifully begins by quoting her description of this fruitful gathering time. In 1942 Welty explained to Robert Van Gelder that the position "let me get about the State [of Mississippi] and gave me an honorable reason to talk to people in all sorts of jobs."[2] But it is scarcely an exaggeration to say that critical understanding of this exposure to the geography, folkways, lore, legends, and history of Mississippi has not surpassed Welty's first statement of regional self-discovery. Invariably, discussions of her use of place are conducted on a high level of generality, relieved only by brief asides concerning Welty's fine ear for southern speech or her sharp eye for southern landscape. Without inquiring into the specific, local sources of her art, commentators just as dutifully conclude such treatments by echoing Welty's truism that "place undoubtedly works upon genius."[3] This study agrees, of course, but at first its approach to place will be more detailed and particular, for only by observing the constant flow of Mississippiana into Welty's fiction can one pose the more revealing questions of how and perhaps why place "works upon genius." Even a modestly successful answer will locate Eudora Welty more firmly in her world and will begin to disclose the underlying cultural unity of stories and novels that now span five decades. In claiming support for this kind of study, I would turn to the distinguished editors of *Southern Literary Study* (1975); they are unified in advocating as scholarly objective "the study of the writer *in* and *of* the South, and that of the South *in* and *of* the writer."[4]

In reviewing *Delta Wedding*, Hamilton Basso expressed fear that Eudora Welty's new novel had not "been praised for the right reasons." There is "no doubt," he wrote in 1946, that "she can do things with the English language that have all the unpredictable wonder and surprise of a ball of mercury rolling about in the palm of one's hand. But the point . . . is not whether Miss Welty can write but what she has done with her writing."[5] With notable industry, readers for three decades have responded to this challenge and have discovered in Welty's numerous stories, novels, novellas, and sage criticism the mark of an estimable, if not major, literary reputation. This study both respects and depends upon earlier critics who identified Welty's special thematic concerns, who described the formal excellence of her work, or who patiently followed a labyrinth of mythological allusion until touching the inviolable domain of inspiration. I do, however, continue to share Hamilton Basso's uneasy feeling that Welty has not often "been praised for the right reasons." Quite recently an admirer of Welty described her as a "secret" Southerner and advised that she be read "aloud" to reveal the essence of her "Southern music."[6] This is fine personal advice, but as a model for criticism it again separates technique from vision and continues to obscure the substantial, weighty, unitary quality of Welty's extended reflection upon her southern homeplace. If this distinct quality has been seldom expounded, it is because friend

Introduction

and foe alike have not provided the "informed historical and cultural scrutiny" (in Louis D. Rubin's phrase) needed to open Welty's "secret" and thus to establish a full circulation of meaning among her memorable texts. The "secret" Welty is more often a consequence of scant research than a genuine mystery.

The obscure perception of Welty's underlying cultural unity— "what she has done with her writing"—can be attributed to the recent prominence of formalist and mythological criticism, to staunch defenders who feared that emphasis upon a "local" Welty would either convict her of regional writing or would charge her with scholarly intention, and to Eudora Welty herself, whose penchant for drawing a curtain across the working imagination is well known. More inhibiting than these, however, has been the confusion surrounding her practice of lyrical fiction. No one has described this subtle expression better than Katherine Anne Porter in her preface to Welty's first collection of stories, *A Curtain of Green* (1941). In the most successful stories, Porter claims, "external act and the internal voiceless life of the human imagination almost meet and mingle on the mysterious threshold between dream and waking." Eudora Welty's antecedents in the lyrical vein include Turgenev and Chekhov, Henry James, Katherine Mansfield and Virginia Woolf, and Sherwood Anderson and Porter herself, although here we must draw a sharp historical breath and recognize that the designated analogue between lyric poet and the writer of narrative is at least as old as *Tristram Shandy*. Under such a lyrical dispensation, the suspended moment of personal vision becomes the seeing eye of fiction. It not only dictates the story's pace, shape, and texture but also absorbs the sensible outer world and recasts it as a delicate web of emotional awareness. In 1943 reviewers of *The Wide Net,* Welty's second collection of stories, lamented her apparent extreme departure from the canons of traditional realism, but actually much greater damage to the wholeness of Welty's vision has been accomplished by admirers of her lyrical method, who typically underestimate its cultural amplitude.

One commentator has recently exemplified this familiar confusion regarding Welty's object of imitation. "Miss Welty is concerned . . . with the individual perception of the passing moment, the interaction of a single consciousness with each unique moment of passing time, . . . not with the historical effect or the social consciousness that evolves from a continuum of time's changes."[7] Perhaps by selecting an instant of time and isolating the individual within his own consciousness, the lyrical writer may seem to enforce this narrow conception of the author's motive, but a deeper view of the form, such as Ralph Freedman has achieved in *The Lyrical Novel* (Princeton: Princeton University Press, 1963), reveals no essential antipathy between personal and cultural experience. The intense subjectivity that Welty portrays in her most characteristic work may indeed be historic in origin, although it finally rests upon a "mysterious threshold between dream and waking." Failing to probe this realm, critics not only deny themselves a fascinating excursion into Mississippi's vivid past and present life but also dismiss the primary source of Welty's fictional coherence. As "each unique moment of passing time" assumes social and historic dimension, it implicates adjacent moments and thus forms a chronicle of events which reaches from the earliest days in the Mississippi Territory until the present. This larger story embedded in Welty's discrete fictions not only exerts a cumulative, unifying pressure upon the canon but also reveals the presence of a complex historical imagination, one which has remained an unmistakable, if subtle, signature since Welty's first important publication in 1936.

The present study is not an introduction or inclusive guide to the works of Eudora Welty. Ruth M. Vande Kieft and Michael Kreyling have satisfied these needs and have accomplished still more with high energy and intelligence.[8] My purpose is twofold: to reconstruct Welty's Mississippi chronicle and to define the structure of her historical imagination by studying selected relevant texts.[9] Focusing upon *A Curtain of Green* (1941) and *The Robber Bridegroom* (1942), chapter 1 will identify local sources, will speculate upon the literary importance of Jackson, Mississippi, where Eudora Welty has remained "underfoot" since her birth there in 1909, and will examine Welty's historical aesthetic in relation to Southern Agrarianism of the 1930s and to national patterns of historiographical thought. In chapter 2 the term "historicism" will be introduced to explain how Welty's imagination gives structure and value to the elaboration of her chronicle in *The Wide Net* (1934). Of special importance in chapter 3 will be an attempt to create a sounder basis than we now possess for identifying and evaluating the distinctively southern quality of Welty's historical imagining. The deepening southern quality which informs *Delta Wedding* (1946) and persists thereafter leads in chapter 4 to the most perplexing questions of southern historiography, which treat regional distinctiveness and continuity, and to Welty's most resourceful creations, Virgie Rainey (*The Golden Apples,* 1949) and Laurel McKelva Hand (*The Optimist's Daughter,* 1972). As Welty's chronicle moves through the post–World War II years and into a contemporary South of racial turmoil and drastic commercialization, their imaginative response to the reality of a diminished local community recapitulates in dramatic terms Eudora Welty's superb control of rich, although potentially coercive, regional materials. A concluding chapter further substantiates Welty's aesthetic control by briefly examining her literary kinship with a corps of modernist writers, chiefly Yeats, Joyce, and Virginia Woolf. Lewis P. Simpson's conception and articulation of a modern "Republic of Letters" will be instrumental in establishing this subtle affiliation.

Finally, one cannot write seriously about Welty without recognizing her extensive collection of literary criticism, journalistic reviews, personal reflections, and interviews. Distributed over forty years, these expressions betray a literary intelligence marked by wide reading, by unfailing respect for the talent of other writers, and especially by a reverence for the act of literary creation itself. Indeed, it is only in defending this act from misapprehension that Welty may be said to strike a disputatious note of correction or even chastisement. Usually, such misapprehension imposes upon the creative imagination a logic of means and ends which is rigid, preordained, and constant in operation. When this occurs, the critic or scholar has in effect projected his or her own analytic method onto the "blessedly open" art of the storyteller. Welty has explained this reversal in "How I Write" (1955):

> Analysis, to speak generally, has to travel backwards; the path it goes, while paved with good intentions, is an ever-narrowing one, whose goal is the vanishing point, beyond which only "influences" lie. But writing, bound in the opposite direction, works further and further always into the open. The choices get freer and wider, apparently, as with everything else that has a life and moves. [10]

As a corollary of this dynamism, Welty adds that it is "hard" for her "to think that a writer's stories are a unified whole in any respect except perhaps their lyric quality." Stories, she concludes, are not "written in any typical, predictable, logically developing, or even chronological way." [11]

In writing about Welty, one can easily pay undue attention to her critical voice, although she herself reveals no inclination to control or otherwise direct students of her work. Nonetheless, Welty's characterization of the "blessedly open" act of writing is apt and bears importantly upon the means and ends of the present study. At first glance, these means and ends would seem to violate Eudora Welty's wisdom, both by assimilating discrete novels and stories to the implied order of chronicle and by seeking therein an underlying unity or coherence produced by Welty's distinctive historical imagination. The "glance," however, is illusory. By tracing a chronicle in Welty's work, I do not attribute to the writer the same intentionalism that presumably guided Ellen Glasgow in composing her social history of Virginia. The reconstruction of Welty's Mississippi story follows roughly the chronological progression of her fiction, especially in the last phase, which includes *The Golden Apples* and *The Optimist's Daughter,* but my emphasis upon chronicle is directed more at the comprehensiveness of Welty's attention to history. The entire history of Mississippi, reaching from territorial days in the early nineteenth century until the present, resounds throughout Welty's fiction, but this constant presence has scarcely, if at all, been recognized by her many diligent readers.

As noted above, Welty's reluctance to believe that "a writer's stories are a unified whole" is a corollary of her general principle that "the *way* of writing" defies analysis. The "main lesson" that Welty has "learned from work . . . is the simple one that each story is going to . . . pose a new problem; no story bears on another or helps another, even if the writing mind had room for help and the wish that it would come."[12] What, then, is the rationale for pursuing the underlying cultural unity or coherence of Welty's work? She, I believe, provides the answer. It is indeed "hard" for Welty "to think that a writer's stories are a unified whole . . . except perhaps [in] their lyric quality." By "lyric quality," Welty means an "impulse" of the writer's mind, "the impulse to praise, to love, to call up, to prophesy," which is the unchanging "source"[13] of vision and creativity. Welty's historical imagination is adept at assimilating, selecting, and transforming local materials into satisfying aesthetic forms. This process, however, is not without coherence and consistency; it is governed by a "lyric quality" which has remained an unmistakable, if subtle, signature of Eudora Welty since the 1930s. Throughout her Mississippi chronicle, Welty praises, loves, and even prophesies, but the nature of her cultural-historic materials precipitates a more special "lyric quality." She celebrates the resourcefulness of the human imagination, not to evade or alter temporal necessity, but to discover *within* time changeless human values. It is this characteristic "impulse" of Welty's mind that unifies her extended reflection upon the vivid past and present life of Mississippi.

Notes to Introduction

1. Quoted by Marion C. Michael, "Southern Literature in Academe," *Mississippi Quarterly* 32 (winter 1978–79), p. 11.
2. "An Interview with Eudora Welty," *Writers and Writing* (New York: Scribner's, 1946), p. 289.

3. "Place in Fiction" (1956), in *The Eye of the Story: Selected Essays and Reviews* (New York: Random House, 1978), p. 123.

4. *Southern Literary Study: Problems and Possibilities,* ed. Louis D. Rubin, Jr., and C. Hugh Holman (Chapel Hill: University of North Carolina Press, 1975), p. 3.

5. "Look Away, Look Away, Look Away," *New Yorker,* 11 May 1946, p. 89.

6. Daphne Athas, "The Woman Writer in the South" (Paper delivered at the Modern Language Association convention, San Francisco, 28 December 1979).

7. D. James Neault, "Time in the Fiction of Eudora Welty," in *A Still Moment: Essays on the Art of Eudora Welty,* ed. John F. Desmond (Metuchen, N.J.: Scarecrow, 1978), p. 35.

8. Ruth M. Vande Kieft, *Eudora Welty* (New York: Twayne, 1962); Michael Kreyling, *Eudora Welty's Achievement of Order* (Baton Rouge: Louisiana State University Press, 1980).

9. All quotations from *A Curtain of Green and Other Stories, The Wide Net and Other Stories, The Golden Apples, The Bride of the Innisfallen and Other Stories,* "Where Is the Voice Coming From?" and "The Demonstrators" follow *The Collected Stories of Eudora Welty* (New York: Harcourt Brace Jovanovich, 1980). Other quotations from Welty are taken from the following texts: *The Robber Bridegroom* (New York: Doubleday, Doran, 1942), *Delta Wedding* (New York: Harcourt, Brace, 1946), *Losing Battles* (New York: Random House, 1970), and *The Optimist's Daughter* (New York: Random House, 1972). Throughout, page references are included parenthetically in the text.

10. "How I Write," *Virginia Quarterly Review* 31 (winter 1955), p. 244.

11. Ibid., p. 241.

12. Ibid.

13. Ibid.

Eudora Welty's Chronicle

1

Eudora Welty's Mississippi
A *Curtain of Green* and *The Robber Bridegroom*

BECAUSE of her long-standing admiration for William Faulkner, Eudora Welty must have rejoiced in 1946 when Malcolm Cowley brought him back into print and began the arduous process of exploring his fictional domain. Faulkner, Cowley argued, was essentially "a creator of myths that he weaves together into a legend of the South," not a mere writer of discrete novels and short fiction. His work falls into cycles treating the important familial, geographic, and chronological distinctions of Yoknapatawpha, but these "cycles or sagas," Cowley maintained, "are closely interconnected; it is as if each new book was a chord or segment of a total situation always existing in the author's mind."[1] Perhaps this is why Faulknerians come to resemble Quentin Compson of *Absalom, Absalom!* They too are "peopled with garrulous outraged baffled ghosts, listening, having to listen," to voices from "old ghost-times."

Eudora Welty has also created many distinctive voices, although it was not her way to locate them in such a reflexive fictional world. Certain stories may be more familiar to specialists, but others, including "Keela, The Outcast Indian Maiden," "A Worn Path," and "Powerhouse," speak to a wide, responsive audience. Each of these stories was printed periodically between 1940 and 1941 and was then collected in Welty's first volume, *A Curtain of Green* (1941). Each story also renders black life in rural Mississippi, but diversity in mode and tone obscures whatever bibliographical and thematic unity this group may possess. "Keela" remains essentially gothic in spirit, while "A Worn Path" embodies the pastoral impulse and "Powerhouse" explores a darker stratum of ritualistic comedy. Temperamentally, this

3

group exhibits at one pole the absurdist's suspicion of meaning and at the other the most traditional humanistic values. Perception of such diversity, expanding beyond this initial group to include the full collection, not only characterized many early assessments of *A Curtain of Green* but also has become a staple of Welty criticism. Writing in 1942, Robert Van Gelder summarizes this attitude.

> Each story is distinct, purely individual, born of its subject and a point of view that is so wide and deeply understanding that it is as though there were no brand of one mind upon the stories. Their outstanding similarity is formed of the intensity that went into their writing. They create moods as powerful as the moods developed by good poetry.[2]

This is meant as high praise and usually would not prompt reservations. In Welty's case, however, acute emphasis upon the distinctiveness of each story has obscured from critical view the formation of a larger social vision. Rarely has anyone thought to accuse this superb stylist of writing "closely interconnected" stories that possess the amplitude of cultural history.

Perhaps this is the fate of any short story writer whose works have been widely anthologized and have thus frequently been studied as separate entities. But for some admirers of Welty, the hovering presence of William Faulkner offered a more persuasive rationale for her apparent lack of historical intention. To "avoid rewriting Faulkner," Robert Daniel suggested in 1953, Welty made a strategic decision early in her career that ensured uniqueness. The critical assumption is that Faulkner's world resounds with "the clash" of mighty historical forces, but its scope and density so militate against intimate depiction of character that one can "seldom think" of his people apart from such categories as Snopes and Sartoris. "Here lay Eudora Welty's opportunity."[3] While Faulkner portrayed the large outer world of historical action, she would paint finer china and poetically evoke the inner world of psychological nuance. When history functioned at all in her work, it would provide atmospheric verisimilitude. Both writers are equally violated by this curious division of the house of fiction, but while the Sartoris-Snopes mythology has been tempered by later, more informed scholarship, early descriptions of Welty's uniqueness persist in the critical literature. In 1960 Leslie Fiedler described two lines of Faulknerian descent: "the masculine Faulknerians," chiefly Robert Penn Warren, who treat "complex moral and social problems"; and such "distaff Faulknerians" as Eudora Welty, in whose work the "masculine vigor of Faulkner" tends "to disappear among the more delicate nuances of sensibility." A dozen years later, Welty still provided (for Elmo Howell) a "feminine counterpart" to Faulkner's complex world of "men and ideas and the course of history." In 1980 Richard King framed only a thinly disguised corollary of the Fiedler thesis. Welty, Carson McCullers, Flannery O'Connor, and Katherine Anne Porter are excluded from *A Southern Renaissance* because they do not "take the South and its tradition as problematic."[4]

Commentators speak according to their several abilities, but even the more valuable discussions of Eudora Welty have not redressed this faulty critical balance of inner and outer weather. Her best stories do weave a pattern of imagery around experience and evoke "moods as powerful" as those "developed by good poetry." But these inward states ultimately reflect a solid world, governed by time and causality and beset by social pressure. For purposes of analysis, the "lyrical" Welty may be allowed to recede for a moment. The initial search is for a novelistic self which found enough "edges and corners" to make its native Mississippi as "treatable" as William Faulkner's. Her work has not cohered with either the frequency or the intensity needed to create a Yoknapatawpha, but in contending with the problematic relations of past and present, Eudora Welty has developed a cohesive view of historical reality. Very early in her career, she assumed what Henry James termed "the tone of the historian."

2

Perhaps one reason *A Curtain of Green* appealed to northern reviewers is that it seemed to conform to a prevailing image of the benighted South. In 1917 H. L. Mencken had ridiculed this "Sahara of the Bozart" for its "Baptist and Methodist barbarism," for its commercial boomers "inoculated with all the worst traits of the Yankee Sharper," and for its racist political economy. This "picture" not only gave Mencken "the creeps"[5] but also caused the rest of the nation to shudder while it watched a procession of southern grotesqueries. During the 1920s this carnival stopped in Dayton, Tennessee, for the Great Monkey Trial, where (as Mencken reported) "holy rollers" and other "gaping primates" battled the leviathan of modern science; and in Florida, where "the world's greatest poker game, played with building lots instead of chips," attracted hordes of eager Americans to this speculative Xanadu. Labor violence accentuated Georgia and North Carolina in the national imagination, but during the 1930s its focus remained most steadily upon Alabama's callous indictment of the Scottsboro Boys. When President Roosevelt asserted that "the South presents right now, in 1938, the Nation's No. 1 economic problem,"[6] he inadvertently summarized the prevailing belief that this region defamed the most cherished American ideals. There was, of course, no reason for assuming that Welty's imagination had responded specifically to any of these episodes, but her northern reviewers did find a situational excess in *A Curtain of Green* that seemed further to propound an image of the benighted South.

Although early commentators reproved Welty's "strong taste for melodrama,"[7] they also thought they detected a satiric attitude that made her a reliable observer of the southern grotesque. What nearly every reviewer termed Welty's preference for the odd or the grotesque appears not only in "Keela," "Powerhouse," and "A Worn Path" but in stories that detail contemporary white experience as well. In "Petrified Man" Leota and her beauty shop patrons are known by their graceless idiom, abrupt intimacies, and shabby materialism. Because they pervert love, these modern Gorgons find their symbolic reflection in Mr. Petrie, a carnival freak who is turning to "pure stone." In "Lily Daw and the Three Ladies," a simple girl worships more enthusiasti-

6

cally at the shrine of romantic love, but Mrs. Carson, the Baptist preacher's wife, decides that Lily's honor can better be guarded at the Ellisville Institute for the Feeble-Minded. Everyone in Victory, Mississippi, comes to see Lily off, but when a red-haired suitor appears on the platform, her guardians cancel plans for commitment and propose a hasty wedding. If the plot of "Lily Daw and the Three Ladies" turns upon the officious, inconsistent nature of middle-class piety, then in "Clytie" we witness a lingering aristocratic order whose pathos is measured finally by suicide. The youngest daughter of a once prominent family, Miss Clytie Farr discovers a truth-telling image in an old rain barrel. To break its hold, she slips into "the kind, featureless depth" of the water.

Perhaps the reviewer who found Welty composing her scenes "almost inch by inch" felt her urge to encompass in these early stories a range of experience peculiar to blacks and whites, to riffraff, to proper maidens, to a fading, if minor, aristocracy. But Louise Bogan revealed more than awareness of Welty's inclusive design when she assumed that these deformed and defeated people could readily issue from "some broken-down medieval scene" governed by "its own obscure decomposing laws." Within this "atmosphere of decaying feudalism"[8] resides the most persistent myth of southern life, but here the plantation legend of the nineteenth century has been stripped of its glamorous trappings and has been presented as a neoabolitionist image of a decadent society. Presumably, Eudora Welty shares the same enlightened attitude toward the South. Her habit of "detached observation," the uniformly "cool distance"[9] from which she views her grotesques in *A Curtain of Green*, would seem to assign to this artist a satiric, defensive pose. Subsequent analysis will reveal, however, that Welty's sensibility is governed not by romantic or critical versions of the plantation legend or by any other rigidly enforced thesis of social change. In attempting to understand her "unfortunates," Welty would adopt strategies more complex and compassionate than those usually employed by the satirist.

We might pause here to sketch a summarizing picture. In

7

1931 Eudora Welty completed several years of formal education in the North and returned to her native Jackson, Mississippi, where she wrote radio copy, reported local society for the *Memphis Commercial Appeal,* and later served as a publicist for the Works Progress Administration. Only the length of her sojourn in Madison, Wisconsin, and New York City has been documented; its personal note remains guarded by an author whose aversion to "the cold fact" of biography is well known. Thus we can only interpret with prudence and suggest that between 1927 and 1931 Eudora Welty could observe closely the formation of a distinct northern attitude toward the apparent excesses of her region. In 1945 Allen Tate reflected upon the past four decades of southern writing and described the usual consequences of such exposure. "Generally," Tate stressed, the familiar northern critique of a benighted South "imposed two limitations upon the Southern writer: first, he must ignore the historical background of his subject; and second, he must judge the subject strictly in terms of the material welfare of his characters."[10] One effect of the present study will be to show that Welty resisted both "limitations." Reaching from the earliest territorial days in Mississippi until the present, Welty's chronicle dramatizes a continuous "historical background" whose degree of verisimilitude is high throughout. At the same time, the profound historical imagination which informs this record of the past with quintessential human values permits a more sensitive authorial judgment than is commonly found in the literature of social reform. In short, for all her apparent exposure and vulnerability, Welty has little kinship with those writers whom Donald Davidson rebuked in 1934 for "producing Southern versions of what New York thought was wrong with the South."[11]

For a southern writer in the 1930s, the more intense pressures, though, were probably home grown. In *Tobacco Road* (1932) Erskine Caldwell argued that "an intelligent employment of his land . . . would have enabled" Jeeter Lester "to raise crops for food, and crops to be sold at a profit. Co-operative and corporate farming would have saved them all" in depression-scarred Georgia. This is not a casual formulation. It follows closely the course of economic recovery advanced by Howard Odum and other well-known regional planners at the University of North Carolina. Perhaps a better measure of this liberal group's influence can be found in the persistent antagonism of a far more "intense and coherent" (in Lewis Simpson's phrase) group of traditionalists associated with Vanderbilt University. Published in 1930, their symposium *I'll Take My Stand* not only assailed the foundations of scientific rationalism by stressing the religious nature of experience but also proposed social, political, and economic reforms needed to restore the South's traditional agrarian life. There is no need to remind anyone that these self-conscious, mutually aware groups often shaped southern discourse in the 1930s and that they in effect provided convenient, if not seductive, vehicles of regional interpretation. Although Welty's freedom from these influential groups has never been seriously challenged, it is nonetheless worthwhile to examine briefly how she defined her uniqueness in the presence of rival southern "schools." This exercise in turn will offer a more positive direction for exploring Welty's uniqueness and for marking the beginning of her Mississippi chronicle. Collected in *A Curtain of Green,* "The Whistle" and "Death of a Traveling Salesman" point respectively, if inadvertently, to a southern climate of opinion fostered by the "new regionalism" and by the conservative values of *I'll Take My Stand.*

To Howard Odum the South was still potentially a garden, possessing the "optimum quartette of temperature, moisture, surface and soil." But when Odum and his colleagues at the Institute for Research in Social Science began to inventory the Southeast, they documented an immense gap between this potential and the actualities of technical deficiency, waste, and outmoded institutions. In 1930 Mississippi was the poorest of the poor. Fifty percent of its population lived on tenant farms that produced an average annual income of $604. Several years later, when debts far exceeded state deposits of $13,000, Mississippi

9

averted bankruptcy only by passing an emergency sales tax. To alleviate such conditions, the regional specialist called for a diverse, carefully planned economy that would effect "a working balance between nature's endowment and its use."[12] By listening closely to "The Whistle," we may, however, hear a faint demur, for in this story man and nature enter an equation that challenges the dictates of scientific optimism.

In the dramatic foreground are the tomato farmers, Sara and Jason Morton; in the historical background is a model experiment that anticipated by sixty years the methodology of Odum's "new regionalism." Progressive farmers living on the Jackson prairie realized that cotton was poorly suited to local conditions and introduced in the mid-1870s the "scientific cultivation of tomato plants." By 1927 the area around Crystal Springs shipped annually some 1,500 carloads of the staple. As summarized in *Mississippi: A Guide to the Magnolia State,* a volume to which Eudora Welty contributed several photographs in 1938, these farmers had turned to diversification and were now among "the most prosperous in the State."[13] To the fictional Sara and Jason, however, this well-being must have seemed a phantom wealth, for during the last thirty years they had slipped into the most irremediable poverty. A local entrepreneur now owns their farm, and as tenants they illustrate the fixity of old economic patterns. But in "The Whistle" nature proves a still more inscrutable force, as it did historically, for example, in April 1916, when temperatures in Crystal Springs fell dangerously near the freezing point.[14] As the title of the story indicates, the threat of such a memorable frost can be announced confidently, but its scope and intensity lead finally to meditations upon our contingency.

"Every night" Sara "lay trembling with cold" (*CS,* p. 57), but on the present occasion she nearly recovers a time of "legendary festivity" that relieves the "chill" of her dismay. Steeped in memory, Sara's mind becomes "a theater," a "place of pleasure" in which joyful farmers, raucous children, and a "parade" of exotic "Florida packers" savor the "heady, sweet smell" of a triumphant harvest. "Let the packers rest," Sara thinks. Let them talk to "the girl wrappers" whose faces remain "forever sleepy and flushed" (*CS*, pp. 58–59). But the cold obtrudes, annulling the perfection of this harvest vision, and calling both Sara and Jason to witness a scene whose spectral desolation creates one of Welty's most perplexing landscapes.

Outside "everything looked vast and extensive to them." Illuminated by "the intense whiteness" (*CS*, p. 60) of a distant moon, the frozen land has become empty space, a strange, silent world that no longer seems habitable or productive. In their confusion, Sara and Jason stare "idly" (*CS*, p. 60) at the field and sky before returning to their cold hearth. At a similar point in *Tobacco Road*, Erskine Caldwell claimed that the people "had so much faith in nature . . . that they could not understand how the earth could fail them."[15] This despair, however, is not Welty's focus at all, for in *A Curtain of Green* the earth remains vital. In the title story, for example, Mrs. Larkin also stares "without understanding at the sky," but her "unknowing face" is touched by a summer rain that now imbues nature with "inexhaustible" (*CS*, pp. 111–112) force. By inference, nature continues to live a mysterious seasonal life, although its phases of creation and destruction, benevolence and villainy, may elude human understanding. Eudora Welty probably encountered the "success" story of Crystal Springs during her tenure as a WPA publicist, but what attracted her to this obscure bit of Mississippiana was its innate historical character. What began in "The Whistle" as a brave venture in diversified scientific farming had narrowed ironically to deprive the Mortons of a future.

Welty's focus in "The Whistle" is dramatic, for the trouble of Sara and Jason always preoccupies her attention. But if the story is read more broadly in cultural terms, then "The Whistle" becomes a subtle critique of regional planning, upsetting in effect Howard Odum's "working balance between nature's endowment and its use." Perhaps "The Whistle" poses obliquely the same rhetorical question as *God Without Thunder* (1930), John Crowe

Ransom's companion volume to *I'll Take My Stand,* which argued for a mysterious universe and human contingency. "Suppose it turned out," Ransom asks, "that the actual universe was essentially undependable, so far as human purposes are concerned?"[16] The implied association of Eudora Welty and Agrarian values is not entirely arbitrary. In 1969 Welty allowed that "perhaps there was something romantic and heroic about *I'll Take My Stand,*" but this symposium had still identified "general, far-reaching, and profound" truths about living and writing in the South. "Their cause is not lost even yet,"[17] Welty concluded of the original Agrarians. But neither this retrospective statement of admiration nor the apparent critique of scientific optimism in "The Whistle" can be construed as aesthetic allegiance to the values, principles, or conclusions of Agrarianism. Although "Death of a Traveling Salesman" has been considered "too suggestive of an 'Agrarian' design,"[18] it actually confirms Welty's independence of this nearly poetic evocation of the lasting South.

In constructing a "counter-myth" to the national credo of progress, the writers of *I'll Take My Stand* agreed that Agrarianism rests upon a series of interlocking dichotomies which culminates in the formula "Agrarian *versus* Industrial."[19] Apparently, Welty adopts a similar tension in organizing "Death of a Traveling Salesman." R. J. Bowman hopes to reach his destination "by dark," but as the "graveled road" gives way to "a rutted dirt path," the painful admission grows that "he was simply lost." A bright winter sun pushes "against the top of his head," intensifying the strange perspective from which Bowman views his unfamiliar world "after a long siege of influenza." When his dusty Ford falls into "a tangle of immense grapevines" (*CS,* pp. 119–121), he can only make the admission complete and seek help at a nearby cabin. Here he finds the same kind of traditional family life, marked by unvarying domestic patterns and lived in conformity with nature, that the Agrarians proposed as an antidote to mass culture. But soon after entering this rustic cabin, R. J. Bowman senses a "quiet, cool danger" (*CS,* p. 123), for the fruitful ways of husband and wife now underline the futility of his own life of relentless travel and brief commercial encounters. In Agrarian terms, this apostle of "personal salesmanship" epitomizes "modern man [who] has lost his sense of vocation."[20] When Bowman traces Sonny's "old military coat" (*CS,* p. 124) to a more distant campaign than World War I, Welty's imagination may seem to be completely captivated by the Agrarian reading of history. In *Jefferson Davis: His Rise and Fall* (1929), Allen Tate boldly, if not wishfully, declared that "all European history since the Reformation was concentrated in the war between the North and the South."[21] With less pomp, the authors of *I'll Take My Stand* endorsed this same judgment, finding in "the irrepressible conflict" between egalitarian and conservative societies a routing of traditional southern values. By asserting its progressive temper, America had deflected the Old South from its agrarian ideal. The "precious thing" that was lost apparently moved Eudora Welty to picture "an alien commercial drive"[22] still assaulting the last reserves of provincialism.

With varying degrees of urgency, *I'll Take My Stand* and "Death of a Traveling Salesman" address the modern credo of progress, but for all its echoing of Agrarian themes and motifs, Welty's text strikes a unique, distinctive note of artistic awareness. In their aggrieved response to modernity, the Agrarians attempted to restore an earlier "consciousness of the webbed order of myth and tradition,"[23] but this pastoral intention never strayed far from the dominant image of man living in a stable, rationalized community. Perhaps the antebellum southern version of this life "was not so fine as some of the traditionalists" claimed, but as John Crowe Ransom judged in *I'll Take My Stand,* the Old South's possession of "a sufficient economic base" and its cultivation of "community arts" had given rise to a culture that was "considered and authorized."[24] Its "prototype," Allen Tate concluded, was "the historical social and religious scheme of Europe."[25] In "Death of a Traveling Salesman," Welty's symbolic pattern leads beyond this vision of a fixed order, rich in social attainment, into a more primitive heritage. R. J. Bow-man's actual destination is Beulah, a hamlet in Bolivar County in northwestern Mississippi, but he also travels "far back" (*CS*, p. 119) into a state of repose that evokes the mythic journey of Bunyan's pilgrim and countless other legendary antecedents. Sonny and his wife rehearse the same round of domestic chores described by Andrew Lytle in *I'll Take My Stand*, but they are not merely attuned to nature or inspired by its endless variety. Instead, its creative principle imbues Sonny's "hot, red face" (*CS*, p. 124) and possesses the shining eyes that reveal to Bowman the miracle of an unborn child. By casting Sonny and his wife as figures scarcely to be distinguished from their environment, Welty blurs the important ontological separation of mind and nature that the Agrarian writer instinctively preserved as a measure of his traditional values. Steeped in myth, legend, and romantic archetypal imagery, "Death of a Traveling Salesman" would seem to posit a more radical pastoralism than the Agrarians usually sanctioned.

Perhaps this examination of "home-grown" pressures can be concluded more vividly by adopting an analogy that places Welty upon the same kind of perilous course followed by Phoenix Jackson in "A Worn Path." The "thorny" bushes that catch her dress are no less insistent than the foregoing ideologies, which might distract a writer who was beginning to gather her most vivid impressions of contemporary Mississippi. Both "The Whistle" and "Death of a Traveling Salesman" suggest, however, that like old Phoenix, Welty completed her humanistic mission with little compromise of integrity or independence. Neither the Chapel Hill nor the Vanderbilt idea of a restored South was sufficiently flexible or capacious to direct Welty's imagination in "The Whistle" and "Death of a Traveling Salesman." These stories, however, finally produce something more important than negative evidence of Welty's uniqueness. They not only contain positive hints that help to unify the stories of *A Curtain of Green* but also point suggestively toward the formation of Welty's larger chronicle. The critic Kurt Opitz can direct the next phase of this discussion by virtue of a brilliant image that he once used to describe the elusive quality of A *Curtain of Green*.

3

In 1964 Kurt Opitz identified the source of thematic unity in *A Curtain of Green*.

> From the surface, fine threads seem to run to a hidden center, suggesting by their trace rather than demonstrating in obvious display a secret core in life. There is a precise and particular face value to everything Eudora Welty writes in those early years, but however active, this face value is also and mainly simile of a vaguely irrational purport.[26]

After briefly discussing "The Key," Opitz veers erratically through several later texts, abandoning his image of "fine threads" running to "a hidden center." Curiosity should lead us back to "The Whistle" and "Death of a Traveling Salesman" where Opitz's paradigm functions with special ability to reveal both the prototypical search of A *Curtain of Green* and underlying patterns of thematic unity.

The goal of Sara Morton and R. J. Bowman is a recovered state of natural perfection. To this end, Sara imagines that "the May sun was shining" again in Dexter Station during the packing season. The "colors of green and red, the smell of the sun on the ground, [and] the touch of . . . warm ripening tomatoes" are composed in memory to relieve "the chill of the here and now." Their faces "forever sleepy and flushed," the "girl wrappers" (*CS*, pp. 58–59) give the accent of eternity to this perfected harvest vision. R. J. Bowman is also drawn by intimations of the eternal as he travels "far back" into the hill country of northwestern Mississippi. " 'What's that noise?' " he asks, to which Sonny's wife "grudgingly" replies, " 'You might hear the stream' " (*CS*, p. 126). In "Looking Back at the First Story," Welty has explained the symbolic nature of Bowman's query. The "soft, continuous, insinuating" sound of water "means a great deal to" Bowman, for "clearly I was trying to suggest that he'd come near, now, to the stream of life."[27]

In their pursuit of "a secret core in life," Sara Morton and R. J. Bowman enact the prototypical search of *A Curtain of Green,* but for all their urgency and dire need, neither reaches this "hidden center" of fulfillment where human contingencies are subsumed into nature's vast articulation. Respectively, the harsh summoning of the whistle and of Bowman's exploding heart casts Welty's protagonists back into a world governed by restricted personal space and harsh temporality. Their deaths imminent, Sara Morton "lay perfectly still in the dark room" as the cold "reached down" like a "pressing hand" (*CS,* p. 59), while R. J. Bowman "covered his heart with both hands" (*CS,* p. 130), sealing the narrowness of his sensibility. The reconciliation of past and present fails here because the filaments of memory and imagination prove too brittle to recover the generative force of life itself. This failure is attested in "The Whistle" and "Death of a Traveling Salesman" by patterns of spatial and temporal imagery that dramatize the characters' isolation from "a secret core in life." These "fine threads" of imagery will guide concluding discussion of *A Curtain of Green.*

Often Welty will endow objects and places with the pathos of restricted personal space—Keela's cage, Lily's hope chest, Ruby Fisher's imaginary coffin in "A Piece of News," the falling tree of the title story, a guitar box which focuses the random murder in "The Hitch-Hikers," the "remote little station" in "The Key," Sister's "little old window" through which she protests her happiness in "Why I live at the P.O." and, most pathetically, the rain barrel from which Clytie's legs protrude "like a pair of tongs" (*CS,* p. 90). To Clytie "the most moving sight in the whole world must be a face" (*CS,* p. 83). But her preoccupation with the hundred or so faces in Farr's Gin is less a product of sheer aberration, as the ladies opine, than a search designed to recall the image of a lost countenance. When had she first seen it?

Perhaps as a child. "Yes, in a sort of arbor, hadn't she laughed, leaned forward . . . and that vision of a face . . . had been very close to hers." But Clytie's search for love and self-esteem is thwarted by other faces "thrust between" (*CS*, p. 86), demanding that she uphold the local preeminence of her family, that in its decline she serve a paralytic father, her imperious sister Octavia, and a neurasthenic brother. As Robert Penn Warren has noted, Clytie is trapped in a "house of pride"[28] whose locked doors and windows forbid intercourse with man or nature. The narrow confines of the rain barrel evoke these long years "of waiting" by giving back to Clytie an image that now bespeaks her deprivation. "Too late, she recognized the face" and realized that "the poor, half-remembered vision had finally betrayed her" (*CS*, p. 90). The experience of restricted personal space that vexes Clytie and her contemporaries in *A Curtain of Green* is unique and dramatic in presentation, but it also assumes historic dimension when measured by the impressions of an early traveler in the Mississippi Territory. "The shores of the Mississippi," Governor Claiborne wrote in 1801, "are fertile beyond description. . . . Its future . . . is beyond the wildest imagination to calculate. This great delta is almost entirely unoccupied."[29] Here apparently was sufficient personal space for even the most immoderate of dreams.

Time in the ruins is finally a measure of tedium. Among Sister's recovered possessions in "Why I Live at the P.O." is a kitchen clock that will reiterate endlessly her loss of Mr. Whitaker (Will-he-take-her?), "the only man [who] ever dropped down in China Grove." Marian detects "a smell . . . like the interior of a clock" when she enters the Old Ladies' Home in "A Visit of Charity." " 'How old are you?' " she asks the "face on the pillow," but it only "gathered and collapsed," appalled that still another birthday has arrived. To Albert and Ellie Morgan, both without speech or hearing, a trip to Niagara Falls holds miraculous promise. There, Albert instructs Ellie "on his hands," " 'You listen with . . . your whole body. You'll never forget what hearing is, after that.' " But in "The Key" the Morgans do not reach this "hidden center" of communication. Its walls "dirty with time," the "remote little station" near Yellow Leaf, Mississippi, immures Albert and Ellie in a sorrowful present. It remains, however, for old Mr. Marblehall, the most enigmatic figure in *A Curtain of Green,* to demonstrate the full tyranny of time abstracted from the flow of history.

By Welty's testimony, there has been a Mr. Marblehall in Natchez since pioneer days, when this outpost on the Mississippi historically assumed its dual character. High on the bluffs, elegant homes and gardens displayed the hopes of Mississippi's first native aristocracy. Natchez-under-the-Hill attracted thieves, gamblers, prostitutes, and all the hardy adventurers who traveled river and Trace in the first quarter of the nineteenth century. Philosophically considered, the present Mr. Marblehall may seek to fill what Robert Detweiler calls "an existential void," but the terms of his bizarre double life are quintessentially historic. By maintaining two establishments, replete with patrician and common wives and heirs, he seeks to recover the duality of his heritage. Either in actuality or in dream, Mr. Marblehall or Mr. Bird pursues both spatial and temporal abundance, "shuttling . . . back and forth" (*CS,* p. 96) between his "ancestral home" (*CS,* p. 92) and the "little galleried" house "under the hills" (*CS,* p. 94). His is the most fertile historical imagination in *A Curtain of Green,* but it is also the most pathetic. Old Mr. Marblehall's secret bigamy reflects both a personal dilemma and the dilemma of a culture that can no longer "assure one a place within a physical or spiritual community."[30] For all the splendor of his vision, it cannot redeem the time allotted to old Mr. Marblehall. He will continue to lie abed, reading pulp *Terror Tales,* to "get through the clocking nights" (*CS,* p. 97). In "Old Mr. Marblehall" the eponymous hero "is killing time" (*CS,* p. 95), not unifying it.

Welty's choice of "time-worn" Natchez is not surprising, given her need to grant Mr. Marblehall a lengthy heritage and an antiquated locale for his wanderings, but several hints in the text suggest that her imagination has been stirred by contemporary events as well. In 1932 the Natchez Garden Club sponsored the first Pilgrimage, an annual tour of antebellum homes designed to promote local history and to restore the area's depressed economy. Echoes of this enterprise punctuate the text of "Old Mr. Marblehall." His dessicated, patrician wife "has gone further than you'd think: into club work," and at innumerable teas she is surrounded "by other more suitably exclaiming women" (*CS*, p. 91). In general, the populace of Natchez is so complacent that "even the thought" of Mr. Marblehall "having a stroke right in front of one of the Pilgrimage houses during Pilgrimage Week makes them only sigh" (*CS*, p. 93). A sharp irony emerges if this disregard for old Mr. Marblehall, who daily performs the historical essence of Natchez, is juxtaposed with the town's sudden, profitable immersion in Confederate ritual. Perhaps something of this critical attitude is conveyed by a photograph of Pilgrimage festivities that Welty has deposited at the Department of Archives and History in Jackson. Penciled on the back is the legend "The Exploitation of Natchez," later canceled and the benign "First Natchez Pilgrimage"[31] substituted. Fascinating as Welty's apparent judgment and recanting may be, it is more important to stress here the attentiveness of her historical imagination. "Old Mr. Marblehall" not only encompasses the origins of a frontier town, "raw and polished, crude and elegant,"[32] but also treats present difficulty in Natchez occasioned by the Great Depression.

A Curtain of Green demonstrates the truth of Paul Tillich's observation that a "mythical element," including "original epochs and final epochs," pervades all serious historical writing. As the "fine threads" of spatial and temporal imagery reveal, Welty's people not only bear the weight of "successive stages of finiteness"[33] but also sense an imminent ending in the collapse of familiar social, economic, and domestic institutions. With Howard, the young husband in "Flowers for Marjorie," they fear that everything in the world has stopped. Such apparent futility does not, however, warrant a recent opinion that Welty the cool observer merely turns from this "sorry cast of characters" with "a shrug of the artist's shoulders."[34] Welty's people continue to dream of "original epochs," as their strenuous exertions to recover nature, to extend personal space, and to give chronology its full body attest, but memories of these abundant times recede all too abruptly into a distant past. Whatever aesthetic distance finally separates these characters from Welty is less a measure of satiric intent than evidence of her comprehensive view of historical process. For all the subtlety of her vision, the patterns of spatial and temporal imagery which unify *A Curtain of Green* announce starkly that the southern frontier of enterprise and opportunity has closed some fifty years after Frederick Jackson Turner made a similar report on the western line of expansion. Open space has given way to "the solid wall"[35] and with it an inevitable internalization of conflict.

Perhaps the lyrical Welty, banished at the outset, can now reappear, for the acute inwardness of her characters in *A Curtain of Green* has assumed a historical as well as an artistic rationale. She has assimilated the ruinous statistical profile of Mississippi in the 1930 census and has reprojected it as intimate personal experience. But like her "unfortunates," Eudora Welty cannot contemplate ends without considering beginnings as well. She, however, possessed the imaginative resources needed to follow the historical tracings of *A Curtain of Green* back to their ultimate source in *The Robber Bridegroom.* Here in Mississippi's original epoch of frontier exuberance she tested the notion of "a hidden center" by imagining spacious contours and by resuming her meditations upon time. Very probably Welty also turned to Mississippi's legendary past with a certain skepticism for epochal theories of history that would impress watershed dates upon our collective memory. Part of the groundwork for this counterview had already been established in the one story from *A Curtain of Green* that remains to be discussed. Both its title and its strategic position in the volume suggest that "A Memory" can help to mend some of the broken circuits that have been observed, but

the vantage point will be improved by considering first *The Robber Bridegroom* of 1942. Set in the Natchez country during the late
1790s, it introduces into Welty's fiction the element of historical
extension needed to launch her chronicle of Mississippi life.
Significantly, it is the only work by Welty for which Faulkner
revealed a strong affinity.

4

In particular, Faulkner probably admired the antic blend of European fantasy, Mississippi lore, and frontier humor that greeted
him in *The Robber Bridegroom,* but other early readers were less
sure of their bearings and thus frequently temporized. *The Robber
Bridegroom* became as "playful" a book as the gossamer forest in
which Rosamond, a beautiful Rodney heiress, and Jamie Lockhart, the bandit of the Natchez Trace, consummate their love.
Apparently, even "Eudora" herself did not know "what she [had]
concocted."[36] Several years ago, Welty emphasized the deliberate
character of this volume, explaining that she sought to make
"working equivalents"[37] of local history, legend, and fairy tale;
but in the meanwhile, this curious novella had been orphaned by
critics who either exaggerated its uniqueness or failed to pursue
an intuition that *The Robber Bridegroom,* for all its capering, did
not necessarily break the pattern of Welty's thought. This continuity is suggested by the dating of *The Robber Bridegroom* itself.
What scant evidence is available indicates that a text was complete and in circulation by 1938.[38] So dated, *The Robber Bridegroom* becomes a still more integral part of the search that Welty
was conducting in *A Curtain of Green.* Even her earliest work
seems tinctured by the sense of "a total situation" guiding choice
and treatment of subject matter.

In 1938 Rodney was designated "extinct" by Mississippi's
official *Guide to the Magnolia State.* Perhaps this was provocation
enough for Welty to restore the old river town to its heyday as
the scene of many festive landings. After disembarking,

Rosamond's father, Clement, is borne on waves of light and sound to a crowded inn where the same spirit of commotion reigns. Never before has Clement Musgrove encountered such an awesome traveler as Jamie Lockhart, whose swaggering manner and prodigious libations astound the unassuming planter. His way home may lie through a wilderness "beset with dangers," but Clement will hear no fiercer cry than Jamie's assertion of independence. " 'Guilt is a burdensome thing to carry about in the heart. . . . I would never bother with it.' " A more thoughtful Clement attributes these sentiments to "a man of the times, a pioneer and a free agent" (p. 27), who has neither recoiled in self-consciousness nor identified space and time as dreadful adversaries.

The Robber Bridegroom is eloquent when it crosses broad fields, passes through fragrant groves of locust, and follows Rosamond into the forest where a dark lover brings her dreams to womanly fruition. "Red as blood," Jamie's horse "rode the ridge," accomplishing "the fastest kidnaping" ever recorded in "that part of the country." Their steep ascent follows the course of the sun, which now "mounted the morning cloud . . . and lighted the bluff" from which Jamie and Rosamond view a resplendent Mississippi River. Then Jamie "robbed her" (pp. 64–65) of a treasure that Rosamond willingly offers. An abundant nature continues to support their idyll in the weeks that follow. At first Jamie "was only with her in the hours of night, and rode away before the dawn" (p. 82) to do his robbing, but once he "did not ride away with the others, and then the day was night and the woods were the roof over their heads." Of course, in a world that "had just begun" (p. 87), there was no reason to "feel deadly faint" and to stagger with Melville's Ahab "beneath [all] the piled centuries since Paradise." Lacking absolute value, the day and the night derive their character from the disposition of Jamie and Rosamond, who both dominate time and claim the vast forest as a personal domain. *The Robber Bridegroom* "sprawls" as a consequence, the action covering a year and wandering almost to

Zanzibar. It seems to defy the extreme concentration of *A Curtain of Green* by inhabiting a "fairyland" (p. 82) where the line separating physical and human nature remains indistinct.[39] But there are ominous signs, too. A wicked stepmother, Salome, vengeful Indians, and the vicissitudes of history threaten to wake Jamie and Rosamond from their "dream of time passing" (p. 87).

The time of *The Robber Bridegroom* is summer, when "myths of apotheosis, of the sacred marriage, and of entering into Paradise"[40] prevail, but as Clement Musgrove realizes, these are "the deep last days of the Summer" (p. 77). He foresees the triumph of a new era, the same "Age of Brass" that Joseph Baldwin described in *The Flush Times of Alabama and Mississippi* (1853). Once dislodged from Spanish control, Mississippi passed rapidly through its territorial phase, achieved statehood in 1817, and entered the "hurly-burly" times which Baldwin, as frontier lawyer and politician, relished and which, as an informal historian, he skillfully described. "Avarice and hope joined partnership" in this new country. Emigrants from every part of the nation sought to mend tattered fortunes or to imagine themselves anew by amassing extensive property. "The times were out of joint," prowled by "unclean beasts of adventure" that affrighted such "retiring men of worth and character"[41] as the fictional Clement Musgrove. For him, the historic "journey down" is a bitter trip, culminating in the murder of wife and child. Even the reason for coming " 'is forgotten now,' " he tells Jamie. " 'I know I am not a seeker after anything, and ambition in this world never stirred my heart once' " (p. 20). Yet at the urging of Salome, his second wife, Clement becomes a wealthy planter. " 'We must cut down more of the forest,' " she counsels, " 'and stretch away the fields until we grow twice as much of everything. . . . the land is there for the taking, and I say, if it can be taken, take it' " (p. 99). Here in this extractive economy is the origin not only of Baldwin's "flush times" but also of the progressive alienation from nature that comes to full effect in *A Curtain of Green*.

So far this description of *The Robber Bridegroom* would suggest

23

that Welty has evoked a golden time—a "hidden center" of innocence and natural fulfillment—only to begin the long downward path to disillusion. Clearly, Welty shares with Robert Frost the knowledge that "nothing gold can stay," and realizes that as "original epochs" beget "final epochs," historical patterns emerge which cannot be swayed from their course. But in the speculative temper of Clement Musgrove, she begins to affirm a counterforce, perhaps not unlike the "strange resistance" to "the stream of everything" that Robert Frost detected in "West-Running Brook."

Clement's meditation is extended and complex, but it follows closely an important development in the relation of Jamie and Rosamond. A rather fanciful plot demands that she wash the berry stains from his sleeping face and discover that Jamie Lockhart, her father's new friend, is also the king of the bandits. " 'Good-by' " he tells Rosamond, for " 'you did not trust me' " (p. 135), but his violation of Clement's trust, although inadvertent, proves a more serious offense. When Clement learns that the man commissioned to find his daughter is also her abductor, he takes to the forest, encloses himself in a circle of stones, and studies "the lateness of the age" (p. 144). Nature appears complex and manifold to Clement, for "here are all possible trees" and "upon each limb is a singing bird," but it reflects order as well, following the discipline of the seasons. That, Clement muses, "was the way the years went by" (pp. 141–142) when he lived with his first wife, Amalie, "in the peaceful hills" of Virginia. But "what kind of time is this," he continues, when change is so rapid that "wrath and love burn only like campfires." For all his brilliance, even the hero is "but a wandering fire soon lost" (p. 143), perhaps a subtle allusion to Aaron Burr and John James Audubon of "First Love" and "A Still Moment," stories also published in 1942 and based upon the historical aspirations of these well-known travelers to the Mississippi Territory. Their experience in the Natchez country would lead them to ask with Clement, "What will the seasons be, when we are lost and dead?

The dreadful heat and cold—no more than the shooting star"
(p. 144). Apparently, "the time of cunning" (p. 142) has frustrated Clement's wish for order and simplicity in nature, but
before he can rediscover permanence in change, he is dragged to
his feet by those who know best "the lateness of the age."

In *The Robber Bridegroom* Eudora Welty's use of the Natchez
Indians involved a solecism that she both recognized and ex-
ploited. Virtually annihilated by the French in 1732, the ghostly
Natchez could roam the forest and could poignantly reaffirm its
spirit. When Salome, a captive with Jamie, Clement, and
Rosamond, defies "the elements," she is commanded by the
Natchez to dance "until the dance was raveled out and she could
dance no more." But "still the sun went on as well as ever" (pp.
161–163), paradoxically confirming the faith of the Indian in the
midst of his historic desolation. *The Robber Bridegroom* moves
briskly to shape this vision into a future for those who survive the
present ordeal. In the following spring Clement returns to New
Orleans and finds a daughter whom he thought dead. Rosamond
points to a new life with her husband, Jamie Lockhart, rich
merchant and father of "beautiful twins." Perhaps Rosamond
"did sometimes miss . . . the rough-and-tumble of their old life,"
but the city, she trills, "was splendid, . . . it was the place to
live" (pp. 183–184). In *The Robber Bridegroom* Eudora Welty has
positioned herself along the Mississippi River and has viewed the
same "procession of civilization" that Frederick Jackson Turner
envisioned at the Cumberland Gap. As Clement now realizes,
"the planter will go after the hunter, and the merchant after the
planter, all having their day" (p. 161). Each in his time and place
is a good, even the nation builder Salome, at whose Faustian
vigor we marvel. But *The Robber Bridegroom* also moves decisively
to restore its comic phrasing. A child named for Clement not
only tempers the bitter loss of the past but also instills a cyclic
sense of life perpetually renewing itself. " 'God bless you,' "
Clement says, before returning to Rodney and what remains of
the planter's life. Should he again enter the forest and occupy a

circle of stones, Clement will speak as one who has descended into time and wrestled with change only to find permanence. According to Michael Kreyling, he "has won an integrating vision"[42] that binds past and present into a moment of full perception. In the process, Eudora Welty has not denied change but has assured herself that wrenching historical developments occur within larger patterns of cyclic duration.

In the present age, Sonny and his wife and old Phoenix Jackson most nearly approximate the pastoral condition of *The Robber Bridegroom*. A "little tree" is etched in the "numberless branching wrinkles" of her forehead, suggesting the same sympathy with nature that underlies the intimacy of Sonny and his wife. As they hear the "soft, continuous, insinuating" sound of a nearby stream, they are transported metaphorically to the same bluff where earlier lovers brought their own sexual expression into harmony with the river of life. But these are essentially simple characters whose wholeness precludes the kind of vigorous striving that Clement Musgrove demonstrates. For his modern counterpart in *A Curtain of Green,* we must turn to the most personal of all Welty's stories.

5

In "A Memory" the time again is summer and the place, although not directly identified, is Livingston Park, a popular resort in the West End of Jackson. The "sun, sand, water, a little pavilion, a few solitary people in fixed attitudes," are enclosed within a "brightly lit" rectangle, no larger than the framing fingers of the young girl who habitually adopts this controlling perspective. It is her need to judge "every person and every event," to anticipate "grimly and possessively" the revelation of "a secret of life." She is in love "for the first time." Later she will realize how "hopelessly unexpressed" this passion for an unknowing schoolmate remained, but now the memory of their "brief encounter" can expand with "overwhelming beauty, like a rose

forced into premature bloom" (*CS,* pp. 75–76). The simile jars
ever so slightly and prepares the reader to follow the course of this
memory when a family of bathers, as gross as they are energetic,
suddenly enters the illuminated rectangle. They not only objectify the young girl's fear of the unknown, "the untoward," but
also penetrate the "retarded, dilated, timeless" quality that
confines her dream of love. "Sprawled close to where" she is
lying, these "loud, squirming, ill-assorted people" (*CS,* p. 77)
cannot be blinked; their images are retained visually even with
her eyes "pressed shut" (*CS,* p. 79). If it is not too fanciful to
superimpose the young girl's spot of sand upon Clement's circle
of stones, then both characters may be viewed in their relationship to "beasts of adventure" that challenge static, sentimental
ideas of human experience.

"A Memory" confirms Walker Percy's surmise that Jackson
"bears more than an accidental relation"[43] to Welty's writing.
Livingston Park opened in 1920 and immediately provoked a
controversy. Mayor Walter Scott half-humorously decreed that
bathing suits must be of opaque cloth and that the "women
folks," in traveling to and fro, must cover their "bare limbs!"
Churchmen were not reassured, however, and criticized the city
for allowing "bathing on Sunday" and "indiscriminate public
dancing." One "well-known Jackson woman" wrote to the *Daily
News* and expressed her inexpressible shock upon seeing women
in "one-piece bathing suits, minus stockings," parading before
"the public gaze. We ought to have a crusade against this
thing,"[44] she concluded.

Traces of "this thing" appear with some unspoken wryness in
Welty's portrait of the family. "They wore old and faded bathing
suits which did not hide either the energy or the fatigue of their
bodies, but showed it exactly." The older brother "protruded
from his costume at every turn," while the younger girl
threatened to burst from her "bright green" suit and go up "in a
rage of churning smoke" (*CS,* pp. 78–79). For the girl of memory, "a peak of horror" is reached when the older woman loosens

27

the front of her suit, "so that the lumps of mashed and folded sand came emptying out" (*CS,* p. 79). Both the editor of the *Jackson Daily News* and, in retrospect, Eudora Welty probably realized that the fundamental issue was not indecency but the threat of modernity to a small provincial capital. The "well-known" woman who visited Livingston Park undoubtedly sensed that this public scene challenged more traditional, exclusive patterns of Jackson society. She may also have guessed that its daring, innovative quality foreshadowed a decade of extraordinary growth when much of the city's "nineteenth-century flavor"[45] would be lost. The young girl of "A Memory" (and Eudora Welty, too, I suspect) moves just as uneasily between these poles. Her sensibility has been formed in the matrix of a traditional family but now is assaulted by insistent, vulgar forces which change "the appearance of the beach like the ravages of a storm." She can only feel pity for the "worn white pavilion" and must confess that her dream, as vulnerable as Clement's untested view of nature, "had vanished" (*CS,* p. 79).

Clement and the girl of "A Memory" are separated by more than a century of cultural change. The ease with which Jamie and Rosamond adapt to a mercantile existence could not be repeated in Welty's more complex modern world. For R. J. Bowman and for Harris of "The Hitch-Hikers," commercial life has become an exercise in futility. But these two periods also produce constants which have the effect of abridging time. Each character has been positioned by Welty at an identical point where change seems to accelerate and to present the human imagination with nearly insuperable difficulty. If Clement's "way" lies through meditation, then the girl of memory formalizes this impulse by assuming the guise of an artist. She is abetted by Eudora Welty, who has infused the structure of "A Memory" with dual perspective. In recording the facts of experience, the "I" of the story speaks from a vantage point that implies personal growth and maturity. She can now gauge the disproportion of her dream to its trivial source, but this retrospective gaze does not dissipate the original intensity. "Even now, I remember unadulteratedly a certain morning when I touched my friend's wrist . . . as we passed on the stairs in school" (*CS*, p. 76). Even now, "I still would not care to say which was more real—the dream . . . or the sight of the bathers. I am presenting them, you see, only as simultaneous" (*CS*, p. 77). Within this unification of time rests an authority which is not granted to any other story in *A Curtain of Green*. Strategically placed as the ninth of seventeen stories, it renders, aesthetically and psychologically, the condition of temporal wholeness sought by each of Welty's protagonists. The blond boy on the stairs is a perennial vision. Aesthetic memory has not only restored the past but has also transformed it into a timeless order of experience. Involvement and detachment, dream and actuality, permanence and change exist as simultaneously within the frame of "A Memory" as they do in Clement's heart.

For Eudora Welty, this aesthetic harmony of opposites probably received no sterner test than one occasioned by the ambush of Medgar Evers in 1963 and its aftermath of violent civil rights demonstration. In "Must the Novelist Crusade?" Welty tells of midnight phone calls challenging the writer to open her mouth and "do [something] about it," but Welty answers that even in these "relentless" days, the writer "works neither to correct nor to condone, not at all to comfort, but to make what's told alive." This "is the continuing job, and it's no harder now than it ever was. . . . Every writer, like everybody else, thinks he's living through the crisis of the ages."[46] What may seem indifference actually reveals a more intense commitment, for Welty continues to be guided by a historical attitude that emerged in her first two volumes. With the civil rights movement, Mississippi entered a phase of historic change which promised to many still another Age of Brass. Those who panicked failed both morally and imaginatively. As one epoch begets another, "externals" change "dramatically,"[47] but the girl of memory confronted by social and sexual change and contemporary Mississippians facing the prospect of a multi-racial society were responding to the same beast that Clement Musgrove discovered in the forest, "slowly and softly and forever moving into profile" (p. 141). From age to age, Welty's people are immersed in their time and their place, but in her imagination they also occupy an extratemporal moment of mysterious relationship.

Source study is no longer tedious when it succeeds in illuminating the shadowy regions of otherwise familiar stories. "The Whistle," "Old Mr. Marblehall," and "A Memory," texts that have been selected from *A Curtain of Green* for more intensive study, reveal themselves in unexpected ways when their formal properties assume cultural significance. Sara and Jason Morton are not merely unfortunate croppers who seek a last desperate warmth in their frigid existence. They become unwitting agents of mystery in a universe that some would define with dogmatic certainty. The bizarre, hallucinatory cloud that follows old Mr. Marblehall is not merely gothic staging. His double life recapitulates a dualism in the historic settlement of Natchez, revealing an unsuspected element of allegorical characterization. Still more surprising is "A Memory." Scrutiny of the Jackson that Welty knew as a child opens this exceedingly personal, private story to more public interpretation. Careful research has brought each of these distinctive stories into a more vivid state of disclosure, but it also reveals a unifying effect that bears importantly upon the formation of Welty's Mississippi chronicle. Embedded in the historical and cultural matrix of "The Whistle," "Old Mr. Marblehall," and "A Memory" is a legacy of abundance that has been attenuated in the present by economic distress, temporal dislocation, or a vulgar ethic of instinctual modern behavior. This same predicament typifies nearly all the stories of *A Curtain of Green.* Together they compose a panorama of deprivation, of isolation from the "hidden center" of life itself, that is scarcely relieved by acts of memory. But in *A Curtain of Green* the present still points to the legendary past and thus ensures that Welty will turn to the fabulous frontier world of *The Robber Bridegroom.* On the surface, its insouciant life comports ill with the troubles that beset *A Curtain of Green*, but these texts are finally inseparable documents, revealing in their historical extension and mutual address the first faint outline of Welty's Mississippi chronicle. Put in slightly different terms, the "fine threads" of *A Curtain of Green* ultimately lead backward in time to the "hidden center" of Welty's frontier epoch. In the process, the discrete lyrical moments that punctuate *A Curtain of Green* are subsumed into a larger epical structure encompassing "original epochs and final epochs."

6

Each of Welty's succeeding volumes reflects this same coherent vision of historical process. *The Wide Net* (1943) and *Delta Wedding* (1946), for example, supply many of the intervening stages in the formalization of Mississippi's pioneer heritage, helping to fill the record of vivid moments from the earliest days in the Mississippi Territory until the present. But Welty's apparent fondness for chronicle is not entirely innocent of more abstract considerations regarding the intrinsic structure and value of history. Perhaps her essential attitude can be approached by identifying and testing two categories of historical thought that may at first seem consonant with *A Curtain of Green* and *The Robber Bridegroom*. Analysis of the plantation legend and Turnerian history, a curious assembly of waning and progressive hypotheses, is inspired in part by their conspicuous reexamination during the time of Welty's early maturity.

In *Cavalier and Yankee* (1961) William R. Taylor distinguishes between "two active periods" of nineteenth-century southern plantation writing: the first, extending from 1824 until the 1850s, presented a "complex and fluid" interpretation of plantation life, while the later, occupying the 1880s and 1890s, employed "saccharine and sentimental" stereotypes too familiar to be listed here. The chief writers of the first group, beginning with George Tucker and John Pendleton Kennedy, were impelled to examine their culture, not because of any special fealty to the "slavocracy," but because vast social and economic changes after 1820 had confronted the educated Southerner with knowledge of his "provincial limitations" and diminished role in determining the affairs of the nation. This painful "new historical consciousness" found its appropriate literary image in "the gentleman as a doomed aristocrat" surveying his desolate fields and hall. The writers of the later period, emboldened by a new national tolerance for the South, were on the whole more nostalgic and less critical or satiric in depicting the person and culture of the planter. Under the guiding hand of Thomas Nelson Page, the literary plantation came to resemble "an idyllic sanctuary, a kind of sunny Shangri-la, into which the cares of the world rarely intruded."[48] Distinctive as these phases may be, they nonetheless share a common origin in the South's historic perception of cultural dissolution and decline which only intensified as the century progressed. From the vantage point of the 1820s, George Tucker (in *The Valley of Shenandoah,* 1824) measured the spiritual distance separating these baneful, contentious days from the cultivated society of Williamsburg that flourished "twenty-five or thirty years ago." From the perspective of Civil War, Reconstruction, and its aftermath, Thomas Nelson Page constructed in *Red Rock* (1898) a legendary antebellum Virginia where "old-time courtesy and high breeding" prevailed. Utopia had become portable, located in time relative to the experience of each generation, but in the literature of the plantation it was invariably an object of memory rather than of anticipation. History, these retrospective writers seemed to say, was essentially a process of decline that could not be resisted by human agency.

As Richard Hofstadter notes in *The Progressive Historians* (1968), Frederick Jackson Turner's paper "The Significance of the Frontier" set out "a very large part of the course that American historiography was to run for the next generation."[49] Turner argued in 1893 that "the existence of an area of free land, its continuous recession, and the advance of American settlement westward, explain American development." This "record of social evolution"

> begins with the Indian and the hunter; it goes on to tell of the disintegration of savagery by the entrance of the trader, the pathfinder of civilization; we read the annals of the pastoral stage in ranch life; the exploitation of the soil by the raising of unrotated crops . . . in sparsely settled farming communities; the intensive culture of the denser farm settlement; and finally the manufacturing organization with city and factory system.

Repeated on successive frontiers, this dynamic process nurtured "a steady growth of independence" in the American disposition and effected the "economic and social consolidation of the country."[50] Hofstadter's assessment of Turnerian thought is most penetrating when he identifies a trace of pessimism that accompanied Turner's well-known address in 1893 and appeared intermittently in later writings. The exhaustion of free land after 1890, the "easternization" of the West, and the prospect of a future governed by urban-industrial civilization violated what Hofstadter terms an element of "romantic primitivism" in Turner's thought and therefore seemed to mark "a gigantic regression."[51] But Turner's pessimism remained latent and in no substantial way altered his faith in progressive American values. The skill of the common man and the flexibility of his democratic institutions would ensure the writing of still another "wonderful chapter" in American life. "In place of old frontiers of wilderness," Turner challenged, "there are new frontiers of unwon fields of science, fruitful for the needs of the race; there are frontiers of better social domains yet unexplored."[52]

Superficially, the plantation legend and the Turner thesis offer a plausible explanation of historiographical attitudes that inform, respectively, *A Curtain of Green* and *The Robber Bridegroom*. In *A Curtain of Green* the spiritual and economic reservoirs of the South are empty, and a cloud of despair appears to have settled over the wasteland. The displaced, the violent, or the merely pathetic search for the old bases of life, but in the present obscurity they can recall only dim, fleeting impressions of a more richly endowed time. In "Clytie" and "Old Mr. Marblehall," this regressive phrasing not only is employed but also seems to be assimilated to the specific mystique of the plantation legend itself. The lingering social preeminence of the Farrs, their patrician form of address to inferiors, and the aura of classical decorum invoked by Octavia conspire to produce in "Clytie" a latter-day image of the plantation ethos. A similar association is suggested in "Old Mr. Marblehall" by myriad details evoking his ancestral wealth, aristocratic lineage, and the leisurely past of Natchez-on-the-Hill. Reflecting its generic heritage, each story seems chiefly notable for its measuring of the decline of the plantation ideal. As the main actor in this literary tradition, the southern gentleman has descended again from his eminence and is rendered by Welty as a paralytic or as one who does not "know what to do" (*CS*, p. 94). In view of such circumstantial evidence, one may pardon the reviewer who embraced the nostalgic premise of the plantation legend and found in *A Curtain of Green* the remains of a "medieval scene" governed by "its own obscure decomposing laws."

If Welty's first collection was a book of decline, then *The Robber Bridegroom* seems a boisterous paean to frontier times along the old Natchez Trace and to its peculiar virtues of daring and optimism. Clement Musgrove, the reluctant pioneer, will often strike a retrospective note, contrasting his turbulent migration with a more pacific time in the hills, but his daughter Rosamond and Jamie Lockhart possess only the present in which nature seems new and lovers have no "memory of meeting in the past" (p. 68). The dynamic, evolutionary process that projects them into the future seems nearly to recapitulate Frederick Jackson Turner's celebrated "procession of civilization" observed at the Cumberland Gap. As Clement muses, "the savages have only come the sooner to their end; we will come to ours too. . . . The planter will go after the hunter, and the merchant after the planter, all having their day" (p. 161). Perhaps the apparent influence of Turner's thesis upon the chronological schema of *The Robber Bridegroom* can be advanced by noting that when Welty studied at the University of Wisconsin, the scene of Turner's most fruitful research between 1889 and 1910, both the history curriculum and the campus at large were still permeated by the influence of "the most celebrated American history professor of the day."[53] In its depiction of an open, fluid society, of characters who adapt confidently to more complex stages of social evolution, of a future alight with optimism, *The Robber Bridegroom* would seem to be philosophically attuned to the democratic, progressive surge of Turner's frontier history.

For this study, it is a useful coincidence that the retrospective plantation legend and Turner's progressive history were critically reexamined during the 1930s when Eudora Welty was gathering materials and forming attitudes that compose her chronicle of Mississippi life. In the 1930s the writing of southern history reached a "take-off point." Older histories that were "unscholarly, romanticized treatments" had encouraged H. L. Mencken's kind of South baiting. A more rigorous historiography, guided by the examples of Virginius Dabney and others, moved to reevaluate "many hypotheses" once "regarded as axiomatic."[54] In particular, the more extravagant claims of the plantation myth were checked by demographic, economic, and racial studies that questioned the romantic definition of the Old South as a static, homogeneous culture disposed to courtly behavior. The same process of simplicity giving way to a more complex historical judgment can be observed in the 1930s assault upon the Turner thesis. "Turnerism came under fire," to follow Hofstadter's analysis, chiefly "because its premises seemed incongruous with the realities of the great Depression and the Second World War." To a new generation of urban historians, many Marxist in sympathy, "Turner's Middle Western loyalties began to seem quaint at best" when confronted by "economic collapse" and "global ideological struggle." By 1940 the "self-doubting and self-critical" mind of the modern American intellectual had discounted the frontier

35

thesis as too naive "to be reliable in any survey of world history or study in comparative civilization."[55] Almost in concert, the critical historians of the 1930s attacked the postulates of the Old South and Turnerism by identifying their factual inadequacies and demanding a more precise, scientific approach to complex problems. It is not inconceivable that Welty's attitudes were affected by these twin streams of revisionist history, but they are finally more helpful in defining her distinctive, independent "critique" of plantation and frontier mythology.

When *A Curtain of Green* and *The Robber Bridegroom* are viewed separately, their circumstantial evidence seems to affirm respectively either regressive or progressive theories of social change. But when they are viewed as texts that address each other within the confines of Welty's emerging chronicle, they reveal quite a different attitude toward our life in time. Clement Musgrove and the girl of "A Memory" occupy distinct points in time whose historicity Welty guards with the eye of an antiquarian seeking the perfect local, temporal detail. But their historic dilemmas and the imaginative vigor they summon in transcending trouble are structurally indistinguishable, producing constants which abridge the procession of time and manifest Welty's reliance upon a universal theory of human nature. Neither the frontier nor plantation mythology is sufficiently flexible or capacious to embody this paradoxical relationship between past and present, change and stasis, which forms the crux of Welty's Mississippi chronicle. Her "critique" of these potent mythologies is, then, implicit, inadvertent, surely not the product of any ideological weighing and balancing or choosing among rival schools of history. As Faulkner has suggested, "art is simpler than people think." In fact, no one has defined better than Faulkner the attitude toward time which guides Welty's historical imagination. While preparing *The Portable Faulkner*, Malcolm Cowley found the characters and events of *Absalom, Absalom!* composing themselves into "a tragic fable of Southern history." Without specifically rejecting this reading, Faulkner told Cowley that "art is simpler than people think because there is so little to write about." He wrote that "life is a phenomenon but not a novelty, the same frantic steeplechase toward nothing everywhere and man stinks the same stink no matter where in time."[56] Revising this formulation, Welty would probably choose less skeptical language but would still register complete approval of the timeless, changeless image of human nature propounded by Faulkner. He and Eudora Welty have unified their work and have endowed it with social significance by instinctively adopting the only view of historical reality that can ensure the artist's freedom and create intense human drama.

This study has accepted as truism Eudora Welty's statement that "place undoubtedly works upon genius"[57] and attempts instead to show how and perhaps why her long exposure to Mississippi formed a distinctive literary intelligence. The chain of evidence begins with careful research that not only illuminates the individual story but also establishes a basis for membership in what Welty has recently termed "the general family of my work."[58] From this mutual attachment of texts emerges a chronicle of events and a complex attitude toward historical change that will involve further description and much sharper definition, but some glimmer of how place affects genius has already been seen in chapter 1. In the 1930s, Welty's opportunity to travel widely in Mississippi and to see "for the first time the nature of the place" that she had "been born into"[59] did not produce a brittle satirist or an urgent defender of southern tradition, an Agrarian reformer or a proponent of the "new regionalism," a lamenter of the depression or racial injustice or a booster of facile schemes to enhance tourism. Instead, the Mississippi landscape and its folkways and institutions encouraged a habit of historical reflection by presenting images both suffused with time and redolent of changeless human drama. Frustrated by local zealots, the distinguished sociologist Howard Odum once declared that it was "impossible for an individual of independence to work in freedom"[60] in Mississippi. Welty's achievement does not necessarily

37

set aside this judgment of a "closed society," but it does identify the different means and object of literary artists and suggest that they are nurtured by culture in surprising, unpredictable ways.

Notes to Chapter 1

1. Introduction to *The Portable Faulkner* (New York: Viking, 1946), p. 7.

2. "An Interview with Eudora Welty," *Writers and Writing* (New York: Scribner's, 1946), p. 289.

3. "The World of Eudora Welty," *Hopkins Review* 6 (winter 1953), pp. 50, 57.

4. Leslie Fiedler, *Love and Death in the American Novel* (New York: Criterion, 1960), pp. 449–50; Elmo Howell, "Eudora Welty and the Use of Place in Southern Fiction," *Arizona Quarterly* 28 (autumn 1972), p. 248; and Richard H. King, *A Southern Renaissance: The Cultural Awakening of the American South, 1930–1955* (New York: Oxford University Press, 1980), p.8.

5. The revised 1920 text of "The Sahara of the Bozart" is reprinted in *Southern Writing: 1558–1920,* ed. Richard B. Davis, C. Hugh Holman, and Louis D. Rubin, Jr. (New York: Odyssey, 1970), pp. 971–79.

6. For the image of a "benighted South" and for its illustrations, see George Brown Tindall, *The Ethnic Southerners* (Baton Rouge: Louisiana State University Press, 1976).

7. "New Writers," *Time,* 24 November 1941, p. 111.

8. Louise Bogan, "The Gothic South," *Nation,* 6 December 1941, p. 572.

9. Bogan, p. 572, and Arthur J. Carr, "Among Recent Books," *Accent* 2 (spring 1942), p. 188.

10. "The New Provincialism," in *Essays of Four Decades* (Chicago: Swallow, 1968), pp. 543–44.

11. "Dilemma of the Southern Liberals," *American Mercury* 31 (February 1934), p. 233.

12. Howard W. Odum, *Southern Regions of the United States* (Chapel Hill: University of North Carolina Press, 1936), pp. 23–25.

13. Federal Writers' Project of the Works Progress Administration, *Mississippi: A Guide to the Magnolia State,* American Guide Series (New York: Viking, 1938), pp. 100, 393.

14. For descriptions of an April "flareback," see the *Jackson Daily News,* 9 April 1916, p.5.

15. "After Ten Years," Introduction to *Tobacco Road* (New York: Modern Library, 1940), pp. viii–ix.

16. *God Without Thunder: An Unorthodox Defense of Orthodoxy* (New York: Harcourt, Brace, 1930), p. 33.

17. "From Where I Live," *Delta Review* 6 (November-December 1969), p. 69.

18. Frederick J. Hoffman, *The Art of Southern Fiction* (Carbondale: Southern Illinois University Press, 1967), p. 59.

19. "Introduction: A Statement of Principles," *I'll Take My Stand,* ed. Louis D. Rubin, Jr. (1930; reprint ed., New York: Harper and Row, 1962), p. xix.

20. Introduction, *I'll Take My Stand,* pp. xxviii, xxiv.

21. *Jefferson Davis: His Rise and Fall* (New York: Minton, Balch, 1929), p. 301.

22. Alexander Karanikas, *Tillers of a Myth: Southern Agrarians as Social and Literary Critics* (Madison: University of Wisconsin Press, 1966), p. 46—a useful study that has guided my thought at several points.

23. Lewis P. Simpson, "The Southern Republic of Letters," p. 70.

24. "Reconstructed But Unregenerate," *I'll Take My Stand,* pp. 12–13.

25. Allen Tate, Letter to Donald Davidson, 10 August 1929. Quoted by Lewis P. Simpson, "The Southern Republic of Letters and *I'll Take My Stand,*" in *A Band of Prophets: The Vanderbilt Agrarians after Fifty Years,* ed. William C. Havard and Walter Sullivan (Baton Rouge: Louisiana State University Press, 1982), p. 67.

26. "Eudora Welty: The Ordeal of a Captive Soul," *Critique* 7 (winter 1964–65), p. 82.

27. "Looking Back at the First Story," *Georgia Review* 33 (winter 1979), p. 754.

28. "The Love and the Separateness in Miss Welty," *Kenyon Review* 6 (spring 1944), p. 255.

29. J. F. H. Claiborne, *Mississippi as a Province, Territory and State* (1880; reprint ed. Baton Rouge: Louisiana State University Press, 1964), p. 221.

30. Robert Detweiler, "Eudora Welty's Blazing Butterfly: The Dynamics of Response," *Language and Style* 6 (winter 1973), pp. 59, 61.

31. State Department of Archives and History, Jackson, Mississippi, Z 301.2, folder 9.

32. *Mississippi: A Guide to the Magnolia State,* p. 238.

33. *The Interpretation of History* (New York: Scribner's, 1936), pp. 96–97. Quoted by Harold P. Simonson, *The Closed Frontier* (New York: Holt, Rinehart and Winston, 1970), a useful book that has widened the allusive range of chapter 1.

34. Barbara Fialkowski, "Psychic Distances in *A Curtain of Green:* Artistic Successes and Personal Failures," in *A Still Moment: Essays on the Art of Eudora Welty,* ed. John F. Desmond (Metuchen, N.J.: Scarecrow, 1978), p. 70.

35. Simonson, *The Closed Frontier,* p. 38.

36. Reviews by Charles Shattuck in *Accent* 3 (winter 1943), p. 124, and Henry Harrison Kroll in the *Memphis Commercial Appeal,* 25 October 1942, p. 10.

37. *Fairy Tale of the Natchez Trace* (Jackson: Mississippi Historical Society, 1975), p. 13.

38. See Whit Burnett to Welty, 17 October 1938, Welty Papers, State Department of Archives and History, Jackson, Mississippi, Z 301.1, folder 1.

39. My thought is guided here by Carol P. Smith, "The Journey Motif in Eudora Welty's *The Robber Bridegroom*," *Shippensburg State College Review* 6 (1973), p. 20.

40. Northrop Frye, "The Archetypes of Literature," in *Twentieth Century Criticism,* ed. William J. Handy and Max Westbrook (New York: Macmillan, 1974), p. 240.

41. *The Flush Times of Alabama and Mississippi* (1853; reprint ed., New York: Hill and Wang, 1957), pp. 59–66.

42. *Eudora Welty's Achievement of Order* (Baton Rouge: Louisiana State University Press, 1980), p. 50.

43. "Eudora Welty in Jackson," *Shenandoah* 20 (spring 1969), p. 37.

44. See the *Jackson Daily News,* 30 May, 1 June, and 29 July 1921.

45. Gwen Ann Mills, "A Social History of Jackson, Mississippi, 1920–1929" (M.A. thesis, University of Mississippi, 1966), p. 66.

46. "Must the Novelist Crusade?" (1965), in *The Eye of the Story: Selected Essays and Reviews* (New York: Random House, 1978), p. 157.

47. Welty, "Must the Novelist Crusade?" p. 154.

48. William R. Taylor, *Cavalier and Yankee: The Old South and American National Character* (New York: Braziller, 1961), pp. 51–52, 148–50.

49. *The Progressive Historians: Turner, Beard, Parrington* (New York: Knopf, 1968), p. 71.

50. "The Significance of the Frontier in American History," in *The Frontier in American History* (New York: Holt, 1920), pp. 1–38.

51. Hofstadter, pp. 74, 109.

52. "The West and American Ideals" (1914). Quoted by Hofstadter, p. 110.

53. See David Kinnett, "Miss Kellogg's Quiet Passion," *Wisconsin Magazine of History* 62 (summer 1979), pp. 267–99, for an informed estimate of Turner's influence upon former students and the Madison campus at large.

54. See James P. Hendrix, "From Romance to Scholarship: Southern History at the Take-Off Point," *Mississippi Quarterly* 30 (spring 1977), pp. 193-211, and F. Garvin Davenport,*The Myth of Southern History* (Nashville: Vanderbilt University Press, 1967), pp. 106–15.

55. Hofstadter, pp. 92–93, 149–150.

56. *The Faulkner-Cowley File,* ed. Malcolm Cowley (New York: Viking, 1966), pp. 13–16.

57. "Place in Fiction" (1956), in *The Eye of the Story,* p. 123.

58. "Looking Back at the First Story," p. 751.

59. Preface to *One Time, One Place: A Snapshot Album,* in *The Eye of the Story,* p. 349.

60. Quoted by Tindall, *The Ethnic Southerners,* p. 96.

2

The Wide Net

Welty's Historicism: Method and Vision

REVIEWERS of *A Curtain of Green* may have regretted Eudora Welty's "strong taste for melodrama,"[1] but the extremity of event and character recorded in this volume also had a potentially liberating effect in November 1941. These "dark, weird and often unspeakably sad" stories did not proceed from literal observation or possess the abrasive certitude of statement.[2] Welty's beleaguered commentators rejoiced that there were "no wars going on behind the scenes, no revolutions or headline-disasters" to nag the political conscience.[3] Her "sensitiveness" was that "of an artist . . . and not a political theorist."[4] As a corollary, the only allegiance was to aesthetic sensibility, for Welty's "highly imagined" stories were "to be apprehended as metaphors."[5] Perhaps it was inevitable that notions of a problem South would supply many of her northern reviewers with an invidious key to submerged metaphoric referents, but they agreed that the poetic structure of *A Curtain of Green* was purposive and substantial, revealing "meticulously the author's mode of acute evaluation."[6] At a time when literature was often asked to assume immediate social responsibility, *A Curtain of Green,* for all its apparent poetic indirection, still had "nothing to do with escapism."[7]

In 1943, reviewers of *The Wide Net* could readily identify a preferred story or two, but generic classification of the volume proved elusive and finally exasperating. One admiring notice strained willingly beyond the limits of narrative art to find an apt critical language. Eudora Welty's "sentences have the timbre of bells," while her stories in their cumulative stylistic effect "resemble brilliantly colored illustrations in a medieval manuscript."[8] But more frequently these were the terms of indictment. Of the eight stories in *The Wide Net,* many seemed "too visibly studied in diction and hence inclined to be lifeless." "First Love" and "A Still Moment," in particular, succumbed to "the threat of the pseudo-poetical" and led finally "to mere words, not to a story."[9] Punctuated by the "nervous little hooves" (*CS,* p. 207) of goats, the epiphany of "Asphodel" belonged more properly "to ballet or to case histories than to literature." Eudora Welty was "not writing stories" at all but was lodging her private fancies in a form that comprehended "lyric poetry, painting, the still untouchable possibilities of color photography, and dancing."[10] For Diana Trilling, whose remarks appeared regularly in *The Nation,* this betrayal of narrative fell nothing short of "the sin of pride."[11]

Diana Trilling's harsh review of *The Wide Net* provoked Robert Penn Warren to begin serious evaluation of Welty's work,[12] but this intemperate document is equally valuable for revealing the state of the reviewer's art as practiced by Trilling during 1943. Printed on October 2, her estimate of *The Wide Net* would not have surprised any attentive reader of *The Nation* who was following the expression of her attitudes in this perilous year. Temperamentally, she was ready to reject "primitivism in any of the contemporary arts" (17 July) and to see regional writing as a sentimental exercise that presumed the existence of "gold in the heart of your rural neighbors" (21 August). The southern heart, however, was more often tarnished by accretions of "violence, prejudice, [and] myth-making." The still "rankling bitterness" that Trilling detected in the South both frightened this self-defined "liberal Northern reader" (15 May) and propelled its reactionary literature into an orbit of European fascism. Her most pronounced antipathy, though, was reserved for a virulent strain of "exaggerated subjectivity" that had "corrupted modern short fiction." Derived from Katherine Mansfield, whose practice first "separated the flesh from the bone of Chekhov" (9 October), this influential school of lyrical writing continued to sacrifice plot and action to mood, to reduce character to a shadowy projection of the author's "excruciatingly precious" (12 June) sensibility. Eudora Welty's harshest reviewer found *The Wide Net* to be the epitome of "a very crafty literary period" which bred "exhibitionism and insincerity" (2 October).

In reviewing *The Wide Net,* Trilling confessed admiration for the "healthy wit" used to evaluate "actual life" in *A Curtain of Green.* But now Welty spoke to the same reviewer with diminished artistic and ethical authority. As a southern book with a penchant for primitivism and fancy writing, *The Wide Net* managed to rasp against each of Diana Trilling's prejudices, nearly ensuring its defeat, but the nature of the times also helped to harden a still deeper bias that Welty's puzzling collection offended as well. Particularly in "these days," Trilling frequently warned in 1943, we have ample proof "that to be soft with words and sentiments is to be irresponsible with ideas and eventually dangerous."[13] By seeming to prefer the rhythms of language to its "precise meaning," by turning her "gifted" eye from the sensible outer world to some illusory dreamscape, Welty not only blurred generic distinctions and deprived the unsuspecting reader of conventional gratification but also evaded the fiction writer's traditional "moral-intellectual"[14] duty when culture itself was threatened. Although *The Wide Net* probably explores "a season of dreams" more avidly than *A Curtain of Green,* there is also good reason to conjecture that pressure of the home front, peaking in 1943, conditioned even the more sensitive journalism critics to mistrust the subtlety of lyrical fiction. Apparently, Eudora Welty's transformation of manners and the density of history into delicate subjective patterns now constituted "escapism." This critical view of *The Wide Net,* we shall see, not only belied its rich sense of place but also neglected a dynamic, reflexive quality that unites the two historical stories, "First Love" and "A Still Moment," with those that employ a contemporary Mississippi setting. Had early readers discerned this underlying unity, they would have sensed that Welty's lyrical method possessed the same cultural authority it revealed in *A Curtain of Green.* They

43

would also have placed *The Wide Net* within Eudora Welty's Mississippi chronicle.

2

With the exception of "The Purple Hat," which traipses off to New Orleans for a ghostly turn or two, the five contemporary stories in *The Wide Net* gain portentousness through Welty's allusion to river and to the old Natchez Trace. In the title story, William Wallace and his companions drag the Pearl River for an overwrought wife, but their somber excursion gradually brightens into a joyful rite that marks the adjustment of lovers to a more complex relation. A second river story, "At The Landing," moves some miles to the west and shares with *The Robber Bridegroom* the dense, exotic watershed of the Mississippi. "Heavy with its great waves of drift" (*CS,* p. 257), the stream periodically floods The Landing, overtaking its immured inhabitants with promises of journey. For Jenny Lockhart, this annual turbulence permeates Billy Floyd, an atavistic creature who dispels her timidity and prompts Jenny to seek "the next wisdom" (*CS,* p. 256). Violations, either achieved or anticipated, propel "Livvie," "Asphodel," and "The Winds" along a similar course, but these contemporary stories turn from river to road for their primary symbol. A deeply etched path once used by Indian and settler, the remnants of the old Natchez Trace continue to guide human destiny, bringing the black girl Livvie her vision of Cash McCord, strategically signifying the enmity of Miss Sabina and her husband Don McInnis, and foretelling Josie's womanhood. To date, consideration of these stories has often been couched in the language of myth criticism. Under its aegis, river and road have become "long, winding, difficult" (*CS,* p. 201) avenues that approach finally the self. Seldom, however, has this mythologizing process been supple enough to admit cultural or historic knowledge into its formulary design. For now, it is sufficient to note that both the Natchez Trace and the Mississippi River con-

44

tributed conspicuously to public discourse, not only during Welty's time, but also in the early 1800s, the setting of "First Love" and "A Still Moment," when a more complex, modern state was emerging from territorial Mississippi.

Published periodically in 1942, "First Love" and "A Still Moment" are unique, independent works of art that derive their completion from the fullness of Welty's distinctive voice. And yet, in a certain sense, the stories merge. Both share a common setting in the Natchez country and treat historical figures whose "romantic readiness" makes a permanent contribution to the literature of the Old Southwest. In "First Love" Aaron Burr descends the Mississippi River and encounters in Natchez a program of Jeffersonian bias that many historians now consider petty and unwarranted. He is joined by Harman Blennerhassett, an eccentric Irish national, and by a small band of followers, but the dramatic action is not defined exclusively by the politics of Burr's alleged conspiracy. In "First Love" his imposing presence briefly touches the obscurity of Joel Mayes, a young orphan without speech or hearing, who finds in Burr a personal idol. Much the same sense of awe and veneration marks the encounter of "A Still Moment." Assembled by Welty along the Natchez Trace, John James Audubon, Lorenzo Dow, and James Murrell follow the arc of "a solitary snowy heron," their eyes "infused with a sort of wildness" (*CS*, p. 195). Although each man brings to this chance meeting a unique perspective, Welty so blends the aspiration of artist, priest, and bandit that they find a unified expression within the heron's echoing symbolism. Examination of these stories not only will permit closer study of Welty's continued assimilation, selection, and transformation of historical matter into satisfying aesthetic design but also will reveal the presence of a dynamic, reflexive quality that unites "First Love" and "A Still Moment" with the contemporary dimension of *The Wide Net*. This relation of past and present, repeating more concisely the "fine threads" that lead from *A Curtain of Green* to *The Robber Bridegroom*, discloses in turn Welty's continuing chronicle in *The*

45

Wide Net and encourages a more precise description of its implied historiographical attitudes. Finally, Welty does not seem to have resented harsh reviews of *The Wide Net* that failed to connect her present self with the (presumably) more "healthy" authorial image of *A Curtain of Green*. Her composure in 1943 and thereafter may indeed be the best indication that she understood both the uniqueness of her texts and the subtle circulation of meaning between this long-planned Mississippi book and her earlier stories. *The Wide Net* is pure imaginative act, free from any undue purposiveness, but it also has the effect of testing patterns of historical continuity that emerged from the interplay of *A Curtain of Green* and *The Robber Bridegroom*. Assessing this test, however, depends upon a lengthy procedure, for only by identifying Welty's sources in "First Love" and "A Still Moment" can the foundation of her vision be reached. Welty's method is not nearly so tidy as the categories assimilation, selection, and transformation imply, but they offer a relatively undistorted path through each story.

3

Although Welty has never disclosed what formal research precedes her stories, there is evidence in "First Love" that she had assimilated relevant historical data regarding Burr's Mississippi expedition. She accurately places his small flotilla on the Bayou Pierre, thirty miles above Natchez, and carefully numbers its nine bateaux, each so "delicate" that even Joel Mayes is "shocked" (*CS,* p. 162) by their lack of the anticipated military threat. Numerous sources, including Harman Blennerhassett's journal, record that each boat was searched for guns and ammunition, but instead of contraband, local officials uncovered "a large supply of flour, pork [,] whiskey, and corn meal,"[15] stores which tend to reinforce Burr's claim that his goal was colonization, not disruption of the Union. Welty stresses these same domestic staples, mentioning "barrels of molasses and whiskey," but also under-

stands that Burr, even in the midst of anticlimax, inspires en-
thusiastic commitment. A "young dandy" (*CS,* p. 162) dragged
by militia recalls the order of Cowles Mead, acting governor, to
apprehend those "restless spirits"[16] about Natchez who aggres-
sively support Burr, while more mature partisans—perhaps the
same Colonel Osmun and Major Guion with whom Burr met
daily—are dressed by Welty in their Revolutionary War uni-
forms, demonstrating solidarity with the man who "fought once
at their sides as a hero." Even Burr's hasty retreat from Natchez
reflects firm authorial control. After enacting his celebrated
farewell scene with Madeline Price, Burr is accurately placed on
the Liberty Road, riding "a majestic horse" whose "silver trappings" contradict the "dirty and ragged" (*CS,* pp. 166–167)
clothes he wears in disguise. Historically, this same disparity
revealed Burr's true identity to Nicholas Perkins, a young attor-
ney living in Wakefield, who precipitated his capture on February 19, 1807.[17]

But Welty's facticity is even more impressive when it serves
formal literary ends. She takes care, for example, to correlate
historical data and the prevailing imagery of "First Love." "The
north wind struck one January night in 1807" and was followed
by a "strange drugged fall of snow." Venerable trees wearing
"blue and shining garlands" of Spanish moss were deeply entranced, while "the glassy tunnels of the Trace" stripped travelers
of "all proportion," making their progress slow and surrealistic.
For Joel Mayes, however, this intense cold occasions a "new
transparency," a marvelous kind of perception whereby "infinite
designs of speech" emerge "in formations on the air" (*CS,*
pp. 153–154). Such delicate architecture perfectly conveys the
illusory quality of "First Love," but it also claims a base in hard
historical fact. On January 17 Harman Blennerhassett's journal
records an unexpected storm. "This day was remarkable for a
heavy fall of snow, perhaps four inches deep." William Dunbar,
noted geologist, surveyor, and leading citizen of Natchez, also
records the same storm, but adds precise meteorological data

which substantiate the conditions of "First Love." From January 17–20 prevailing winds were northerly, skies clear, and the lowest temperature in this "bitterest winter of them all" (*CS*, p. 153) an unseasonable nine degrees. [18]

It is important for the historical integrity of "First Love" that Joel Mayes's expanded perception have a verifiable base, but examination of pertinent records also led to an unforeseen source both for the title of the story and for its persistent meteorological imagery. In 1917 Elizabeth Brandon Stanton published a full-dress historical romance treating Aaron Burr's Mississippi expedition. Pious references to "first love—the holiest, purest emotion of the soul" are scattered throughout the text of *"Fata Morgana": A Vision of Empire,* [19] but chapter 25 bears most closely upon the present discussion. Subtitled "The War of the Ice King on the Forest Primeval of the Sunny South," it extravagantly records Burr's arrival in January 1807, "the coldest winter ever known in the South." Thereafter the Stanton and Welty texts are often parallel. Stanton mentions trees glazed with ice, "long drips of Spanish moss festooning their boughs" (p. 247). She also seems to anticipate Welty's "new transparency." For Stanton, "the sun arose resplendant [*sic*] the following morning on a scene of glacial brilliance and sublime devastation" (p. 249). Both authors note the prosaic fact that the Mississippi "grew heavier and heavier from the ever increasing ice" (Stanton, p. 247), but Welty enriches this pictorial image, personifying the river as "a somnambulist" who, driven to seek new ways, "shuddered and lifted from its bed" (*CS*, p. 153). Many additional details support a strong, if circumstantial, case of indebtedness, but a larger lesson confronts the Welty enthusiast, for this obscure source can be useful in demonstrating the resonance of her distinctive voice. While Mrs. Stanton invokes a predictable trope, explaining that nature had given Burr "a glacial, Arctic welcome" (p. 247), Eudora Welty fully exploits this natural imagery, locating its unique significance within the consciousness of Joel Mayes. Her brilliant evocation of "speech [made] visible" is an index both to the modesty of Stanton's achievement and to the intensity of Eudora Welty's poetic imagination.

The historical basis for "A Still Moment" is more difficult to establish, not because Welty is a lesser historian in this tale, but because the lives of its characters are at times remote and poorly documented. It is clear, however, that in "A Still Moment," John James Audubon, Lorenzo Dow, and James Murrell assume their historic roles of artist, priest, and bandit, and that their highly charged, although fictitious, encounter along the Natchez Trace possesses at least a hypothetical historicity. As Victor Thompson notes, "it is conceivable" that Dow, in his tireless itinerancy, "might have met Audubon—who actually did visit Natchez— and Murrell, who reached the peak of his career in the 1820's."[20] The dramatic structure of "A Still Moment" confirms that Welty not only realized the possibility of such a meeting but also was stimulated by the historical personalities of its participants. Although there is no firm evidence that she knew *The History of Virgil A. Stewart*,[21] a repository of information regarding Murrell's career, Welty accurately recreates his vicious and vain conversational style. As recorded by Stewart, John Murrell (designated James by Welty) would rehash his evil deeds with ritualistic precision, speaking anonymously of the violence which had been tried on numerous victims. Significantly, when recast in "A Still Moment," "Murrell riding" is "Murrell talking." His "long tales," recounted anonymously, build slowly, inexorably, to the shocking revelation of their author's true identity. Then "it would only take one dawning look for the victim to see . . . that he too was about to recede in time" (*CS,* p. 192).

Sources for Audubon and Dow can be discussed more confidently. Welty quotes, for example, from the journal of Audubon's decisive sketching trip to New Orleans. On January 5, 1821, he notes that "the Mocking Birds [are] so gentle that they Scarcely would move out of the Way—"; and then on January 28, after a day of hard, though fruitful, labor, adds he is "only sorry that the Sun Sets."[22] Both entries are quoted verbatim, but

49

Welty also makes larger, more imaginative use of an important motif in Audubon's journal. There the noble Indian remains "free from Acquired Sorrow"[23] and prompts the artist to ponder the splendor of God's creation. In "A Still Moment" he uses this same primitivistic norm to gauge the constricted heart of James Murrell, whose burden of " 'acquired sorrow' " (*CS*, p. 194) now leads Audubon to the brink of personal and artistic despair. Lorenzo Dow is also viewed within an authentic framework. On June 20, 1803, while traveling the Natchez Trace, he encountered a small band of hostile Indians but readily escaped after noticing that they "had ramrods in the muzzles of their guns as well as in their stocks."[24] In "A Still Moment" these same frustrated Indians again fail to discharge their "new guns," not from comic ineptitude, but because the resourceful itinerant, with his head pressed against "the horse's silky mane," has made horse and rider equally vulnerable. By banishing the fairly mechanical escape recorded in "Lorenzo's Journal," Welty heightens the degree of actual danger and prepares Dow for his realization that divine grace has again been thwarted by a prideful "admission to strength . . . and not frailty" (*CS*, p. 190).

Although such analysis may illuminate the composition of "First Love" and "A Still Moment," it finally raises a more basic question regarding the incisiveness of Welty's historical imagination. Each story repays close examination, revealing numerous details that enclose the dramatic action in a discernible air of authenticity. In turn this verisimilitude reveals some authorial diligence, for Welty probably consulted a wide variety of sources, ranging from the journals of Dow and Audubon to the eccentric *"Fata Morgana."* But such scholarship can be used defensively. When the historical eye is uncertain or unknowing, a writer may, for example, recreate all the local color of an exotic Natchez Trace but fail to isolate those timeless values which animate history and align our personal lives with the aspirations of long-forgotten progenitors. If "First Love" and "A Still Moment" are to have more than passing antiquarian interest, they too must communicate this texture of significance, invoking a stern principle of selection designed to identify and heighten the dramatic potential of human history. Close examination of "First Love" will reveal the operation of this principle and prepare for more intense consideration of "A Still Moment."

Aaron Burr's brief sojourn in the Mississippi Territory is handled surely by Welty, but the historical facts come alive only by marking off a decisive period in his experience. Historically, Burr's decline in political fortune begins with the disputed presidential election of 1800, is nourished by his duel with Hamilton in 1804, and finally displays all the hubris of classical tragedy when he next begins to form dreams of empire. Although specialists still debate the exact nature of this design, it is clear that by January 1807, Aaron Burr had reached precisely that point where illusions of public esteem and influence could be supported only with intolerable strain. Jefferson's presidential proclamation of November 27, 1806, had enjoined "all faithful citizens" from participating in Burr's "unlawful enterprise," and as noted above, territorial officials responded to this warning by searching his small flotilla and forcing its harassed leader to submit to civil authorities at Cole's Creek. During the remainder of January Burr becomes a celebrated, although equivocal, figure in Natchez. As "First Love" attests, each evening the public inn "shook with debate," while more elegant entertainments given in his honor are marked by an undertone of argumentation regarding Burr's "good or evil" (*CS,* p. 161) intentions. Perhaps it was this ambiguous status which led a contemporary observer to note that Burr, notwithstanding his "splendid talents" and "transcendant [*sic*] address," lacked "that inestimable boon, content and tranquility."[25] With the special significance of January 1807 in mind, Welty now begins to construct a scene which postulates Burr's private response to an abrupt expression of public censure.

Welty carefully sets the scene for Burr's last encounter with Harman Blennerhassett. On the evening preceding their trial, the conspirators again meet furtively in Joel Mayes's tiny room, but their conversation is interrupted by Margaret Blennerhassett, who, fiddle in hand, comes to lure the weary husband home. Although her "insect-like motions" at first appall Joel, the "endless tunes" soon foster a sense of communion, reminding all "how far they were from home, how far from everywhere that they knew." Then Aaron Burr and Joel Mayes are alone. While pacing before the fire, an anxious Burr "turned each time with diminishing violence," until finally, with "almost a limp," he went and stretched himself upon the same puncheon table often used to bear the bodies of men killed in duels. Now the surviving duelist begins to toss wildly. His face, no longer a mask of wit and confidence, records the pain of thwarted dreams, but Joel does not dare to silence the delirious ramblings of his famous guest. Instead, he thrusts his hand into Burr's "spread-out fingers" and calms the "lonely man" (*CS,* pp. 162–165).

What remains permanently striking in this extended scene is Welty's subtle use of interpretive keys to fix the historical context and reveal the intense human drama that it possesses. In this regard her staging is functional. The puncheon table, cured by the blood of failed duelists, naturally recalls the fiasco of Weehawken Heights, where both Hamilton and his adversary received mortal wounds of different kinds. But to place a now vulnerable Burr upon this same fateful table is to evoke the whole series of faulty judgments and actions whose course has led inevitably to the retribution of January 1807. In turn Margaret and Harman Blennerhassett are touched by these same destructive forces, having sacrificed their personal fortune and settled way of life to follow Burr down the Mississippi River. But this displacement only suggests an earlier one. In 1796 the historical Blennerhassetts hastily embarked for America, not because of political intrigue in Ireland, but because they hoped to elude the family scandal occasioned by uncle and niece in their married state.[26] Accordingly, the fictional melodies played by Margaret Blennerhassett, "still a child and so clearly related to her husband that their sudden movements . . . were alike," assume new resonance and invite us to picture the "hills and valleys" (*CS,* p. 163) that dot her native Irish landscape. But Burr too is poignantly reminded of a faraway country, and again the active reader will supply the historical context. In all probability Burr remembers the lost serenity of Richmond Hill, a magnificent estate overlooking the Hudson, where his genuine capacity for familial devotion had found ripest expression. Indeed, Burr's painful separation from his beloved daughter Theodosia may have afforded Welty a rationale for associating this aggrieved father with a pathetic child who had lost his parents along the Natchez Trace. In any event, the selective process implied by this scene makes enormous demands upon the reader. If he can understand that these interpretive keys delimit a crucial period and probe its human emotion, then he will have conspired more richly with the artist-historian of "First Love."

Hypothetically, Lorenzo Dow, James Murrell, and John James Audubon might have met along one of "the little intersecting trails" (*CS,* p. 191) of the Natchez Trace, but textual evidence in "A Still Moment" suggests that their fictional meeting embodies a more complex principle of selection. By locating each quester at a decisive point in his career, Welty both ensures his uniqueness and draws upon the dramatic potential of not one but three distinct periods. Historically, Lorenzo Dow's encounter with vengeful Indians occurred on June 20, 1803, during his first extended tour of the Mississippi Territory. It was the next tour, begun in September 1804, that separated him from Peggy, the new bride "with whom he had spent [only] a few hours of time" (*CS,* p. 190). Because Welty cannot resist the piquancy of Lorenzo Dow's abrupt departure from either hostile Indians or his wedding bed, she has merged events of 1803 and 1804 and has thus created a discernible "now" for the aspiring evangelist. Occurring nearly twenty years later, Murrell's first foray into the Mississippi Territory is also marked by striking incident, not an Indian uprising, to be sure, but the rumor of a slave revolt that had paralyzed inhabitants of a small town through which he passed in 1821. According to Robert M. Coates, a popular historian of the Trace writing in 1930, the lucrative potential of such a revolt "lay in the back of his mind fermenting,"[27] but actual plans for the "Mystic Rebellion" would emerge only during the last few years of the decade. Had they met, Audubon might have secretly admired the extension of Murrell's design, for he too had recently defined a vast project. His business ventures in Kentucky badly compromised, Audubon settled his family in Cincinnati and then undertook a sketching trip down the Ohio and Mississippi rivers, entering New Orleans on January 7, 1821. After a number of desultory experiences, punctuated by disagreements with inconstant patrons, he spent the summer of 1822 in Natchez, giving frequent lessons and searching the Trace for additions to his projected *Birds of America*. Dow, Murrell, and Audubon had wanted, respectively, "to save all souls, to destroy all men, to see and to record all life" (*CS,* p. 196), but understanding the intense pressure occasioned by their dreams again hinges upon our ability to utilize interpretive keys that fix the historical context and reveal its emotional coloration.

If Lorenzo Dow seems troubled in "A Still Moment," it is because his ministry lacks firm establishment. Riding along the Trace, he is guided by voices and lights, but "ocean sounds" also intrude, a cryptic reference to Dow's "failure in Ireland" (*CS,* p. 191). Dismayed by the censure of his Methodist colleagues, Lorenzo Dow had traveled to Ireland in 1799 to convert the Romish and win an international reputation. But by 1801 even the "Eccentric Cosmopolite" saw the improbability of his dream, and a sorrowful Dow returned to America, "without accomplishment . . . , without a definite purpose."[28] Historically, the southern tours of 1802–1805 did relieve this obscurity, but even in the midst of his new success, Dow believed that a still greater mission would be revealed to him. During these years "Lorenzo's Journal" often refers in passing to the abortive Irish tour, lending credence to Welty's allusion, but more relevant is the heightened emotional state which marks the conclusion of his second Mississippi expedition. Confessing that his heart again "feels drawn and bound to Europe," Dow records much the same spiritual apprehension that controls his responses in "A Still Moment." Fits of gloomy depression, a sense of "insurmountable" discouragements, and prophetic dreams auguring "severe trials" deepen the journal account of Dow's return to the North in February 1805, creating a crisis on the eve of his second Irish tour. Accordingly, Lorenzo prays for divine sanction, seeking precisely the same revelation of "thy will and disposal"[29] that he asks of the "solitary snowy heron" (*CS,* p. 195).

On the evidence of "A Still Moment," James Murrell is no longer the impulsive youth who detained travelers by shouting " 'Stop! I'm the Devil!' " Instead, he now accompanies potential prey, "drawing out his talk," and "by some deep control of the voice" (*CS,* pp. 191–192) slowing the frenetic pace of even Lorenzo's Spanish racehorse. Additional internal evidence further sharpens the chronological focus. When Murrell tries to shade his eyes from the heron's radiance, "the brand 'H.T.' on his thumb" suddenly "thrust itself into his own vision," evoking "the whole plan of the Mystic Rebellion" (*CS,* p. 195). Court records for Williamson County, Tennessee, show that in 1826 Murrell was publicly whipped, branded, and imprisoned for stealing a mare. The experience, no doubt, was shocking, and from that moment he claimed the American people as an enemy. "They have disgraced me. My life . . . shall be spent as their devoted enemy." Devotion would characterize the next five years of Murrell's life. Ceaselessly, he rode up and down the Trace, "directing and managing"[30] the bloody rebellion of slaves that he would unleash on December 25, 1835. Insofar as Murrell is concerned, it is this intense period of preparation, when he is poised on the edge of a consuming dream, that Welty reconstructs in "A Still Moment."

When Audubon first sees James Murrell, he is so oppressed by the bandit's dark, narrow eyes that this "sure man" (*CS,* p. 194) momentarily questions the epistemological base of his art. Is it true "that the openness I see, the ways through forests . . . , the wide arches where the birds fly, are dreams of freedom?" (*CS,* p. 195). Historically, this troubling question is not without point. In February 1822, while preparing to sail for Natchez, Audubon wrote of his recent work in New Orleans. "Every moment I had to spare I drew birds for my ornithology, in which my Lucy and myself alone have faith."[31] But the Natchez period would severely test his guarded optimism. Although the deep forests of the Trace were readily available, much of Audubon's time during the summer of 1822 was consumed "in the hard and glittering outer parlors" (*CS,* p. 193) of the rich, where the trivia of lessons, hackwork, and patronage obtained. After recovering from a fever exacerbated by these distractions, he wrote in July that prospects for completing his book had darkened appreciably, and now "full of despair," he feared that all "hopes of becoming known to Europe as a naturalist were destined to become blasted."[32]

To focus these historical crosscurrents of hope and despair, Welty exploits an old controversy regarding Audubon's birth that had been revived in the late 1930s. Reacting to the cryptic and often contradictory statements made by Audubon about his origins, Constance Rourke and Alice Janes Taylor entertained the notion that he was indeed the dispossessed son of Marie Antoinette and Louis XVI. In 1938, however, Francis Herrick would deflate this Lost Dauphin thesis, showing that Audubon had sought only to obscure the fact of his illegitimacy, which he considered a hindrance to artistic recognition.[33] Because the question of his birth did trouble Audubon, it is, then, with a certain historical realism that Murrell's dire image not only leads the artist to doubt the actuality of his vision but also prompts a related question whose reverberations are far more important. "O secret life. . . . If my origin is withheld from me, is my end to be unknown too?" (*CS,* p. 195). Although the text of "A Still Moment" does not reveal how closely Welty followed the controversy implied by this question, she apparently identified the historical trauma surrounding Audubon's birth and surmised that its continuing effects might be used to objectify his uncertain motivation in 1822.

Commentators have frequently examined the encounter scene of "A Still Moment," debating the comparative levels of frustration or growth informing each viewpoint, but it has not been recognized that the dramatic unity and coherence of this scene rest upon a historical base shaped by Welty's selective process. At first Lorenzo finds solace in the heron's transcendent beauty, proclaiming the revelation of divine love at this crucial juncture in his spiritual odyssey, but because such assurance would contradict the finitude of existence, Welty subjects him to a more challenging vision of God's inscrutable nature. The heron's tragic death denies Lorenzo an easy salvation, but it also elicits a final, perhaps desperate, gesture of faith. When time elapses, Dow trusts that "all hearts shall be disclosed" (*CS*, p. 199) in a unity of divine and human perspectives. With paradoxical effect, much the same procedure is repeated in Murrell's case. In an "instant of confession" provoked by the heron, he not only doubts the reality of his "Mystic Rebellion" but also seeks inclusion within the human community. Wearily throwing himself upon the ground, Murrell pleads silently with Dow and Audubon: " 'How soon may I speak and how soon will you pity me?' " (*CS*, pp. 196–197). But soon the stillness is broken by Audubon's gun, and Murrell, alone again, assesses the effects of this potentially humanizing experience. Has his faith in the "innocence" of travelers, or his knowledge "of ruin," been shaken? Based upon evidence of the heron's mortality, the answer is a joyous no, and Murrell concludes confidently that the "Mystic Rebellion" can now be resumed, for nothing "could possibly be outside his grasp" (*CS*, p. 198).

Audubon too is immersed in the radiance of the "solitary snowy heron." He first feels "the old stab of wonder" and questions "what structure of life bridged the reptile's scale and the heron's feather?" Identification of such an evolutionary principle would perhaps relieve any lingering psychological tension between Audubon's inauspicious origins and the potential richness of his artistic sensibility. Continuing his reverie, Audubon next asks how only "the intensity of its life" could sustain the fragile heron within a hostile universe. His answer, at once simple and enormously complex, posits a saving freedom, for the tranquil bird finds "nothing in space or time to prevent its flight" (*CS,* p. 196). By implication, man, too, through the intensity of creative endeavor, may more perfectly adjust his relations to a world governed by the inevitable categories of time and space. For now, it is enough to conclude that those commentators who would measure the relative success of each quester should understand that historical materials under Welty's hand provide more than a static backdrop.[34] In "First Love" and "A Still Moment," the emotional projections of each figure are quintessentially historic and should always be evaluated as such.

To write serious historical fiction is to encounter a paradox. Through the assimilation and selection of pertinent data, the writer convinces us that the attitudes of each historical character reflect the causative principles of his age. But while this particularity constitutes a basic source of verisimilitude, it may also frustrate the proper ends of the artist. If fact qua fact begins to dominate the formal structure, then its range of suggestion and applicability will be severely limited. It is for this reason that Welty herself distrusts the contemporary historical novel, a form (to her mind) that typically retreats into the past and abolishes the essential "here and now"[35] of fiction. To speak with authority, fiction that essays a historical method must draw the past into the present, creating a new order of experience which is both historic and timeless. In "First Love" and "A Still Moment," the transformation effected by this third dimension of Welty's historical method emerges from her stunning experiment with point of view and narrative time itself.

On the simplest level Joel Mayes's disability permits striking synesthetic effect, but this technique represents only a part of the full strategy whereby his exceedingly private world is used to transform the historical framework of "First Love." Because the entire story is filtered through his consciousness, there is a predictable lack of auditory imagery. For example, when Burr and Blennerhassett meet in Joel's room on the night of the first snowfall, his sleep is broken not by the warning approach of heavy boots or the opening of a reluctant door, but by the eerie illumination of a fire already "high in the grate." The sudden manifestation of Burr and Blennerhassett so deeply stuns the young boy that he assumes the preternatural descent of "two men [who] had seemingly fallen from the clouds." Welty quickly extends this magical dispensation of fantasy. One of Burr's gestures, apparently fraught with nobility, transfixes Joel and opens upon "a panorama in his own head." Entranced by the contours of this mysterious world, he now loses all sense "of how long" (*CS*, pp. 156–157) Burr and Blennerhassett occupied his room before their departure. The element of fantasy, used to insinuate timeless qualities into the historical structure of "First Love," depends paradoxically upon the impairment of Joel Mayes's sensibility.

Point of view continues to serve Welty in a later scene whose importance has already been assessed from a different perspective. Seized by loneliness, Burr paces before the fire in Joel's room and then rests briefly on this his "last night." An unrecognized companion, Joel first adopts a protective stance, but while approaching the puncheon table, he forgets both "the time and place" and compulsively directs his gaze upon "the sleeping face" of Aaron Burr. Words, torn "by some force out of his dream," now terrify Joel, who barely resists the impulse to silence Burr and shield him from "eavesdroppers." But he need not be apprehensive, for Welty herself has ensured Burr's privacy by locating this historic encounter within a medium that is powerless to record its shaping language, "whatever words they were" (*CS*, pp. 164–165). Did Burr in this unguarded moment clarify the ambiguity surrounding his mission? History, of course, cannot answer this extraliterary question, its will to preserve frustrated by the dreamy ambiance of a deaf-mute. Welty's use of such a narrator may imply doubt regarding the efficacy of history, but in a more comprehensive way Joel actually serves the past. His timeless perspective draws us into the center of a discrete historical situation, so that the human aspirations of Aaron Burr, Joel Mayes, and their subsequent observers are rendered coeval.

In "A Still Moment" Eudora Welty predicates the dramatic structure upon historical emotions, but she also wishes to make these materials more flexible and resonant. Although the Natchez Trace retains its identity as a trade and travel route, under the force of her imagination it also assumes near-legendary status. Riding "as if never to stop" (*CS*, p. 189), Lorenzo first encounters the misty shapes of saints and sinners, next "a serpent crossing the Trace, giving out knowing glances." With "a courteous sort of inflection," birds speak of "divine love" (*CS*, p. 190) and break the reverie of an "evening still with thought" (*CS*, p. 193). Such heightened diction anticipates the symbolic interpretation of the Trace offered by each traveler. "Driving back and forth upon the rich expanse of his vision," Lorenzo tells an imaginary congregation that "these trails of awesome loneliness lie nowhere . . . but in your heart" (*CS*, p. 191). Murrell, who "observed no world at all," is nevertheless assaulted by "the two ends of his journey." With willful malice, they "pulled at him always and held him in a nowhere . . ." (*CS*, p. 192). Although trained to "see things one by one," John James Audubon ultimately finds in the Trace a unity of all creation. Majestic cedars both tower above and reach into the "deepness" of this place, while the Trace itself accommodates "all life" (*CS*, pp. 193–194). To the extent that the lone heron intensifies each projection, it both extends this symbolizing process and further idealizes Welty's universe, but its appearance also occasions a complex organization of time which she has termed "the precipitous moment" (*CS*, p. 196). In viewing the heron, each quester invokes the emotional terms of a given historical period, ranging from Dow's travel in 1803–1804 to the tours of Audubon and Murrell during the mid and late 1820s.

We have, then, the same historicity which marks the central dramatic scene of "First Love," but instead of relying upon a Joel Mayes to interrupt its temporal rhythms, Welty uses narrative time itself with stunning effect. By joining artist, priest, and bandit in a fictive present, she again creates a timeless perspective from which the intense personal drama of historical action may be viewed. We now share "the precipitous moment" of Burr, Dow, Murrell, and John James Audubon, but through the mediating influence of the creative imagination, its peril has been transformed into an aesthetic experience whose challenge can be met "with a storehouse of hope and interest."[36]

Like Audubon, the reader who studies Eudora Welty's historical method sees "his long labor most revealingly" where it meets the outer limits of its utility. Such categories as assimilation, selection, and transformation may adequately describe "a sum of [the] parts" (*CS,* p. 198), but the essential life of "First Love" and "A Still Moment" remains perennially fresh. Several conclusions have been earned, however, in the course of these remarks, and at the same time directions for further study may be indicated. Careful research shows that these presumably "pseudo-poetical" stories were not composed in the "stumbling sleep"[37] that Jean Stafford claimed, but with intent to reconstruct accurately the local Mississippi past. Careful research also reveals Welty's selection of four equally intense historic moments. The excursions of Burr, Dow, Murrell, and Audubon, although impelled by the usual cares of our quotidian lives, allow Welty to saturate her fables with human drama. In a brief coda, Diana Trilling's strictures upon lyricism will be reconsidered, but for now it seems clear that the third dimension of Welty's method does not defy time, historical causality, or the fiction writer's traditional "moral-intellectual" duty. Her transformation of actual experience into a "precipitous moment" of vision creates an intersection that is at once public and private, historic and lyrical, in composition. Only by understanding the essential historicity of this intense subjective state can one reach the true foundation of

Welty's vision. Its solidity in *The Wide Net* is no less impressive than the substantial sense of the times which marks *A Curtain of Green* and pervades the most intimate experience of its protagonists.

4

Such conclusions reflect a primary concern with describing the "how" of Welty's method, but the attempt to follow the process of her assimilation and selection has the important effect of raising more theoretical questions that turn chiefly upon "why" she may have chosen the particular time and historical figures of "First Love" and "A Still Moment." Given the rich and varied history of Mississippi, neither was an inevitable choice. After completing *The Robber Bridegroom,* Welty might, for example, have returned to a glittering Spanish rule of the 1780s or might have moved forward in time to record the cultural ascendancy of antebellum Natchez. Instead, she focuses upon the intervening period whose drama, while finally compelling, is less concentrated, and upon historical figures who, although celebrated, make only a modest contribution to their immediate culture. Clearly, these decisive choices represent a more inclusive rationale than their successful dramatization in "First Love" or "A Still Moment" can alone provide. Addressing this question of authorial intent is a necessary first step in identifying the dynamic, reflexive quality that unites the historical and contemporary stories of *The Wide Net* and leads in turn to the twin goals of chapter 2: to trace the further disclosure of Welty's Mississippi chronicle and to define more precisely its guiding historiographical attitude.

It is doubtful that Welty needed to consult Mrs. Stanton's "*Fata Morgana,*" Robert Coates's *The Outlaw Years,* or even the compendious *Guide to the Magnolia State* to identify Aaron Burr and his coevals as locally relevant actors. Their florid gestures had long since passed into the memory of any Mississippian at all prone to value the past. These readily available figures also promised to be responsive to artistic form. Like Styron's Nat Turner, Welty's historical people were sufficiently remote and mysterious to free the writer's imagination of undue facticity. Ready as these explanations may be, they do not, however, preclude seeking a more inclusive rationale that can mediate between the historical and contemporary stories of *The Wide Net*. Historically, each of Welty's questers turned to the South after opportunities in more settled regions had narrowed. By 1805 Aaron Burr was systematically excluded from political preferment in Washington and remained a fugitive from justice in New York and New Jersey. Lorenzo Dow, never approved for Methodist ordination, disobeyed superiors by leaving his assigned circuit in New England to tour the Mississippi Territory. In part, Audubon's sketching trip was occasioned by the disgrace of bankruptcy and imprisonment in Kentucky, while Murrell soon realized that his brand of economic individualism implied a simpler society than that found in Middle Tennessee. Threatened by an encroaching world, each man sought in Mississippi a moral arena whose physical extension and simplified dynamic would sustain even the most exorbitant dreams. Quite literally, Burr, Dow, Murrell, and Audubon follow on the heels of Governor Claiborne and share his vision of a "great delta" rife with new opportunities. This is Eudora Welty's point of departure in "First Love" and "A Still Moment," but her continuing story explores the vulnerability of such dreams when engaged by the inevitable rhythms of change.

Between 1800 and 1830, the time span fixed by both stories, Mississippi codified its laws, grew from territorial to federal status, and developed an agricultural system that began to dispel the wilderness character. Significantly, the normative course of these developments is adumbrated in *The Robber Bridegroom*, but the pace and logic of Welty's gradually unfolding chronicle leads her to reserve the deeper psychological effects of historical time for the questers of "First Love" and "A Still Moment." In 1807

Aaron Burr descends the Mississippi River under primitive conditions, but his goals are checked by a wilderness government which served to transport Jeffersonian bias into remote, provincial Natchez. Fifteen years later, when Natchez had entered its mansion-building phase, John James Audubon experienced both the sterility of urbanization and its threat to the artist, whose concentration is easily broken by the demands of a highly rationalized society. But it remains, paradoxically, for James Murrell to articulate most fully this dread vision of progress. When the wilderness is reclaimed and the labyrinthine protection of the Trace lost, a process well under way by 1830, "poor Murrell" (*CS*, p. 196) understands that increased communication will disclose his "Mystic Rebellion." In "First Love" and "A Still Moment," Eudora Welty chooses both the time and the circumstances of her questers because she finds them to be historically piquant. They fix precisely the moment in Mississippi's past when the will of the individual is challenged by the emergence of a centralized authority. The experience derived from *A Curtain of Green* and *The Robber Bridegroom* taught Eudora Welty that this kind of juncture would produce intense human drama.

Welty's selection of this historic moment contributes notably to the elaboration of her chronicle and to the testing of its implied historical values, but Welty's emphasis in "First Love" and "A Still Moment" upon romantic assertion and the concomitant formalization of Mississippi's pioneer heritage holds more immediate significance for the contemporary dimension of *The Wide Net*. Soon after its publication, Robert Penn Warren reflected upon Welty's growing shelf of Mississippi stories and correctly identified their existentialist core. He explained that "it is in terms of the effort, doomed to failure but essential, that the human manifests itself as human." The "vital effort"[38] of protagonists such as Clytie, Powerhouse, and old Mr. Marblehall supplants any other measure of success or failure, rightness or wrongness, that might be invoked. The same is true of "First Love" and "A Still Moment." Before leaving Natchez in "mock

Indian dress," Aaron Burr points defiantly "toward the West" (*CS*, p. 167), reaffirming his dream in the face of dispiriting setbacks. Shocked and "leaning a-tilt" (*CS*, p. 197) on his horse, Lorenzo rides slowly from the scene of his ruin, but he professes faith in a day of divine disclosure and then hurries to his next appointment. Murrell, who "had gone through the day," now anticipates a nocturnal world in which the "dark voice" (*CS*, p. 198) of his rebellion and the myriad wilderness sounds will coalesce. Having perceived the inherent limitations of his artistic medium, Audubon too walks deeper into the forest, seeking the beneficence of "a particular beast or some legendary bird" (*CS*, p. 197). By even the most generous estimate, Welty's historical figures contribute only modestly to the ravelment of national and international aspiration that traveled river and Trace to converge on Natchez after 1800. They neither (in Sidney Hook's terms) cause great events nor have the innate power to exploit existing circumstances. Their impact is more nearly personal and dramatic, bound up with the morality of "vital effort." When Aaron Burr penetrates the enclosed world of Joel Mayes, he not only inspires our surrogate figure to continue his lonely search along the Natchez Trace but also bequeaths to the contemporary characters in *The Wide Net* a vivid gesture of resistance. Nowhere is the effect of this dynamic, reflexive quality stated explicitly by Welty; it is conveyed instead by recurrent aesthetic patterns that draw historic and contemporary life along river and Trace into a simultaneous order of existence.

5

Eudora Welty frequently employs temporal and spatial imagery in *The Wide Net* to describe its contemporary phase. If the book has a reigning spirit, then it is Old Biddy Felix, an eccentric in "The Winds," who warns the protagonist Josie that " 'the time flies!' " (*CS*, p. 215). A profusion of calendars, clocks, and "ticking" watches, of "old circus posters" and houses shabby with age, records in mechanical, material terms the inevitable prosecution of time. When Jenny and Billy Floyd ("At The Landing") enter a pasture, their brief, although intense, course as lovers is signaled by the "whirring" of "two black butterflies" that circle each other "rhythmically" (*CS,* p. 244). Still more ephemeral, "pears lying on the ground warmed and soured" in the deep summer, as Jenny, bent upon adventuring, leaves The Landing to seek "the next wisdom" (*CS,* p. 256). In "Livvie" Solomon's death liberates his young wife from the nets of domestic servitude, but the silver watch he bequeaths continues to tick ominously as she and Cash McCord, an insistent lover, embrace in "the brightness of the open door" (*CS,* p. 239). For Josie, Jenny Lockhart, and the eponymous black girl Livvie, for the newly married Hazel and William Wallace in the title story, *The Wide Net* is potentially a book of beginnings; but each journey is governed by the same temporal necessity that attends the last days of Solomon, who "was surely wearing out in the body" (*CS,* p. 230), or Miss Sabina, whose death in the dusty P.O. is no less grotesque than Clytie's. " 'Time came for the tyrant to die' " (*CS,* p. 206), intones the chorus in "Asphodel," whose mythological reference to the Elysian Fields perfectly reveals the inexorable character of time in *The Wide Net.*

Its spatial sense, too, is pronounced and is conveyed by strategically placed images of physical and spiritual confinement. Livvie, Jenny, and Josie are each immured in "a good strong house" (*CS,* p. 211) whose windows are either closed or guarded by prisms and "wiry lace." The protective familial structures implied by these staunch dwellings are complemented by community voices that also enforce a rigid decorum and design. In "Livvie" Miss Baby Marie interrupts her commercial mission to tell the naive girl that " 'it is not Christian or sanitary to put feathers in a vase' " (*CS,* p. 233). Similar counsel is offered by a chorus of pious ladies in "At The Landing." They "trudged through the sun in their bonnets" to denounce "the wild man" Billy Floyd and to warn Jenny of her "ruin" (*CS,* p. 254) at his hands. In "Asphodel" Welty plays ironically with the same pattern. Long tyrannized by Miss Sabina, the normally censorious group of ladies now celebrates her death with a memorial picnic, only to be affrighted by the alternate spector of her lewd husband Mr. Don McInnis, "naked as an old goat" (*CS,* p. 207). Livvie's more dignified husband owns an impressive farm along a remote part of the old Natchez Trace, but the effect of his diligence and personal control is tangled, isolating the acquisitive husbandman from nature and trapping his young wife in "a lonely house" built like "a cage" (*CS,* p. 237).

In *The Wide Net* these restrictive categories of time and space not only enforce an air of authenticity in the physical environment but also precipitate the dramatic conflict which advances each story. A patient, conscientious wife of nine years, Livvie suffers intense sexual frustration on this "the first day of spring" (*CS,* p. 231). Solomon's violation of Livvie's youth and vigor is repeated by Jenny's patrician grandfather, who also seeks to arrest in the spring the expression of a passionate nature. Josie is brought to the living room, where her protective family has assembled to resist a fierce equinoctial storm that portends the end of summer and of the young girl's naivete. In October, a time of gathering, William Wallace and Hazel descend, either actually or figuratively, into the Pearl River to gird themselves for parenthood and its inevitable burden of responsibility. Even Miss Sabina responds to a seasonal imperative of sorts by banishing her unfaithful husband during the summer at the height of his sexual enthusiasm.

The foregoing analysis of historic and contemporary persons in *The Wide Net* reveals that Welty has observed the same principle of selection. Each figure has reached a decisive point where visions of personal attainment intersect with a stern institutional authority. It is curious, then, that the contemporary figures in *The Wide Net* have been deemed by critics so antic and barren of historical reality, when they not only are inhabitants of time and space but also share the same human search that drew Burr and his coevals to the Mississippi Territory. F. Garvin Davenport has recently identified "a concept of historical consciousness"[39] residing within this perennial seeking of emotional satisfaction, but because his critical design does not include Welty's chronicle, he only partially recognizes the operation of a dynamic, reflexive quality uniting past and present in *The Wide Net*. Only by following the further disclosure of Welty's Mississippi story in *The Robber Bridegroom* can one experience this structural continuity and place her contemporary questers in their proper relation to the past.

In *The Robber Bridegroom,* Jamie Lockhart's romantic dreams and assertive motto—"Take first and ask afterward" (p. 69)—presume the innocence of a "world [that] had just begun" (p. 87), but he adjusts with remarkable ease to signs of progress along the Natchez Trace. Instead of making his banditry anachronistic, Clement Musgrove's expanding plantation system provides a convenient, new outlet for Jamie's vaunting heroism, necessitating a commercial class in New Orleans which he enthusiastically joins. It is Clement's part to view modernity more starkly and to feel the pull of a temporal order that he knows to be inexorable, but as the book's philosophic center, he enjoys the perspective of age in which nature is both permanent and changing. By returning to his plantation, Clement need not submit himself again to the vicissitudes of history. This instead is the rich fate of the historical questers in "First Love" and "A Still Moment," to whom the stylized solutions of pastoral romance are no longer available. Burr, Dow, Murrell, and Audubon must run "the races of the coming century" (in Henry Adams's phrase) that Clement Musgrove foresaw, protected neither by mythic innocence nor by the wisdom of age, but feeling historical time as the inevitable attenuation of their dreams of power and prominence. By dramatizing this ensuing segment of territorial and federal Mississippi, Welty not only extended her role as annalist or chronicler but also began the gradual accumulation of moments that now weigh so heavily upon the contemporary inhabitants of *A Curtain of*

Green and *The Wide Net.* They are all historically sanctioned characters by virtue of their inclusion in the same underlying epical pattern that unites Welty's first three volumes.

6

Discovery within *The Wide Net* of this dynamic, reflexive quality helps to assemble the progression of events in Welty's chronicle, but it also points to a latent historiographical attitude that shifts the ground from a consideration of the content of history to its inherent structure and value. A second set of recurring aesthetic patterns, encompassing river and road, not only reinforces the epical structure of *The Wide Net* but will also prove indispensible in defining more rigorously Welty's idea of history.

In traveling to the Natchez country, Joel Mayes and his party of Virginians must flee "into the dense cane brake, deep down off the Trace," while Indians pass "in solemn, single file" (*CS*, pp. 154–155). Their guide, Old Man McCaleb, raises his axe in threatening gesture when Joel cries out and tempts one of the several forms that fate historically took along the violent Trace. Later, when Joel travels up the Trace to the Bayou Pierre, he shares in the community disappointment at the size of Burr's fleet, but his expectations are revived when McCaleb gestures a second time and points "in the direction of upstream," prophesying "the arrival of the full, armed flotilla" (*CS*, p. 160). As "First Love" (and "A Still Moment," too, for that matter) historically attests, both the Natchez Trace and the Mississippi River became a public cynosure of adventure and enterprise during this time of migration to the Old Southwest. In Eudora Welty's own time, river and Trace also remained visible and again contributed prominently to the public life of the immediate region.

In 1927 the Mississippi River followed its immemorial practice and flooded the lower valley, but in this spring the devastation was so convulsive that Congress agreed to support a long-delayed flood control plan. The "prize," explained Hodding Carter of Greenville, Mississippi, was "the fertile earth" that the federal government at last decided to protect "in the interests of national prosperity."[40] At approximately the same time, national and local interests again converged in the construction of the Natchez Trace Parkway, a modern road that crisscrosses remnants of the old Trace in its progress from Tupelo, Mississippi, to Jackson. As Jonathan Daniels explains, some early credit for the project must go to the "patriotic ladies and energetic historians [who] built interest in the story of the Trace,"[41] but it was fomented chiefly by the political alignment of Sen. Pat Harrison, Finance Committee chairman, and President Roosevelt, who needed southern support for New Deal spending. In 1936 a state historically resistant to federal allocations for internal improvement received fifteen million dollars in highway funding.

Invariably, flood control and highway construction were comprehended by the same kind of progressive language that Governor Hugh L. White used in 1936 in announcing the BAWI program. By balancing agriculture with industry (BAWI, that is), Mississippi would rejuvenate its economic expectations so sadly depressed in the 1930 census. Although the effect of culture upon the literary mind is finally mysterious, the following hypothesis regarding Welty's selection of river and Trace at least has the virtue of being discussible. In the 1930s, there was no little proof that these historic avenues had maintained an ability to engross public attention and thus to measure the distinct, vivid life of Mississippi. Paradoxically, the hard optimism of political rhetoric that Welty undoubtedly heard did not warn her away from river and Trace but may indeed have taught her that these familiar landmarks could serve a more complex aesthetic purpose, focusing the aspirations of the contemporary figures in *The Wide Net* and at the same time embodying a changeless human significance.

Presumably descended from the Natchez Indian, Billy Floyd (in "At The Landing") not only affronts the ladies by his irregular habits but also threatens Jenny's grandfather, who knows that the young man's return to The Landing at flood time will culminate in his death. For Jenny, Billy's "shining eyes" contain "the whole flood" (*CS*, p. 250), while his insolent embrace reflects its triumphant turbulence. This "shock of love" (*CS*, p. 253) prepares her to leave The Landing after the spring waters subside and to travel west through a dense wilderness to the Mississippi. Soon after Miss Baby Marie's departure, Livvie wanders down the old Trace, where her aimlessness is dispelled by the "vision" of Cash McCord perched atop a bank of the seldom traveled road. Cash has just returned from Natchez, but in his bright Chicago shoddy he seems more an emanation of the "spring winds" (*CS*, p. 235) that ruffle his Easter finery than one of Solomon's black tenants. In "The Winds" Josie's assertion of womanhood promises to be more conventional, but her entry into the life of "the big girls" (*CS*, p. 213) will no doubt occur along "the Old Natchez Trace," now a "Lover's Lane" at "the edge of her town" (*CS*, p. 209). Even Miss Sabina's fervid renunciation of life is preserved by the fabled road. Her restrictive house is forever separated from the "golden ruin" of Don McInnis's Asphodel by "a curve of the old Natchez Trace" (*CS*, p. 201).

In *The Wide Net* both historic and contemporary persons have reached an archetypal juncture in human experience, but what finally unites these questers more decisively than a shared sense of time passing or the similarity of their personal dilemmas is a capacity for spiritual growth. In both the territorial and modern Mississippi, this prime drama occurs along the Trace and river. After embracing in "the still leaves," Cash and Livvie return to Solomon's cabin to confront the "old and strict face" of the dying man. Freed by Solomon's death, they embrace passionately, move "around and around the room," and emerge "into the brightness of the open door" (*CS*, p. 239). When Jenny reaches the fishing camp in search of Billy Floyd, the men come to her "one by one." At first, a "rude laugh covered her cry," but "somehow both the harsh human sounds could easily have been heard as rejoicing, going out over the river in the dark night" (*CS*, p. 257–258).

Her learning heart, cherishing the hope that "more love would be quiet" (*CS,* p. 255), is instructed by violent rape. Through the symbolic medium of river and Trace, the "vital effort" of Burr, Dow, Murrell, and Audubon spans in a moment a century of drastic social change and is received by Livvie and Jenny Lockhart, who have also gravitated to these timeless arteries to assuage "man's old undaunted cry."

As the evocation of an exotic, faraway place, "Some Notes on River Country" more than fulfilled the expectations of the national audience for which it was intended by Welty in 1944. She would contribute at least one more southern piece to *Harper's Bazaar,* but this first exercise in reminiscent local color writing still offered an intense philosophic reflection upon the familiar landscape of *The Wide Net.* The "little chain of lost towns between Vicksburg and Natchez," Welty explained, may no longer produce tumultuous scenes of actual life, but this ancient corridor of Mississippi still enforces "a sense of place as powerful as if it were visible and walking."

> A place that ever was lived in is like a fire that never goes out. It flares up, it smolders for a time, it is fanned or smothered by circumstance, but its being is intact, forever fluttering within it, the result of some original ignition.[42]

In *The Wide Net,* river and Trace embody this paradoxical reflection upon the vicissitudes and constancy of natural and human history. Having changed its course, the Mississippi now touches The Landing only in flood time, while the steep, over-arching banks of the old Trace continue to measure its gradual decline. Such details of geography attest to the tenacity of temporal "circumstance," but in *The Wide Net* river and Trace are also immune to time, maintaining their intrinsic structure as perennial facts of the landscape. In their mutability and constancy, these natural symbols express both the complex organization of human nature, which is at once finite and spiritual, and its incarnation as the reality of history. By uniting past and present and forecasting a time of renewal, Welty's meditation in *The Wide Net* not only has satisfied any element of test that may have remained from *A Curtain of Green* and *The Robber Bridegroom* but also has advanced a distinct interpretation of the essential form and value of history.

7

At least initially, Allen Tate's contribution to *I'll Take My Stand* provides a useful instrument for examining the structure and values of Welty's Mississippi chronicle. In "Remarks on the Southern Religion," Tate begins by describing two extreme versions of history before developing his own more traditional, Christian interpretation. On the one hand is the view of history as "a locus of unpredictable and immeasurable qualities," in which each culture possesses nothing "regular" and thus remains "unique beyond cure." Tate selects the Symbolist poets and M. Henri Bergson as the most notorious exemplars of this stubborn indeterminacy. Tate is more dismayed, however, by the influence of scientific history, by which he means the imposition of an "all-embracing principle" derived from a priori reasoning. This view, which Tate attributed to Hegel, produces "an abstract series" of events that banishes "sensation, accident or contingency." Consequently, "the particular instance fades away into a realm of phenomena related as cause and effect," and one culture becomes no better than, or different from, another. In 1930 Tate considered his own view to be "quite unfashionable." History is not an idea or abstraction, he claimed, but the "image" of "a concrete series that has taken place in a very real time" and thus remains "as full of sensation, and as replete with accident and uncertainty," as the present. Lest this record of "the doings of specific men" appear hopelessly fragmented, Tate also emphasizes the universal character of history. His hypothetical antebellum Southerners, for example, "knew little history for the sake of knowing it, but simply for the sake of contemplating it and seeing in it an image of themselves."[43] Perhaps this is the crux of a remarkable scene in Tate's Civil War novel *The Fathers* (1938) when the impressionable Lacy Buchan is visited by the ghost of his grandfather. By relating "the pathetic tale of Jason and Medea" to contemporary strife, this courtly specter consoles his young grandson with the knowledge that evil is not a recent invention.

Following Tate's formulation, it is clear that Eudora Welty's delineation of history as chronicle allows "the particular instance" to retain its unique, contextual quality and to form an image of human enterprise that is both "full of sensation" and "replete with accident and uncertainty." In Tate's well-known phrase, the historic and contemporary persons in *The Wide Net* act "their parts in a rich and contemporaneous setting which bewildered them."[44] At the same time, however, Welty is also a contemplative historian who finds *within* chronology a spiritual essence as immutable as river and Trace. Clearly, in characterizing history, Tate and Welty reject the extremes of naturalism and mysticism to define a more balanced position, but it would be misleading to conclude that the similar structure of their historical imaginations necessarily transforms Welty into an Agrarian. As creative artists, she and Tate would instinctively embrace the historical aesthetic that offered the greatest freedom from discourse, but if the development of historiographical thought is to be more specifically consulted, then both writers reflect forces and controversies that antedate Southern Agrarianism of the 1930s.

In discussing "Historicism and Its Problems" (1928), Friedrich Meinecke identifies "two great tendencies" in post-Enlightenment historiography: the search for causality and the quest for values. The positivist schools of the later nineteenth century defined "a value-neutral, purely causal history" that inclined to a "mechanistic conception of collective forces." In reaction, a "younger generation" of historians emphasized the search for spiritual values, seeking "to rise above the trivia of causal inquiry" in order "to extract the 'eternal' and the 'timeless' from the past." Their tendency to "rarefy the spiritual atmosphere"

Meinecke views as "a reaction of the soul . . . against the monstrous mass forces which broke loose in the world war and the Collapse of 1918." Meinecke laments that "as matters stand today," balance in "these tendencies will no longer be achieved," but as consolation he points to the distant ideal of Leopold von Ranke, the great mid-nineteenth-century historicist, under whose influence he continues to write. In defining the Rankean tradition of historicism, Meinecke stresses its rigorous methodology, which is governed by a scrupulous respect for the historical record and is reinforced by an "inborn aversion" to "preconceived ideas." But while the Rankean method closely examined "the root domains of causal processes," it also regarded "artistic intuition" as an "indispensable technique" in penetrating "the depths of reality." Recognizing that the pursuit of causality and values is "bipolar," the historicist can witness "break-throughs and revelations of the spiritual within the causal" that not only confirm his own quest for "life-values" but also reassure him of "the continuity and fertility of the spiritual element in history." Meinecke concludes that the "highest instruction . . . history can give . . . consists in nothing else than the corroboration of the infinitely creative power of the spirit."[45]

The choice of Meinecke is not entirely arbitrary. In 1928 he was ideally positioned to summarize both the immediate sources of modern historiography and the peculiar inheritance of the intellectual who lives in the wake of World War I. Of course, Welty's fiction is no more a product of the Rankean tradition than of Agrarianism or the "new regionalism" considered in their formal sense. But Meinecke's profile of the historicist seeking "closer contact" with the past "through living form" does address the modern artist who proceeds along similar lines. For Welty, the historical persons in *The Wide Net* remain influential, not because they are epochal figures, but because by resisting the inevitable dictation of their age, they affirm immeasurable human values. This is the timeless "spiritual element" that binds Clement Musgrove and the young girl of "A Memory" in an

75

extratemporal moment of perception. It is the same historical essence that permeates *The Wide Net,* locating all journeys along river and Trace within the same prolonged instant. Perhaps any rashness of assimilating Welty to a historicist vision of reality can be lessened by stressing finally its paradoxical terms. Historicism entails a methodology that is both conceptual and intuitive and a view of human nature that is at once relative and universal. It bears the mark of early-nineteenth-century romantic and idealist philosophies and at the same time eagerly travels (in Meinecke's phrase) "the road of causality . . . to its utmost limits." This is the same paradox that gives common design to Welty's first three volumes. Her people speak to us because they cannot be transported from their proper sphere. It is only by penetrating their unique time and place that she discovered the timeless aspect of individuality. The value which history creates, then, does not rest in any progressive view of human nature, nor in narrow lessons to be culled from the past, but in the full resonance to ourselves of passionate men and women who acted from a perpetual "springtime of the soul."[46]

The strictures of Diana Trilling upon lyrical fiction can now be reconsidered in light of Eudora Welty's revealed historical method and vision. In reviewing *Citizen Tom Paine,* Diana Trilling admitted that she was "profoundly antipathetic" to the usual run of historical novels, but in May 1943 she could nevertheless "heartily recommend" Howard Fast's most recent excursion into Americana. The theme of *Citizen Tom Paine* was timely and patriotic, and its assumptions concerning historical process corrected what Trilling regarded as a tendency in American writing to dissociate one epoch from another. "Mr. Fast," Trilling concluded, "is the only contemporary historical novelist I know who works on the premise that even people who were born two hundred years ago were really people."[47] Ironically, in approving *Citizen Tom Paine,* Diana Trilling has embraced the same personal, dramatic view of history that informs *The Wide Net,* but in October 1943 she was ill prepared by temperament and circumstance to identify the source of this continuity. Its basis in *The Wide Net* is nothing else than Welty's capacious, resourceful lyricism. Rather than obscuring the recurrent drama of history, Welty's lyrical method actually ensures its preservation by entering the consciousness of those who animate the otherwise impersonal record of man's "doings." If anyone could reform the writing of historical fiction in 1943, Eudora Welty was a more apt candidate than Howard Fast.

Notes to Chapter 2

1. "New Writers," *Time,* 24 November 1941, p. 111.

2. Marianne Hauser, "*A Curtain of Green* and Other New Works of Fiction," *New York Times Book Review,* 16 November 1941, p. 6.

3. Hauser, p. 6.

4. Fredrick Brantley, "*A Curtain of Green:* Themes and Attitudes," *American Prefaces* 7 (spring 1942), p. 251.

5. Arthur J. Carr, "Among Recent Books," *Accent* 2 (spring 1942), p. 189.

6. Carr, p. 189.

7. Hauser, p. 6.

8. Martha Read, "Eudora Welty," *Prairie Schooner* 18 (1944), p. 76.

9. "In the Deep South," *Times Literary Supplement,* 5 May 1945, p. 209.

10. "Sense and Sensibility," *Time,* 27 September 1943, p. 101.

11. Diana Trilling, "Fiction in Review," *Nation,* 2 October 1943, p. 386.

12. "The Love and the Separateness in Miss Welty," *Kenyon Review* 6 (spring 1944), pp. 246–59.

13. "Fiction in Review," *Nation,* 27 February 1943, p. 321.

14. "Fiction in Review," *Nation,* 27 March 1943, p. 461.

15. Dunbar Rowland, *Third Annual Report of the Director of the Department of Archives and History of the State of Mississippi* (Jackson, Miss., 1905), appendix 2, p. 70.

16. Rowland, *Third Annual Report,* Appendix 2, p. 62.

17. J. F. H. Claiborne, *Mississippi as a Province, Territory and State* (1880; reprint ed., Baton Rouge: Louisiana State Univ. Press, 1964), pp. 288–89.

18. *The Blennerhassett Papers,* ed. William H. Safford (Cincinnati: Moore, Wilstach and Baldwin, 1864), p. 188. Among the William Dunbar Papers at the State Department of Archives and History in Jackson, Mississippi, is a volume of "Meteorological Observations, 1799–1810."

19. Elizabeth Brandon Stanton, *"Fata Morgana": A Vision of Empire* (Crowley, La.: Signal, 1917), p. 324. Subsequent page references are included parenthetically in the text.

20. See "The Natchez Trace in Eudora Welty's 'A Still Moment,'" *Southern*

Literary Journal 6 (fall 1973), p. 61. Several of my remarks concerning Welty's use of source material in "A Still Moment" are indebted to this fine study.

21. *The History of Virgil A. Stewart,* comp. H. R. Howard (New York: Harper, 1836).

22. *Journal of John James Audubon, 1820–1821,* ed. Howard Corning (Cambridge, Mass.: Business Historical Society, 1929), pp. 108, 121.

23. *Journal of John James Audubon,* p. 72.

24. Lorenzo Dow, *History of Cosmopolite; or, The Writings of Rev. Lorenzo Dow: Containing His Experience and Travels, In Europe and America, Up to Near His Fiftieth Year* (Cincinnati: Anderson, Gates and Wright, 1859), p. 166.

25. Rowland, *Third Annual Report,* appendix 5, p. 171.

26. "The True Story of Harman Blennerhassett" was first told by his descendant Therese Blennerhassett-Adams, in *Century Magazine,* July 1901, pp. 351–56. A closer source for Welty is *Mississippi: A Guide to the Magnolia State,* p. 327.

27. *The Outlaw Years: The History of the Land Pirates of the Natchez Trace* (New York: Literary Guild, 1930), p. 212.

28. Charles Sellers, *Lorenzo Dow: The Bearer of the Word* (New York: Minton, Balch, 1928), pp. 61–62.

29. *History of Cosmopolite,* pp. 223–27.

30. *The History of Virgil A. Stewart,* pp. 60, 110.

31. Quoted by Stanley Clisby Arthur in *Audubon: An Intimate Life of the American Woodsman* (New Orleans: Harmanson, 1937), pp. 245–46.

32. Arthur, p. 254.

33. See Constance Rourke, *Audubon* (New York: Harcourt, Brace, 1936); Alice Jaynes Tyler, *I Who Should Command All* (New Haven: Framamat, 1937); Francis Hobart Herrick, *Audubon the Naturalist: A History of his Life and Time,* 2nd ed. rev., 2 vols. in one (New York: Appleton, 1938).

34. In "Eudora Welty and the Quondam Obstruction," *Studies in Short Fiction* 5 (spring 1968), pp 209–24, Daniel Curley provides an excellent reading of "A Still Moment," but his conclusion that only Audubon matures as a result of the encounter reflects the absence of a firm historical perspective upon Welty's materials. Her process of assimilation, selection, and transformation suggests that she is reluctant to enhance one quester at the expense of the other.

35. Eudora Welty, "Place in Fiction" (1956), in *The Eye of the Story* (New York: Random House, 1978), p. 117.

36. Eudora Welty, "The Reading and Writing of Short Stories," *Atlantic Monthly,* March 1949, p. 49.

37. "Empty Net," *Partisan Review* 11 (winter 1944), pp. 114–15.

38. "The Love and the Separateness in Miss Welty," p. 256.

39. "Renewal and Historical Consciousness in *The Wide Net,*" in *Eudora Welty: Critical Essays,* ed. Peggy W. Prenshaw (Jackson: University Press of Mississippi, 1979), p. 199.

40. *Lower Mississippi,* Rivers of America Series (New York: Farrar and Rinehart, 1942), pp. 350, 357.

41. *The Devil's Backbone: The Story of the Natchez Trace* (New York: McGraw-Hill, 1962), pp. 254–56.

42. "Some Notes on River Country" (1944), in *The Eye of the Story,* p. 286.

43. Quotations follow the revised text printed in Tate's *Essays of Four Decades* (Chicago: Swallow, 1968), pp. 560–63, 573.

44. *Essays of Four Decades,* p. 563.

45. Friedrich Meinecke, "Historicism and Its Problems," in *The Varieties of History,* ed. Fritz Stern (New York: World, 1956), pp. 267–88.

46. William Carlos Williams, *In the American Grain* (Norfolk, Conn.: New Directions, 1925), p. 196. Welty could easily agree with Williams's rationale for resurrecting Aaron Burr: "A country is not free . . . unless it leave a vantage open (in tradition) for that which Burr possessed in such remarkable degree" (p. 197).

47. "Fiction in Review," *Nation,* 8 May 1943, p. 676, and 17 July 1943, p. 81.

3

Delta Wedding

A Southern Aesthetic

I F one were asked to categorize the recurrent themes and motifs in Welty's first three volumes of fiction, the term "revolt from the village" would probably offer the most inclusive "rubric of historical criticism." First used in 1921 by Carl Van Doren, the term identifies an element of protest against the pieties of small-town life that often infuses socially conscious literature of the 1920s. In *A Hoosier Holiday* (1916), Theodore Dreiser struck the keynote by acknowledging the existence of "a great revolt against all the binding perfection" of middle-class society. As Anthony C. Hilfer suggests, "the condition of a healthy American literature was to reject and destroy the myth of the village," for its "genteel ideals" and "false optimistic assurances" were "profoundly hostile to the imagination."[1] In the work of such diverse figures as Sherwood Anderson, Sinclair Lewis, and Thomas Wolfe, this imaginative freedom revealed unsuspected depths of alienation and repression beneath the placid surface of white Anglo-Saxon Protestant culture. Between 1900 and 1930, such earlier ideal communities as Sarah Orne Jewett's Dunnet Landing, Zona Gale's Friendship Village, and Tarkington's Plattville, Indiana, gave way to the harsher locale of Winesburg, Ohio, Gopher Prairie, and Altamont. Eudora Welty also examines critically the communal myth of small-town living, reserving various degrees of pathos and satire for Victory, Mississippi, China Grove, Farr's Gin, The Landing, and smug, complacent Natchez. In *A Curtain of Green* and *The Wide Net,* these and other fictional towns provide the atmosphere of "binding perfection" that precipitates awakening and renewal or simply a vision of personal defeat. Eudora Welty's own "revolt from the village" may not possess the same high level of environmental determinism, polemical warning, or bitterness that respectively impels Anderson, Lewis, and Wolfe, but it does permit a comprehensive description of her major themes and motifs, firmly locating Welty within a national pattern of literary decorum. Indeed, all but the most ingenious reader of Welty's first three volumes would be hard put to identify many distinctive southern qualities that transcend the localism of speech, place names, or topography. Even that alleged benchmark of southern literature, the grotesque, had been appropriated by Sherwood Anderson in his depiction of the Midwest.

If a classification of themes and motifs produces only unsureness regarding Welty's regional identity, then her chronicle and its underlying historiographical attitude are not too much more helpful in this respect. As careful research demonstrates, a strong, well-informed localism guides Welty's imagination in the assimilation and selection of men and events that compose her chronicle of Mississippi life. But neither this impulse to chronicle nor the literary intelligence that discovers a recurrent story in the midst of seriality can be attributed solely to regional factors. As the historian George Tindall has noted, consciousness of accelerated change in the South undoubtedly influenced "the regional self-discovery of the 1930's, reflected in agrarianism, regionalism, and the vivid documentary literature of the period,"[2] but the structure of Welty's historical imagination (and Tate's, too, for that matter) reflects at the same time a much older and more comprehensive locus of change, subtly shaping the modern artistic sensibility in international terms. It is at this point that *Delta Wedding* (1946) becomes a crucial document in following the development of Welty's chronicle. Her long-awaited first novel is set in 1923 in the Mississippi Delta and focuses upon the frantic preparations of Battle and Ellen Fairchild and their vast family to marry Dabney, the traditional belle of Shellmound Plantation. On the surface, Welty's choice of plantation may appear surprising, for in "Clytie," "Old Mr. Marblehall," "Asphodel," and "At The Landing," she had apparently rejected regressive patterns of history for a more flexible, comprehensive design. Welty has never been "a bit interested in preserving the home of Jefferson Davis,"[3] as she tartly informed William Buckley on "Firing Line," but in composing *Delta Wedding,* she recognized that the plantation fit cogently into a constellation of historical concerns. In 1946 the paradoxical environs of the literary plantation remained aesthetically useful to Welty, permitting the extension of her Mississippi chronicle and allowing still more intense intersections of the public and private spheres to develop. At the same time, however, its adoption also possessed a much larger significance. In choosing the plantation as scene and mythos, Welty attempted for the first time to fuse her historical aesthetic with a distinctively southern institution. As the national myth of the small town gives way to the unique southern plantation, we are provided with the best opportunity to understand how place contributes to the definition of a regional imagination.

2

In studying Eudora Welty, one encounters no greater challenge than defining the effect of regional culture upon her mind and art. Some years ago, one of Welty's ablest critics employed a biographical method with regional ramifications to account for Welty's objectivity. Presumably, her "simultaneous attachment to and detachment from" a southern homeplace reflects the fact that "neither of Miss Welty's parents came from the deep South." Welty thus escaped "that strong sense of a blood inheritance of southern tradition which is to be found in so many of her distinguished contemporaries."[4] By 1972, this rationale for literary objectivity had gained enough authority to be repeated by one interviewer who asked Welty to comment upon its validity.[5] Her hesitant response implies that she also may be troubled by a logic which seems to overlook the aesthetic character of the Southern

Literary Renascence itself. Allen Tate, for example, finds the inspiration for this flowering of letters in "a crossing of the ways" that occurred after the First World War. Isolated for nearly sixty years, "the South reentered the world—but gave a backward glance as it stepped over the border." This propitious circumstance enabled the southern writer to adopt a complex attitude, neither apostrophizing his lost heritage nor protesting an inelegant future, but experiencing "the past in the present."[6] It is curious indeed that those "distinguished contemporaries" of Eudora Welty, burdened by their own "blood inheritance," enjoyed the same "simultaneous attachment to and detachment from" a southern world composed of lore, legend, and such intimate family history as forms the matrix of Allen Tate's *The Fathers* (1938). Indeed, this ironic perspective forms the distinctive intelligence of Faulkner, Ransom, Tate, and Warren, and it would be equally implausible to argue that any congeries of biological factors had specifically determined their achievement. In order to temper Welty's southern character, the critic has unwittingly invoked the same paradoxical frame of mind that Allen Tate describes as the crux of the Southern Literary Renascence. "It just does not explain," Mr. Compson would be tempted to conclude in *Absalom, Absalom!*

In several well-known letters, Eudora Welty herself has further troubled this perplexing issue of a regional identity. Writing from Jackson, she observed on December 15, 1948, that Mississippi had fared poorly of late in *The New Yorker*. She may have remembered a column of November 13 in which Cong. John Rankin, the vehement states' rights Democrat from Mississippi, is pictured as a prime buffoon in the Alger Hiss affair. She was more deeply disturbed, though, by Edmund Wilson's earlier review of *Intruder in the Dust*. A generally admiring notice, it had nonetheless pointed to Faulkner's address and had asked how a practitioner of the modern novel, "with its ideal of technical efficiency," could function in such an "antiquated community" as Oxford, Mississippi. Welty's surreal vision of an urbanized William Faulkner, lunch pail in hand, being docked by "Boss Man Wilson,"[7] is perhaps the price that condescension must be ready to pay. There is no such restraining fantasy at work in her excoriation of Richard Gilman, who has more recently extended all the implications of Wilson's urbanity. *The Surface of Earth,* a "mastodon" of a novel by the North Carolinian Reynolds Price, convinces this *New York Times* reviewer that southern literature is no longer "an ongoing cultural reality." Today, Gilman argues, the more decisive moral energy informs the "detached" intelligence of Barth, Pynchon, or Hawkes. " 'Home' is wherever . . . humanness can begin to rediscover its outlines against a backdrop of ruins." Under different circumstances, Welty might not find this formulation completely unattractive, but the sharpness of her reply to the *Times* editor precludes any picking or choosing. Richard Gilman's offerings are uniformly "shabby,"[8] not only because they would deny a serious writer (and Welty's long-time personal friend) his subject, but also because they make a vice of his being heir to a tradition of local southern wisdom.

If at all prudent, the modern southern writer has learned to be wary when he or she hears the word "regional." At best, it only ill disguises condescension; at worst, it can harbor imprecision, confusing a richly placed literature with (in Welty's terms) the superficial "Isle of Capri" novel. Welty has said that as a descriptive term it "means little"[9] and that as an evaluative term it fails to bare completely "the big root" of vision. She is, however, a "proud partisan"[10] of regional writing, if by this designation its range of moral implication is not narrowed. When such narrowing occurs, Welty responds vigorously, but perhaps the pressure of the moment unduly influences both her thought and language. Such virtues as Faulkner possessed would probably "identify themselves anywhere in the world,"[11] but in so answering Edmund Wilson's critique of *Intruder in the Dust,* Welty fails to extend the reviewer's own admission that southern provincialism may have nourished Faulkner's art by exposing him to a relatively whole community. In defending *The Surface of Earth,* she concedes a similar point. If Gilman finds the southern locale of this novel to be irrelevant, then he simply does not know that Price's "territory is interior to greater extent than it is exterior."[12] This description may not be entirely untrue, but Welty's more considered criticism has explored the relations of place and vision with far greater subtlety than either of these well-known letters would imply.

If Welty's biography is ever written, its author will be hard pressed to explain how the prosaic rituals of her middle-class southern childhood, including piano lessons, summer camp, and the fondly remembered night-light, derived their aesthetic intensity. The china night-light, in particular, has encouraged Welty to explore the function of place in literature. "The outside," she recalled in 1957, was "painted with a scene, which is one thing; then, when the lamp is lighted, through the porcelain sides a new picture comes out through the old, and they are seen as one." In a better frame of mind, Welty would have rejected defensive, quantitative language and would have reminded Edmund Wilson and Richard Gilman that "the good novel," like "the lamp alight," is "the combination of internal and external, glowing at the imagination as one."[13] As categories, then, interior and exterior cannot survive the "double thunderclap" of artistic creation. The "living world," having penetrated all that "is stirring inside the mind," provokes an "answering impulse that in a moment of high consciousness fuses impact and image."[14] As noted above, *Delta Wedding* offers an excellent opportunity to observe this organic process, not as a general aesthetic truth, or even as a function of Welty's local attention, but in terms that are now distinctively southern. Ultimately, this chapter will create a sounder basis for defining the nature of Welty's southern character, but more immediate goals include further study of her assimilation and selection of pertinent Mississippi sources as well as delineation of Welty's continuing chronicle and its implied attitude and values. All of this work depends, however, upon a preliminary conceptual statement describing the literary resourcefulness of the plantation myth.

3

Since the appearance in 1832 of John Pendleton Kennedy's *Swallow Barn,* few plantation novels of either northern or southern origin have been able to resist the affecting spectacle of lovers' complications solved and marriage vows rehearsed. In *Swallow Barn* the gallant and the heroine are ideally suited by class and fortune but remain temperamentally alienated until Ned Hazard learns discretion and Bel Tracy moderates her exaggerated notions of chivalry. Then their marriage is no less inevitable than the goodwill and unremitting labor of admiring servants. When Dabney Fairchild falls in love with her father's overseer in *Delta Wedding,* she precipitates what would have been a crisis in the Old Dominion world of *Swallow Barn.* Nearly a century later, in the delta of the Yazoo River, the effect, however, is noticeably diminished. Dabney's brothers and sisters spit ritualistically when they pass Troy Flavin's house; and Battle, the exuberant master of Shellmound, grieves recklessly at the prospect of his daughter's equivocal wedding. The whole tribe of Fairchilds, including aunts and great-aunts, regrets Dabney's "wildness for Troy" (p. 33), but their dismay remains an undercurrent of gibe and innuendo rather than confrontation with the deliberate hill man from Tishomingo County. In *Swallow Barn* marriage provided essentially a convenient thread to unify the narrator's disparate impressions of a gracious era along the James River. In *Delta Wedding* marriage also serves a primary narrative purpose, ordering the week-long events that culminate in Dabney's wedding, but by marrying the radiant belle of Shellmound, the aspiring, individualistic Troy Flavin also dramatizes the antagonistic inner life of the plantation itself. The terms of this historic tension can be briefly identified by consulting the articulate master of Westover, William Byrd.

In describing "the advantage" of colonial Virginia to Lord Orrery, an Englishman who stayed at home, Byrd explains that "we who have Plantations . . . abound in all kinds of Provisions":

> I have a large Family of my own, and my Doors are open to Every Body. . . . Like one of the Patriarchs, I have my Flocks and my Herds, my Bond-men and Bond-women, and every Soart of Trade amongst my own Servants, so that I live in a kind of Independence on every one but Providence. However, tho' this Soart of Life is without expense, yet it is attended with a great deal of trouble. I must take care to keep all my People to their Duty, to set all the Springs in motion and to make everyone draw his equal Share to carry the Machine forward. But then 'tis an amusement in this silent Country and a continual exercise of our Patience and Economy. Another thing, My Lord, that recommends this country very much—we sit securely under our Vines and our Fig Trees without any danger to our Property. We have neither publick Robbers nor private, which your Ldsp will think very strange, when we often have needy Governors, and pilfering Convicts sent among us.[15]

Byrd's remarkable letter of 1726 contains two distinct, although entangled, skeins of thought. One reveals a communitarian sense that depicts the plantation as a cohesive social entity. Through the benevolence of the patriarch, family, friends, and retainers are drawn into a circle of mutual, organic relations. But William Byrd's somewhat facetious hymn to Virginia also belongs to an old allurement literature that pictured the southern garden as a realm of personal freedom and economic self-interest—thus Byrd's litany of personal and possessive terms and his wry assurance that real property in Virginia is safe, notwithstanding the institutional threat posed by "needy Governors." A more resolute critic might dismiss this as a contradictory, even cynical, document, for Byrd seems to flaunt his absolute independence while remaining the fount of social harmony. The present writer is restrained, however, by David Potter's apt, intriguing image of the South as "a kind of Sphinx on the American land"[16] whose ambiguity resists easy understanding. In a later discussion, Byrd's enigmatic letter will be reconsidered once the proper historical context has been developed, but for now Byrd's description can serve as a revealing, if inadvertent, statement of tensions that render the southern plantation unique. If his creative imagination is not dulled by partisanship, then the modern southern writer inherits in pure form the same tangled, discordant association of community and self that William Byrd described to his English correspondent. By 1946 Eudora Welty was prepared to exploit this material. The experience of her early volumes not only defended Welty from romantic excess or any other kind of partisanship but more importantly directed her to the true aesthetic resources of the literary plantation itself. In *Delta Wedding* Eudora Welty realized that it could focus with still greater intensity the dilemma of freedom and order that marks her chronicle with timeless human value. To establish a base for this continuing story, however, Welty's assimilation and selection of pertinent Mississippiana must be observed again.

4

In designing her fiction, Eudora Welty has always respected but never bowed to the physical geography of Mississippi. A tiny hamlet on the Tallahatchie, Shellmound is transported in *Delta Wedding* to the southern part of Leflore County and is placed near the more exotic, mysterious sounding Yazoo River.[17] In many other particulars, though, Welty provides an ample verisimilitude, assimilating names and topical allusions that are confirmed by files of the *Jackson Daily News* for 1923. It is one of the book's minor ironies that Shelley Fairchild, Ellen and Battle's unfashionable first daughter, should occasion a flurry of modish reference. A "King Tut sandal" (p. 84) lies in the middle of her room while Shelley labors at her diary, awaiting a facetious beau who will call up the stairs, " 'I'm the Sheik of Araby' " (p. 89). Thickening the aura of forbidden romance, Welty reports that Shelley yearns to read *The Beautiful and the Damned* in bed, but she is frustrated by poor lighting and by a bluff father who could easily endorse the literary opinion of the *Jackson Daily News*. Its editor, piqued by the vogue of Fitzgerald's novel, asked querulously, "Why must we read 'The Beautiful and the Damned?' " and then delayed his answer for ten years on the grounds that "a really good book defies time."[18] Dapper young "Sheiks," advised the same editor, might be encouraged to forgo the current "matinee-idol" pose by a course of "hard work."[19] Tut styles, exploiting the discovery of Tutankhamen's crypt in 1922, had dominated the next year's spring fashion, but by June the bemused editor of the *News* could sense a "waning of the popular interest" and could signal "Vale! King Tut."[20] Although brief, his appearance after millennia of solitude affected the Delta cotton market by stimulating demand for "printed Egyptian patterns."[21] This welcome bit of economic news was published in Welty's hometown paper under the byline of the Fairchild News Service.

The compounding of these and many other similar details accords *Delta Wedding* at least a superficial fidelity to the local truths of time and place, but this circumstantial facticity only begins to reveal Welty's more profound assimilation of sources pertinent to the Delta. Paradoxically, Welty's admitted unfamiliarity with this region of large plantations in west central Mississippi did not inhibit but may actually have enhanced her assimilation of its distinctive ethos. In a very useful 1972 interview, Welty distinguished between a familiar setting that is known "down to the bone" and a strange place whose "*impression*" can "equally well be true" for the writer. If Eudora Welty's Jackson is intimately known, then the "rich and visually striking" Delta, "seen in a flash" by Welty during infrequent visits, possibly "smote"[22] her with aesthetic promise. Perhaps the best way to define this more profound level of verisimilitude is to follow another Jacksonian traveling north from her native city to the mysterious Yazoo country and briefly record impressions.

In *Delta Wedding* Laura McRaven feels a drastic alteration when the tiny, impromptu Yellow Dog train drops from the hills onto the flat Delta, a rich alluvial plain that "begins in the lobby of the Peabody Hotel in Memphis and ends on Catfish Row in Vicksburg."[23] A drummer "across the aisle" groans at the illimitable prospect, but the nine-year-old Laura is prepared to savor "her first journey alone." "Thoughts went out of her head," displaced by a vision of buzzards wheeling "as wide and high as the sun," clouds even "larger than boats or churches or gins," and the "endless fields" of cotton that "glowed like a hearth in firelight." Laura's Delta cousins are no less vivid or expansive than the countryside. With "Fairchilds everywhere," she is "lifted down among flying arms," instructed to kiss baby Bluet, and then "half-carried along like a drunken reveler" (pp. 4–5) back to Shellmound Plantation, where sister Dabney's wedding has quickened the normally hectic pace of life for Shelley, Orrin, India, Roy, Little Battle, and Ranny. Soon the wedding guest from Jackson will feel a curious inversion that Welty may also have experienced in the Delta. Here it is Laura, the sophisticated city dweller, who is abashed by her exhilarating rural kin and made to feel the timid "country cousin." By her own testimony, Welty too found the Delta exhilarating, laughed once to think that "anything having to do with a wedding" there "couldn't be compressed into one day," and more recently explained that its inhabitants were "richer . . . , had so much . . . , did so much,"[24] more than other Mississippians. As the avid, overflowing life at Shellmound reveals, Welty's deepest impression of the Delta was one of inexhaustible bounty, a view that coincides with several bizarre, although not entirely surprising, contemporary estimates of this singular region.

Late in 1923, the *Jackson Daily News* recounted an article that had been printed in June "based on the theory that the Yazoo Delta was the original Garden of Eden." But now in November, the *News* went on to report a still more astounding mythological interpretation advanced by Prof. Clinton McMickle, who designated the Yazoo Delta "cradle of the white race" and located the capital of Plato's lost Atlantis on Lake George, a dozen or so miles above Vicksburg. His imagination stimulated by the local remains of an ancient mound-builders' culture, the archaeologist from Topeka, Kansas, concluded that "America was Eden and the Delta its garden."[25] McMickle's enthusiasm may have overwhelmed professorial restraint, but in a sense he was only responding to the same geological signs that any Deltan or even casual traveler such as Laura McRaven or Welty could read in the landscape. Its flat expanse, numerous lakes and bayous, remnants of vestigial forests, and the soil made "endlessly deep" by periodic flooding not only project an image of unfailing resources but also confront the observing eye with evidence of such vast geological time as to make change appear nearly imperceptible. While there is no evidence that Welty specifically assimilated any of these contemporary sources, it is clear that she seeks to satisfy the demands of verisimilitude by evoking both the superficial aspect of Delta life and its informing myth of timeless bounty. What needs further clarification is that Welty's pursuit of this verisimilitude also implies an act of selection, for in 1923 the myth of timeless bounty forms part of a complex tension that renders the Delta aesthetically feasible. No one has described this circumstance more sensitively than David Cohn of Greenville, Mississippi, in his reminiscent volume *Where I Was Born and Raised*.

For David Cohn, no rhetoric was too fervid nor claim too extravagant to describe his Delta homeplace in part 1 of *Where I Was Born and Raised* (1935). "Here are no hills, no rocks, no thin earth barely hiding the stones beneath, but pure soil endlessly deep, dark and sweet, dripping fatness." In such a prodigal land, the industrial revolution was "an alien device scarcely comprehended." Apparently immune to time, "the patient mule lost in prehistoric thought, followed by a plodding Negro down a turnrow, remains the machine age of the Delta." Other patterns of continuity that Cohn remembered include a tradition of easy, expansive manners rooted in white paternalism and black observance of racial etiquette. In 1935 the languid Delta seemed "a strange and detached fragment thrown off by the whirling comet that is America."[26] A dozen years later, however, Cohn returned to his native Greenville and found that this "long Indian summer of the community" had ended in "convulsive change."[27] Part 2 of *Where I Was Born and Raised* (1947) recounts the deterioration of race relations, caused in part by the demise of noblesse oblige and by the political dominance of poorer whites who now inhabit the Delta. The plantation system could still assume the fertility of the Delta, but in the 1930s the growing of cotton was made precarious by a depressed world market, while in the 1940s the planter was asked to meet unusually high wartime standards of production. The mule, which seemed inseparable from the field he plowed; the Negro, who patiently followed down a turnrow; and the landowner, who observed this solemn procession—all were forced to readjust their traditional relations when the mechanization of agriculture turned time into a form of money. Under the circumstances, David Cohn advised that we "pity the poor white man searching for a security that does not exist. Sing a sweetly sad little song for him who fails to live fully today because he is morbidly concerned with the morrow."[28]

Her greater personal distance from the Delta aside, in the 1930s and 1940s Eudora Welty shared much the same vantage point with David Cohn and with William Alexander Percy, a still more poignant elegist of the Delta, who was "oppressed by vanished glories" and foresaw only "catastrophe."[29] Welty too realized that the old ways of Shellmound were "doomed," a fate that was "implicit," she claims, in the conception of *Delta Wedding*,[30] but her approach to the Fairchilds would not be governed by pity, melancholy, or dejection. The chronicle of Mississippi life constructed in earlier volumes had prepared Welty to see the inevitability of change and had convinced her that it was a positive condition of human growth. Tracing the further development of this chronicle in *Delta Wedding* will provide the same kind of historical context for the changes that beset Shellmound, although Welty's use of the southern plantation to juxtapose again personal and communal motives introduces a new source of intensity. For now, however, it is more important to realize that in focusing upon the "precarious"[31] world of Shellmound in 1923, Welty has selected the same dramatic juncture that occurs in each of her earlier volumes. As the Delta myth of timeless bounty is confronted by the harsh terms of modern history, the human imagination must assume the task of reconciling nearly insuperable change with what remains constant in an ancient land. By her careful assimilation and selection of sources pertinent to the Delta, Welty has established the needed base for prolonging her chronicle of Mississippi life and imbuing it with complex tension.

5

Unfortunately, many reviewers of *Delta Wedding* assumed that the memorabilia cluttering Shellmound merely affirmed Welty's sentimental regard for the old order instead of creating a visible guide to the chronicle of the Fairchild family since pioneer times. In passing from room to room, contemporary Fairchilds might interrupt their headlong pace to follow the progress of history. In the dining room, they sit on "old walnut-and-cane chairs" (p. 18) and play at a card table made by Great-Grandfather, "the original Mr. George Fairchild" (p. 97), who cut a path into the dense Yazoo wilderness during the 1820s. His portrait hangs in the parlor, undisturbed by the froth and ferment of plans to marry his great-granddaughter Dabney. Great-Aunt Mashula's dulcimer hangs by a "thin ribbon" (p. 98) in the same airy room at Shellmound. Sixty years ago, Mashula Hines watched patiently for her husband, but neither the second George Fairchild nor his brothers Gordon and Battle returned from the Civil War. Family legend holds that Mashula "put her dulcimer away" and, although she continued to hope for George's return, "was never the same" (p. 45). Grandfather's dueling pistols, displayed among other firearms in the parlor, extend the Fairchild adventure through 1890. Tragically, the ornate pistols "had not saved his life" when James accused a rival gin master, old Ronald McBane, of compromising the meager fortune of his neighbors. Even a more recent generation has begun to produce artifacts. A pistol carried by Grandmother Laura Allen rests on the same gilt table in the parlor and is scored by the "little toothmarks" (p. 99) of her son, Battle. *Delta Wedding* is richly furnished, even by the capacious standards of southern domestic fiction, but informed readers will discern within this apparent clutter a subtle extension of Welty's Mississippi chronicle. So composed, the memorabilia of Shellmound first evoke the same wilderness days that engaged the imagination of Clement Musgrove and tested the enterprise of Aaron Burr and then project this embedded story of settlement through successive generations of Fairchilds that culminate in the present life at Shellmound. In effect, *Delta Wedding* completes the chain of historical events that leads from the earliest days in the Mississippi Territory to the contemporary setting of *A Curtain of Green,* but as one might suspect, Welty's continuing chronicle represents something more resourceful and profound than a mere procession of colorful personages. In *Delta Wedding* each historical phase is stamped with an arresting image of intense human subjectivity.

Perhaps the image that best conveys the restless character of pioneer days is a memorial portrait of Great-Great Uncle Battle, who was killed by bandits of the old Natchez Trace while traveling to join his brother George. Poised on his great horse, Florian, Battle still surveys the library at Shellmound, a historic emblem of aspiration. It has been estimated that Mississippi lost more than one-third of its soldiers during the Civil War. In tabular form, the deaths of Gordon, Battle, and George tend to validate this cold statistic, but again family legend preserves the more intimate character of history. Aunt Jim Allen, who lives with Primrose at the nearby Grove, reminds India that Mashula's face was etched by lightning on the windowpane and that her ghost, still waiting for George, can be heard "crying" (p. 45) in the night. In 1890 Grandfather James Fairchild completed and occupied an elegant home on a nearby bend of the Yazoo River, but his "dreadful trouble" with old Ronald McBane made Marmion "too heart-breaking" for the survivors. Now empty for more than a generation, Marmion projects the image of "a hypnotized swamp butterfly, spread and dreaming where it alights" (p. 120) on the sluggish river. The vivid presence at Shellmound of old Battle, Mashula Hines, and James Fairchild, their frustration at once unique and yet structurally identical, again imbues Welty's chronicle with recurring moments of subjectivity that establish a solid, evocative core of timeless grief. Throughout, however, it is the image of the plantation, evolving from the mud house that Great-Grandfather built for his wife Mary Shannon, that best focuses the dramatic intensity of Welty's chronicle.

Presumably lured by tales of a "new El Dorado," George Fairchild and his dependents hastened to occupy rich alluvial lands ceded to the new American government by retreating Choctaws. Their tenacity as pioneers established the material welfare of the family but in turn exposed successive generations of Fairchilds to the large-scale violence of Civil War or the more intimate duello. Each generation has experienced a decisive, if not catastrophic, alteration in the conduct of its life. The imagery of death associated with old Battle, Mashula Hines, and James Fairchild asks that we follow a subtle drama whereby the individual is drawn into support of an institution perpetually threatened by change. In the present, Dabney Fairchild feels most acutely the burden of this historic drama. As she anticipates the beginning of a new life with Troy Flavin, Dabney meditates upon the tragic past and affirms silently that "all the cotton in the world was not worth one moment of life!" (pp. 120–121). Her resistance to such abstractions as honor and responsibility, virtues that Grandfather James defended in his fatal duel, works simultaneously on several levels. In her "eagerness" for self-fulfillment, Dabney's aspiration recalls the seeking of Welty's protagonists in other phases of the chronicle, a unified, continuous story that makes their desire a common one. But Dabney's resistance is measured more specifically by the communal needs and dictates of the plantation, an institution whose internal complexity, adumbrated by William Byrd in 1726, brings together with heightened effect the components of Welty's recurring drama of the individual confronting a larger external authority. Later, the distinctively southern roots of this drama will be explored, but as preparation it is necessary first to report two critiques of *Delta Wedding* that betray little knowledge of its place in Welty's chronicle or of its relation to earlier plantation fiction.

6

Diana Trilling continues to be an antagonistic reader of Welty. In reviewing *Delta Wedding* for *The Nation,* she again finds an "exacerbation of poeticism" marring the Welty text but now concludes that her "style and her cultural attitude are not to be separated." Welty's depiction of intimate personal states in *Delta Wedding* is a method that allows her to "cherish" the "aristocratic grace and charm" of the Fairchilds, while leaving any harsh moral judgments "in rosy poetic solution."[32] John Crowe Ransom is a more diplomatic, although ultimately more disquieting, reviewer. Ransom begins by assuring Welty of his "philosophical rapport with her," but his hesitations and equivocations nearly pose the overwhelming question of why the author has lavished her gifts of representation upon the Fairchilds' antique polity. In 1946 *Delta Wedding* is judged by Ransom to "be one of the last novels in the tradition of the old South."[33] At first glance, Shellmound may seem as impervious as the mythical Delta itself to the historic upheavals of the 1920s and may thus become a latter-day synonym for all the timeless, legendary southern plantations that still crowd the American memory. This, at least, is the sub-merged, nostalgic premise that guides Diana Trilling's adverse review and, to a lesser degree, restricts the appreciation of John Crowe Ransom. Both reviewers have attributed to Eudora Welty a sentimental eye, primarily because they are not equipped to follow the extension of her chronicle in *Delta Wedding*. Failing to do so, they do not realize that Welty has selected a time and a place that foresee only difficulties for Shellmound and in retro-spect reveal the historic vulnerability of the plantation to cultural change. No doubt a more timely knowledge of Welty's design would have tempered each reviewer with greater toleration, but it is clear as well that a deeper knowledge of the foregoing plantation literature would have been still more enlightening. A southern writer who adopts the plantation as locale and mythos, Welty stands in direct line of descent from nineteenth-century practitioners of the form. By noting their inclination to address the same problems that attract Eudora Welty, it will be possible to improve generic understanding of *Delta Wedding,* establishing more firmly its social and economic attention and at the same time contributing to the definition of Welty's southern character. George Tucker and William Gilmore Simms do not exhaust or even circumscribe the large body of plantation writing. Con-sidered together, they do, however, express a perennial difficulty which attends the southern conception of community.

In volume 1 of *The Valley of Shenandoah* (1824), young Edward Grayson defines the paradox whereby a healthy culture assimi-lates self-interest to the common good. Having observed the sway of the Virginia planter, his facetious northern friend taunts Edward: "'Indeed what is the love of liberty,'" Gildon asks, "'but the love of doing what we please?'" Edward labels this "'a very ingenious piece of sophistry'" and answers "'that he who has a proper sense of his own rights, has a due respect for the rights of others.'" Still skeptical, Gildon continues to press his friend and implies that local dependence upon chattel slavery violates these republican principles. In answering that domestic slavery is "'an evil,'" though one that "'admits of no remedy that is not worse than the disease,'"[34] Edward speaks for the author, George Tucker of Virginia, who considered slavery to be an intolerable institution. "The doom of its death, though we know not the time or the mode, is certain and irrevocable,"[35] he repeated in 1843. *The Valley of Shenandoah* is a hastily composed, crudely plotted story that stoops to embrace all the banality of popular domestic fiction, but it also depicts the southern plantation community suffering extreme distortion near the end of the colonial period. To a student of southern letters, the book is chiefly interesting because its hero possesses a vision of social harmony that his creator cannot represent in fictional terms.

What purports to be a "veracious history" (vol. 1, p. 91) of the Old Dominion begins with Colonel Grayson's death and the return of Edward to Beechwood, the family's western estate in Frederick County. The main progress of volume 1 is to acquaint Edward with the extent of his father's debts and to ready vengeful plots of foreclosure which banish the Graysons to a small farm aptly named The Retreat. Ironically, the historic conventions defining the gentleman and governing his social responsibility ensure "the ruin of a once prosperous and respected family" (vol. 2, p. 292). Prompted by "his accustomed good nature" (vol. 1, p. 31), Colonel Grayson indulges his Negroes, neglects to supervise fawning, deceitful managers, and assumes the debts of imprudent neighbors by giving his bond in surety. Arrayed against these communitarian ideals of benevolence, trust, and generosity are the parvenu planter, diligent and purse-proud, and the seductive moneylender, "rapacious and unfeeling" (vol. 1, p. 215), who succeed in bringing all the Grayson lands to the hammer. The most affecting image in volume 2 is produced by the aftermath of a daylong auction. Amid the "forlorn and desolate appearance" of Beechwood, Mrs. Grayson is observed by her daughter, Louisa, sitting "with the same serene and resigned countenance." Her composure does not, however, obscure the stains of tobacco which now mark "the bare floors" (vol. 2,

p. 216). In one of the earliest plantation fictions, the image of a defiled manor house has assumed full literary status. Many subsequent writers would color this image with nostalgia, but George Tucker's vision is too resolutely calamitous to permit such indulgence.

From a historical perspective, Tucker accurately portrays what William Gilmore Simms termed "the evil influences of the Revolution."[36] Currency was scarce, encouraging the moneylender to be bold; arable land in coastal Virginia could not support its growing population, pushing the western line of settlement beyond the Blue Ridge; and Virginians had not entirely forgotten the standards of Republican and Loyalist, as contention sparked by the Jay Treaty revealed in 1796. Although each of these circumstances finds an approximate image in *The Valley of Shenandoah,* Tucker reserves special emphasis for the contest between coastal and frontier Virginia. At Stanley, one of few old Tidewater estates that has remained intact, Tucker reveals an insidious "ennui" and "discontent" (vol. 2, pp. 23–24) which mark the erosion of social confidence in the east. In the more progressive, enterprising west of 1796, benevolence and self-interest have been completely prized apart, pitting the effete aristocrat against a new planter class with mercantilist ideals. Although the signs are faint, there is some indication that George Tucker may have considered Edward Grayson to be a potential means of reconciling these discordant features of post-Revolutionary Virginia.

Edward Grayson is endowed with the benevolent instincts of his father, being "all mildness and condescension" (vol. 1, p. 3) to dependents, but he also identifies the pride, folly, and indolence that have made the Tidewater planter nearly extinct in these hard times. By pursuing a legal career, Edward will redeem his father's "deplorable incapacity for business" (vol. 1, p. 113) and will thus earn the right to address the gentle Matilda Fawkner, whose mother remains a shrill exponent of western utilitarianism throughout the book. It is a tidy, consoling package that George Tucker cannot deliver, though, as the plot attests. Unmarriageable without a fortune, Louisa is seduced by the mercenary Gildon; and Edward becomes an indignant cavalier who travels to New York City, where he is killed in a greatly mismanaged duel. By inference, neither Edward's "scrupulous and fastidious honour" nor his "own exertions" to restore the Grayson fortune can relieve the dichotomous note upon which *The Valley of Shenandoah* ends. Only the fond memory of Williamsburg can redeem the faith of an author who wishes to believe that personal and communal aspirations are not necessarily incompatible. In its brief flowering near the end of the eighteenth century, this "sunny spot" joined "the greatest simplicity of character . . . to the greatest polish of manners," producing "a style of delicate and even luxurious living, unaccompanied with that love of show and rivalry, which so often poisons social enjoyment." But from the perspective of the 1820s, a "dreary field of existence" (vol. 2, pp. 48–53) for George Tucker, Williamsburg was merely a receding image of perfection. It remains for Granny Moll, a wise, old slave who reveres the aristocratic past, to provide a fitting legend for *The Valley of Shenandoah:* "Now money makes the mare go" (vol. 1, p. 300). In more pacific times, William Byrd could assure his English correspondent Lord Orrery that "half-a-Crown will rest undisturbed in my Pocket for many Moons together."

The reader who comes next to *Woodcraft* (1852) will no doubt feel in William Gilmore Simms's Revolutionary romance the presence of a more accomplished craftsman who has thought deliberately about the relation of history and fiction. In an earlier essay, Simms described the literary artist as "the true historian" and concluded that he alone "unites the parts in coherent dependency, and endows, with life and action, the otherwise motionless automata of history. It is by such artists, indeed, that nations live."[37] By the standards of contemporary American historiography, this was not a bold claim, for George Bancroft and Francis Parkman commonly assimilated the professional historian to the man of letters. His dramatic technique would keep character in view and would thus help to bring "the Past to life upon the printed page."[38] What is more notable (and pertinent to the present study) than Simms's description of the artist-historian is his failure in *Woodcraft* to summon the confidence that his perceived role would necessitate. In composing *Woodcraft,* Simms only imperfectly achieved the "coherent dependency" of parts whereby nations, especially beleaguered ones, continue to "live." *The Valley of Shenandoah* and *Woodcraft* each revolve around dichotomous terms, but in his more urgent pursuit of reconciliation, Simms ironically portrayed a fissure in the southern plantation community that his historical imagination attempted to deny. Even Simms's most dazzling creation, Captain Porgy, late of Marion's Rangers, could only partially obscure the lapse.

Having defended "the cause of liberty in Carolina," Captain Porgy and several other partisans now return to Glen-Eberley, his desolate estate on the Ashepoo River, and resume an agricultural life. The naive Lieutenant Frampton and the efficient Sergeant Millhouse serve as admirable foils for Porgy, whose "huge bulk" is contorted by ill fortune into a pose of jaded hedonism. Staggered by immense debt, Porgy laments, " 'There is little or nothing now that I should live for,' "[39] but Simms intervenes and endows his fainting hero with the "moral resources" (p. 102) needed to empower the major themes of *Woodcraft:* the reclamation of the gentleman planter and the restoration of his plantation to fertility.[40] Both the choice and the imperative nature of these themes reflect Simms's literary situation in South Carolina in 1852. In the 1840s Simms had produced numerous historical and biographical studies of southern subjects that hastened the growth of his sectional identity. Presumably, Harriet Beecher Stowe perfected this process. It is likely that the composition of *Woodcraft* not only "proceeded in full knowledge"[41] of *Uncle Tom's Cabin,* which appeared concurrently in the *National Era,* but also that Simms viewed his latest romance as an answer to this troublesome book. Mrs. Stowe had not launched an indiscriminate attack upon southern life. In the character of Augustine St.

Clare, for example, she recognized its noble intentions but dramatized instead how this essential goodwill was corrupted by the economic tenor of chattel slavery. In 1852 an adequate answer to *Uncle Tom's Cabin* would hinge upon the creation of a plantation community whose ethical structure might plausibly subordinate fiscal expediency to love. Soon after the publication of *Woodcraft*, Simms claimed success in a letter to James Hammond. The book, he decided, was "probably as good an answer to Mrs. Stowe as has been published."[42]

In deploying his characters, Simms used the same contrapuntal form that George Tucker employed in *The Valley of Shenandoah*. Young Arthur Eveleigh is a noble hearted aristocrat whose promise is unlimited but whose discipline remains incomplete. Accordingly, the plain man Fordham must draw upon his ingenuity and practical experience to help Eveleigh survive in a culture still beset by frontier enthusiasm. This none-too-subtle reflection upon class is repeated in the form of the widows Eveleigh and Griffin, who appeal to Porgy for predictable reasons. The fortune of one might discharge his embarrassing debts and thus ensure Porgy's status as a gentleman planter. By contrast, to follow his heart and address the widow Griffin, the bachelor Porgy must stoop to a fairer form without position or money. This is not even a debatable choice for the efficient, if impertinent, Sergeant Millhouse, whose role in *Woodcraft* is to contest the romantic and Falstaffian elements of Porgy's character. It remains for M'Kewn, the rapacious moneylender, to contest a more benevolent trait: Porgy's humane concern as a gentleman for all fellow creatures, especially his beloved slave Tom. This rather mechanical counterpointing not only functioned for Simms as an artistic strategy but also allowed him to represent the facets of a complicated post-Revolutionary society in South Carolina. Reserved for the gentleman, of course, was the role of mediating between plantation and frontier, aristocratic and republican, in 1782. It is, however, important to note that Simms did not abruptly thrust this role upon the unsuspecting gentleman. In biographical studies of

Marion and Greene, he had defined a prudent yet heroic southern leader by whom Captain Porgy could now be measured.[43]

In drawing Porgy, William Gilmore Simms did not merely execute an honorific design. Frequently, his bulk, loquaciousness, and military ardor become objects of satire and create amusing interludes at Porgy's expense. This satire contributes, however, to a deeper candor regarding the past sins of the planter. Only by disowning his "absurd vanities and excesses" (p. 206), twin products of an indolence that has endangered Porgy's material establishment, can he confront the "great black spider" (p. 456) M'Kwen. Porgy's successful contest with his main creditor finally ensures the restoration of Glen-Eberley, but the fictional vehicle employed by Simms inadvertently reveals his unsureness. Earlier in *Woodcraft* Simms had played with the comic image of Porgy as a plethoric cavalier threatening to burst the seams of his finery. But it is only through recourse to "ancient chivalry" (p. 331) that Porgy and his loyal retainers can now frustrate M'Kwen's intention to foreclose upon Glen-Eberley. In imitation of Chevalier Bayard, whose fictional biography Simms published in 1847, they don armor, fortify Glen-Eberley against siege, and thus buy time until M'Kwen can be defeated on more plausible grounds. In using these courtly high jinks, Simms anticipates the dilemma of Mark Twain, who needed the feverish chivalric imagination of Tom Sawyer to end *Huckleberry Finn.* Simms's fond excursion into medieval fantasy may have satisfied his readers' yen for humor and romance, but it diminished the gentleman's newly won ethical seriousness and set plantation life upon an airy foundation. The promise of a Golden Age, reflected in the renewed communal solidarity of Porgy and his neighbors, is not produced by the literary imagination reconciling cultural antagonisms, but by an urgent, arbitrary act of the political will. In returning Simms's correspondence, James Hammond agreed that his friend had "admirably defended our Institution and elevated it in some respects."[44] For predictable reasons, the former governor and soon-to-be senator from South Carolina had not detected the inner strife of William Gilmore Simms which is the true subject of *Woodcraft*.

George Tucker and William Gilmore Simms practiced the same popular romantic fiction, but because they were located respectively in 1824 and 1852, each inherited a different literary situation. When Edward Grayson reflects upon the economic instability of slavery and attributes the indolence of the planter to his willing bondmen, he recapitulates part of a historic dialogue concerning the fitness of slavery that was conducted by contemporary Virginians. A decade later, such flexibility in southern discourse would become infrequent. By the late 1840s, Simms not only recognized but also accepted his role as a spokesman for southern institutions. As William Taylor notes, Simms's historical and biographical writing in the 1840s and 1850s was intended to create a distinctively southern hero who had supported the Revolution for gentlemanly honor rather than for egalitarian principles.[45] His essay on "The Morals of Slavery," published in 1852 as part of *The Pro-Slavery Argument,* linked the harmony of southern political and social life to its unique system of labor. It is not surprising, then, that Simms rejects any association between Porgy's indolence and prodigal habits and the presence of such beloved retainers as Tom. Instead, their destinies are inseparable, even unto death, as Porgy suggests in a remarkable scene of counsel. Rather than submit to the crass ownership of M'Kwen, he urges Tom, " 'Kill yourself. . . . Put your knife into your ribs . . . and you will effectually baffle the blood-hounds!' " (p. 184). Porgy's angelic solution inadvertently measures what a distinguished southern historian has termed the "spiritual stresses and unremitting social tensions"[46] produced by the plantation culture. Faced with the task of creating a usable history for the beleaguered South, William Gilmore Simms had merely temporized in *Woodcraft* by projecting a fiction alight with fantasy. His literary situation differs markedly from George Tucker's, but each writer reveals a profound skepticism regarding the efficacy of southern community. If Beechwood and Glen-Eberley may be thought representative estates, then each manor house encloses a bitter duality of personal and communal motives that only rarely yields harmony.

In view of this dilemma, it is surprising that so many contemporary readers discuss communal values in southern literature as if they were absolute. Frequently, such an assumption forms the rigid backbone of an argument that makes invidious contrasts between northern-international and southern-provincial literature. To follow a fairly recent commentator, the former literature depicts man as "clown, pervert, or martyr, a stranger in a strange land who . . . finds nothing in objects or in other men to which he can relate himself." By contrast, this same "primordial loneliness and fear is missing in all the writing making up the Southern renaissance." Robert Frost and William Faulkner emerge as predictable test cases, and just as predictably the New England spokesman becomes a regionalist manqué who cannot fill with love and solidarity the "desert places" which terrify his people. Sustained by "a genuine culture," Faulkner, however, speaks of "his land in a noble voice . . . , building his art out of the clay of history and the structure of morality with which his land provided him." Certainly, the literature of the Southern Renascence is guided by "a vision of shared human life,"[47] but as the lessons of George Tucker and William Gilmore Simms suggest, it is misleading to imply that the values of place, family, and community (the terms become nearly interchangeable in such discussions) are not affirmed without grave deliberation and inner strife by the southern literary mind. Although experienced on different levels of awareness, this dubiety connects the modern southern writer to older writers of the region by virtue of their common historical attitude. Granny Moll might be allowed her nostalgic preference for the Old Order, and Captain Porgy might be indulged in chivalric resistance to present vulgarity, but from its inception plantation literature has dramatized the latent complexity of William Byrd's epistle to Lord Orrery. His mind protected by the lull before the ideological debates of the

Revolution, Byrd treats effortlessly, if not innocently, questions of community and self that would progressively trouble later generations of plantation writers. Although Eudora Welty does not think of herself "as writing out of any special tradition,"[48] *Delta Wedding* nonetheless inherits the generic blend of sentiment and social attention peculiar to plantation literature. Perhaps (in Ellen Glasgow's phrase) the "congenial hedonism" of the Fairchilds will be tolerated for a brief season, but suspended in the "rosy poetic solution" of which Diana Trilling spoke are the eventual precipitates of the new woman, the new Negro, and the efficient, modern plantation. The resultant tension between the static perfection of the plantation community and the aspiring individual furnishes Shellmound with a set of extreme counterpressures that George Tucker and William Gilmore Simms could have predicted.

7

To H. L. Mencken, the appearance of the flapper in the teens and twenties was a hopeful sign, if only because she might rescue American women from their tremulous, fainting ways. "This flapper," Mencken assured, "has forgotten how to simper; she seldom blushes; it is impossible to shock her. She saw 'Damaged Goods' without batting an eye . . . and plans to read Havelock Ellis during the coming summer."[49] Shelley Fairchild yearns to read *The Beautiful and the Damned,* a daring, contemporary novel that fixed the literary image of the flapper, but judged by Mencken's code or by Fitzgerald's portrait of Gloria Gilbert, she appears on the surface as obsolete as the high ceilings and poor lighting at Shellmound. By turns, Shelley takes things "hard," goes "white," looks "upset," points "a trembling finger," walks "with excruciating slowness," is "pained," is "carried away," and is nearly deprived of "her breath." She thinks "it's so tacky the way Troy comes in from the side door" (p. 205). Why can't old "Hairy Ears," she laments, "just *quit wanting* to marry Dabney!"

106

(p. 201). Her fear of sexual experience is intensified by the current estrangement of Uncle George and his low-born wife, little Robbie Reid, whose "unhesitant" public tears appall Shelley and send her careening down the aisle of the family store in Fairchilds. As Shelley writes in her diary, sitting amid a clutter of girlish impedimenta, she seems an immature version of Aunts Primrose and Jim Allen, southern Norns who have refined the female sensibility until it becomes a tissue of timid gestures.

This disparaging portrait is not entirely untrue, but it does obscure a nascent self which begins to judge more critically the collective life of the Delta and to envision a larger world beyond the boundaries of Shellmound. At first Shelley makes only the briefest, most pedestrian notations in the diary of a young girl living at home and partaking of Delta social life. Soon, however, Shelley is writing "long entries" that explore hidden rooms in the Fairchild mansion of happiness: "all together we have a solid wall, we are self-sufficient against people that come up knocking. . . . Does the world suspect that we are all very private people? I think one by one we're all more lonely than private and more lonely than self-sufficient" (p. 84). Shelley's unexpected wisdom not only evokes a major thematic concern of *Delta Wedding* but also implies that her apparent remoteness from life may be akin to the artist's perspective of detachment and resistance to his culture. If Dabney fulfills the conventions of plantation romance by marrying Troy and occupying Marmion, then tall, flat, "hipless" Shelley remains the antithesis of the traditional belle. She refuses to attend any more female bridge parties, is beginning to find the renowned dancing of the Delta equally tedious, and as a bridesmaid resists the conformity of ritual by holding her shepherdess crook at the wrong angle. Although mild, these expressions of discontent contribute to the aura of departure that surrounds Shelley. In the near future she will travel to Europe on the *Berengaria,* the trip a graduation present from Aunt Tempe, but this departure only portends still longer and more daring journeys of self-discovery. Shelley is not anxious to follow her

sister in a domestic search conducted "from one room to another";
instead, her "desire" will lead beyond "the line of trees at Shellmound" to "an open place" that is beset "with weather—with
change, beauty." The essence of Welty's new woman resides not
in the flapper's brittle smartness but in a more substantial "vision
of choice" (p. 220).

Nearly every page of Welty's novel confirms the historic pre-
ponderance of Negroes in the Mississippi Delta. The Fairchilds
cannot turn around, enter a room, or play an intimate family
scene without encountering Roxie, Little Uncle, Vi'let, Pinchy,
Howard, or Partheny. As a group, they exhibit the presumed
Negro sins of laziness and thievery but more than atone for these
stereotypical flaws by excessively admiring the Fairchilds. Roxie,
the beaming cook at Shellmound, finds little Ranny's precocious
habit of command engaging and thrills at the prospect of Uncle
George, heroically mounted, drinking from a golden flask. Vi'let
pampers the childish Tempe and tells her "how young and pretty
she looked" (p. 106), while Howard, a bumbling, slow-witted
handyman, agrees with the resolute aunt from Memphis that she
would punish harshly if the wedding cake were dropped. Without apparent design, these black retainers adopt the Fairchild
myth of happiness as a personal credo and thus participate eagerly
in the preparations for Dabney's wedding. Their presence at the
ceremony affirms that all the black Fairchilds, from Partheny the
matriarch to the rudest field hand, possess genuine status in the
extended family of Shellmound Plantation.

In 1919 a Negro newspaper in the South rejoiced that "the
'Black Mammy' . . . is going" and wished her "an affectionate
good-by and a long farewell."[50] The same editor would have been
dismayed, no doubt, by her return four years later when old
Partheny, Dabney's nurse, bursts into the bride's room and takes
command in the familiar style of plantation romance. " 'Git yourself here to me, child. Who dressin' you? Git out, Nothin', and
Roxie, Shelley, and Aunt Primrose all came backing out"
(p. 210). This speech must have caused reviewers to wince in

New York in 1946. Indeed, even in the Yazoo Delta in 1923, it might seem a curious evasion of black unrest reflected in mass migration to the North and hotter tempers among those who stayed behind. A brief contrast of two scenes in *Delta Wedding* will suggest, however, that Welty was more aware of contemporary racial turmoil than her readers have understood. During a morning ride to the Grove, Dabney comes upon Man-Son and remembers a tense encounter eight years earlier when he and another scrapping Negro were separated by George Fairchild. A knife flashed, one child was cut, and then both "cried together melodiously" on Uncle George's chest as he swore in exasperation, " 'Damn you both!' " (p. 36). Later in the week of Dabney's wedding, Shelley is sent to find Troy, but she witnesses a more authentic display of black violence in the overseer's office. Nursing an undefined grievance, Root M'Hook vibrates his arm and aims an ice pick at Troy, who fires deliberately and wounds the field hand. " 'Get the nigger out of here. I don't want to lay eyes on him' " (p. 195). In juxtaposition, these scenes provide the language and symbolism to express a profound social truth. George Fairchild, "the very heart of the family" (p. 33), possesses "an incorruptible . . . sweetness" (p. 47); Troy Flavin, a new man in the Delta, knows exactly "how to handle your Negroes" (p. 95). As a corollary, the innocence of Man-Son and his scrapping adversary gives way to the ferocity of Root M'Hook, whose insolence paints the dark underside of the Fairchild myth of happiness and success. Perhaps it is only an accident of the novel's chronology that World War I stands between these encounters, but in point of fact it did establish a watershed in the historic deterioration of Delta race relations.

During World War II, Mississippians could read of still more drastic changes in the ever notable Delta. In October 1944 *Business Week* reported that "mechanical cotton pickers [had recently] moved onto a . . . field . . . near Clarksdale, Miss., to harvest what is believed to be the first commercial cotton acreage ever raised entirely by machinery."[51] With the development of mechanical tilling, planting, cultivating, and now harvesting, the last American staple crop to be managed by hand was adapting to an unfavorable world market and was preparing for postwar competition from rayon and other synthetics. By 1947, David Cohn could observe that the cultivation of "a crop which only yesterday emerged from its pharaonic swathings" now resembled "the conditions of a factory."[52] As Welty has stated, these and related developments were "implicit" in her depiction of plantation culture in *Delta Wedding*. In 1923 the remote world of Shellmound, only recently guarded by primeval swamp and forest, is easily invaded by the urbane wisdom of Anthony Patch, Fitzgerald's languid hero, who soothes "his hypochondriacal imagination" by "reading in bed"; by the immediate, far-reaching communication of the radio, moving pictures, and the telephone, which rings incessantly at Shellmound; and particularly by the motor car roaring off on sudden trips to Greenwood. But it remains for Troy Flavin, the "high-ridin' low-born" (p. 132) overseer of Shellmound Plantation, to project in his person and manner the drastic changes in the plantation that David Cohn, William Alexander Percy, and Eudora Welty could observe in the 1940s.

During the nineteenth century, settlement in the Delta followed a topographical directive to form large plantations, import Negro labor, and plant cotton. In this "society of gentlemen," David Cohn explains, "there was no room and no welcome for the non-slaveholding farmer who . . . might till a few acres."[53] In the hills of northeastern Mississippi, this yeoman and his large family typically practiced a more diverse agriculture, nursed a distrust of the large planter, and voted against his interests. After World War I, however, adverse economic conditions forced a more cooperative relation between these distinctive groups. The hill farmer sought new opportunities as a tenant in the Delta; and the planter, alarmed by the sudden departure of many black workers, not only welcomed him but, as many contemporary newspaper accounts disclose, actively encouraged his settlement. In *Delta Wedding*, Troy's fictional descent from the Tennessee hills coincides with this historic migration. The vigilant overseer from Bear Creek in Tishomingo County brings to the lazy Delta qualities of efficiency and personal initiative. If the kindly, benevolent Battle slumps into a hammock after dispatching his Negroes to labor, then Troy Flavin rides ceaselessly, displaying the capable, industrious air needed to oversee the harvest of Shellmound Plantation. As Shelley realizes, the impulsive, irresponsible Fairchilds form a strong contrast with this canny, enterprising hill man who has come from nowhere to court and marry Dabney. He "likes to size things up" and "is always thinking of ways in or ways out" (p. 85). For his part, Troy is astounded by the gentility that the Fairchilds can summon, but he is not deterred from contemplating radical changes in the plantation economy. With George Fairchild, another progressive, self-reliant defier of the status quo, he envisions a diversification of Delta agriculture, echoing in his homespun way the advice of contemporary regional planners. Troy Flavin's progressive, independent sensibility forms the essence of the new plantation, imbuing the timeless, artless world of Shellmound with a more rigorous dispensation.

In 1946 Eudora Welty wrote from a vantage point that recognized these changes as fulfilled transformations of an outmoded polity, but two decades earlier this process of modern history bearing down upon a traditional society was imminent and thus occasioned a more intense kind of drama. In *Delta Wedding* the element of personal aspiration implied by the emergence of the new woman, the new Negro, and the efficient, modern plantation exists in tense counterpoint with the communal world of Shellmound Plantation. Often, the visitor, Laura McRaven, the upstart, Robbie Reid, or the intruder, Troy Flavin, serves to express this tension, but Welty finally relies upon a more subtle medium in which comedy and tragedy are brilliantly fused. Ironically, it is the poky Yellow Dog train that summarizes the essential conflict of Shellmound Plantation.

Critics often note with interest the spectacle of George Fairchild rescuing his niece from the oncoming Yellow Dog train, but seldom has this enigmatic episode been discussed as a prolonged authorial reflection upon the contending strains of personal expression and communal solidarity. "'Here's the way it was—,'" explains Orrin to an inquisitive Laura. "'Two weeks ago Sunday,'"

> "The whole family but Papa and Mama, and ten or twenty Negroes with us, went fishing in Drowning Lake. . . . And so coming home we walked the track. We were tired—we were singing. On the trestle Maureen danced and caught her foot. . . . Uncle George kneeled down and went to work on Maureen's foot, and the train came. He hadn't got Maureen's foot loose, so he didn't jump either. The rest of us did jump, and the Dog stopped just before it hit them and ground them all to pieces." (p. 19)

By filtering this episode through the sensibility of Ellen, Dabney, Shelley, and Robbie Reid, Welty permits Orrin's sparse, original narration to expand with lyric significance, but this subtle process of enrichment finally strikes a declarative note when George is goaded by his wife Robbie's exception to his heroism. A lawyer who practices in Memphis, George proclaims with forensic flourish the irreducible singularity of his motivation: "'I'm damned if I wasn't going to stand on that track if I wanted to!'" But ironically throughout *Delta Wedding,* his vaunting heroism must contend with a stern counterwill that is expressed on the present occasion by his sister Tempe. "'Ah!'" she declares, "'Doesn't that sound like his brother Denis's very words and voice?'" (p. 187). Her cry of assimilation, or one like it, resounds throughout the successive narrations of Orrin, India, and Roy. Ellen Fairchild alone recognizes a process of attenuation at work as her family weaves the reckless enterprise of George Fairchild into the family history. They "would forever see the stopping of the Yellow Dog entirely after the fact—as a preposterous diversion of their walk . . . , for with the fatal chance removed the serious went with it forever, and only the romantic and absurd abided" (p. 188). In their telling and retelling, in the soft laughter, low moaning, and "outraged puffing" that the tale elicits, the Fairchilds attempt to transform a vivid personal gesture into a communal possession. The enigmatic tableau of George and Maureen facing down the Yellow Dog contains not only the central tension of *Delta Wedding* but also the same problematic intersection of personal and collective wills that preoccupied earlier plantation writers. In its shaping of conflict, *Delta Wedding* thus reveals the pressure of a long historical foreground that periodically erupts with aesthetic significance. A brief analysis of how the distinctive terms of southern history may inform this complex, socially aware literature will prepare for a concluding discussion of Eudora Welty's emerging southern identity and her unique contribution to plantation writing.

8

In order to distinguish between early southern settlement and its New England counterpart, the historian David Bertelson has examined the relative placement and prominence of personal motives in the formation of each community. Prospective New England colonists were not merely adventurers or entrepreneurs but "lovers of the common good" who, having examined their hearts, accepted a call to labor willingly in the New World. According to Bertelson, their chief work was to build an orderly society whose outward forms consisting of towns, churches, and pious commerce would attest to the inner bonds of love and mutual dependence. If (as the Reverend John White observed in 1630 in *The Planter's Plea*) "callings are employments in which we serve one another through love,"[54] then wealth cannot properly serve as an inducement to emigrate or even as a desired effect of personal labor. Following Perry Miller's study of *The New England Mind* (1937), Bertelson concludes that by the terms of the Puritan covenant with God, the fruits of economic pursuit could be no more than "a sign of moral worthiness."[55]

If the prospect of wealth threatened social unity by fomenting "pride, wantonness, and contention" in the New England community, then the doctrine of allurement peculiar to southern settlement boldly transported personal economic motives into the center of God's design. In his ode "To the Virginian Voyage," Michael Drayton urged Britons not to "lurk here at home" but "to seek fame" in Virginia, "Earth's only paradise," where a temperate climate and "the fruitful'st soil" conspired to produce "without your toil" harvests of surpassing bounty. As David Bertelson has shown in *The Lazy South,* the enticement of Englishmen to this "delicious land" was not accomplished without impressive theological reflection. Edwin Sandys, Archbishop of York and father of a controversial officer of the Virginia Company, reasoned that "with rough commandments" God "joineth oftentimes sweet allurements . . . not enticing men with fair and sweet words only, but pouring His benefits also plentifully upon them." In 1609 William Symonds likened the colonization of Virginia to settlement of Canaan by Abraham's descendents. Each people had been called by the law to possess a rich land; that "the Lord doth allure men to keep it by the abundance of His blessings"[56] neither compromised the divine conscience nor excused men from forming and realizing in the New World distinctly social goals. Indeed, it was the assumption of these and other "attractionists" who celebrated the natural wealth of Virginia that by ensuring personal economic freedom, men would be stimulated to work and thus create a strong cooperative society. In Michael Drayton's words, one could "get the pearl and gold" while serving God and the larger common good as well.

Both Puritan New England and Virginia were conceived as covenant societies, but as David Bertelson's careful analysis reveals, the definition of each agreement with God had profound repercussions upon the actual course of development. The heightened Puritan sense of calling and social responsibility produced (in Perry Miller's terms) "a slow and almost imperceptible evolution" whereby "the Massachusetts Zion was subtly transformed into a mercantile society." By contrast, Virginia passed through the same "cycle of exploration, religious dedication, disillusionment, and then reconciliation to a world in which making a living was the ultimate reality"[57] at a much accelerated pace. This rapidity of transformation should not be allowed, however, to obscure the intense, inherent drama of the southern covenant. Documents pertinent to the colonization of Virginia both betray a lively interest in profit and contain frequent animadversions upon the "careless negligence" of rulers and upon such "miserable covetous men" as only "dream of greater ease and licentiousness." As David Bertelson explains, "the leaders of the Virginia Company wanted their undertaking to be profitable" and "they also wanted to establish a commonwealth in America,"[58] but the record of early Virginia, marked especially by its alternate encouragement and disapproval of tobacco production, shows that personal ambition and social development were seldom reconciled by the doctrine of allurement. The Puritan culture was given to severe internal conflict, as the antinomian crises of seventeenth-century New England attest, but by elevating and sanctioning the acquisitive motive, the southern covenant ensured a still more acute confrontation between the personal and communal realms. The resultant sense of extremity finds no better testimony than the perplexity of an early writer who saw "plenty and famine, a temperate climate and distempered bodies, felicities and miseries," in Virginia and wondered how they "can be reconciled together."[59] A modern observer of the still paradoxical South, "seedbed" of "New South and Old, Cavalier and Yankee, genteel and savage," advises that the historian "investigate the possibility that some obscure dialectic may be at work in the pairing of obverse images."[60] Surely, one might look with confidence to the unique terms of southern settlement for the locus of such ambiguity, but promising as this direction may be, more immediate goals must be pursued on the basis of the foregoing brief and undoubtedly facile differentiation of regional cultures.

As described in an earlier section, one notable attempt to examine Welty's southern character ended in illogic because the critic adopted a doubtful biographical premise. Perhaps now, though, sufficient materials have been gathered to make a more substantial contribution to this considerably difficult undertaking. In Welty's first three volumes of fiction, the conflict occasioned by the individual confronting a larger external authority marked each decisive point in the elaboration of her Mississippi chronicle. The resultant drama, however, lacked a distinctive regional bias, save what might be attributed to the superficial localism of southern speech, place names, and topography. Such hastily composed fictional towns as Victory, Mississippi, and Farr's Gin were little more than stylized shells needed to contain the ensuing action. In *Delta Wedding,* though, Eudora Welty was led progressively deeper into the distinctively southern roots of her vision through the conventions of plantation romance. Every aspect of daily life at Shellmound is richly conceived and extravagantly illustrated, producing an impression of place which is inseparable from consciousness. Troy Flavin's diversification of Delta agriculture, for example, will no doubt prove beneficial, but it will also endanger metaphors of the mind derived from King Cotton. By adopting the plantation as locale and mythos, Welty also achieved a second and still more decisive effect. At Shellmound the aspiration of the individual and the concomitant needs of the community are projected with greater intensity because they now partake of a literary tradition that has preserved and interpreted the central dilemma of southern history. In recalling the china night-light of her youth, Welty noted that "the outside was painted with a scene which is one thing; then, when the lamp is lighted, through the porcelain sides a new picture comes out through the old, and they are seen as one." In *Delta Wedding* the force that lights the lamp of Eudora Welty's imagination is the perennial dilemma of southern history.

9

Often the effect of this dilemma upon the professional historical literature has been to produce such essentially selective writers as Kenneth Stampp and Eugene Genovese. In *The Peculiar Institution*

(1956), Stampp traces the "spiritual stresses and unremitting social tensions" of the Old South to its mercantile philosophy. The "organizational complexity" of the antebellum plantation approached that of "modern factories," while planters "had the businessman's interest in maximum production without injury to their capital." In *The World the Slaveholders Made* (1969), Genovese argues that the same slave system, although "capitalist in its origins," developed into "a way of life, a home, a community":

> The distinctly Southern sense of extended family cannot be understood apart from the social structure at the center of which stood the plantation, and it provided a powerful impetus for social cohesion, ruling-class hegemony, and the growth of a paternalistic spirit that far transcended master-slave and white-black relationships.[61]

Although each recognizes the existence of some diversity in the culture, Stampp and Genovese are essentially selective historians, viewing the South from only one side of the complex of ambivalent attitudes represented by early descriptions of Virginia. Ironically, it is the plantation novel, often popular in rhetorical address and sentimental in execution, that has represented more faithfully the tense intersection of personal and communal motives which forms the basis of southern distinctiveness. But like the observer of extreme "felicities and miseries" in early Virginia, the later plantation writer invariably fails to see how similar distortions in his culture "can be reconciled together." Neither Edward Grayson nor Captain Porgy can satisfy the demand for a southern leader who is at once complete and convincing. Essentially the same dubiety marks *The Deliverance* (1904), Ellen Glasgow's most important contribution to the literature of the plantation. The scion of a dilapidated aristocratic family, Christopher Blake experiences the adversity of hard labor during Reconstruction, but this severe personal discipline cannot banish the essential aristocrat in him, betraying a vein of sentimental pride in Ellen Glasgow's innately ironic disposition. In *Delta Wedding* Eudora Welty's ambivalence is, however, more deliberately controlled, permitting her to endow the plantation novel with unaccustomed resolution of its historic tensions. This unique task of mediation is entrusted to Ellen Fairchild, the efficient mistress of Shellmound Plantation.

As Francis Pendleton Gaines observes in *The Southern Plantation,* the mistress of the literary plantation was cast as a "busy and unselfish woman" whose "domestic efficiency"[62] contrasts sharply with the planter's laxity. Welty's intention both to observe and to expand this conventional role is conveyed by her treatment of an early detail in the characterization of Ellen Fairchild. She detects errors in the plantation payroll, not by laborious accounting, but by dreaming "the location of mistakes . . . that her husband . . . had let pass" (p. 65). Thereafter, Ellen's consciousness is consistently enhanced until it becomes the most discriminating force in *Delta Wedding.* Still something of an "anomaly" at Shellmound, this transplanted Virginian is an especially acute observer of the family's collective, importuning ways as they impinge upon the individual. "She loved George," for example, "too dearly herself to seek her knowledge of him through the family attitude" (p. 26) and, as already noted, foresees the reduction of his "near-calamity on the trestle" to "just a little story in the family" (p. 221). Her "anxiety" (p. 126) for George and for the importuning Fairchilds is released, however, during the remarkable scene of Dabney's wedding and reception. It assembles the extended family of Shellmound, white and black, near kin and distant, including finally "everybody for miles around." The Delta myth of inexhaustible bounty pervades the vast preparations, while the Fairchild legend of happiness guides "gawking and giggling" Negroes, unruly "boys in white suits," and preening bridesmaids through their frantic exertions in "the callingest house" in the Delta. After the ceremony itself, which is accomplished in a brief sentence, "the whole Delta" reverts to its habitual expression of social enjoyment. The dancers cover "the downstairs" and then move "outdoors" to begin a "performance of glory" whose deepest effect is reserved for Ellen. "She peered ahead with a kind of vertigo," seeking each of her daughters, but "they all looked alike, all dancers alike smooth and shorn." First chastened by similitude, Ellen is next redeemed by a vision lurking "in a turn of . . . India's skirt as she ran partnerless through the crowd": "as if a bar of light had broken a glass into a rainbow she saw the dancers become the McLeoud bridesmaid, Mary Lamar Mackey . . . , become Robbie, and her own daughter Shelley, each . . . more different and further apart than the stars." It is at this point that George too appears "among the dancers," and as he approaches Ellen, is rendered "wholly singular and dear" (pp. 221–222) in her imagination. Examined closely, Ellen's perception of her daughters and George *within* this rich communal gathering releases the tension between family and self by affirming the paradoxical relations of diversity and oneness. Just as the shaft of light discloses all the separate colors of the rainbow within the prism, so Ellen's poetic imagination discerns the inviolable self moving at ease within the Fairchild enterprise.

Ellen Fairchild's reconciliation of self and family brings to the plantation novel an unaccustomed relaxation of its bitter duality, one that is achieved by imaginative seeking rather than an urgent act of the political will, but the ultimate source of her vision affords still deeper understanding of Welty's unique relationship with this distinctively southern body of literature. As summarized in chapter 1, nineteenth-century plantation literature dramatizes a painful "new historical consciousness" of the South's "provincial limitations" and diminished national significance after 1820. Only the memory of a golden time, be it Simms's pre-Revolutionary Carolina, Tucker's "sunny" Williamsburg a generation later, or Page's antebellum Virginia, could provide ample solace for the benighted present and still more unpromising future. By temper, then, the literature of the plantation adopts a thesis of decline and fall that is relieved only by the memory of a static moment of perfection. That *Delta Wedding* possesses a different attitude toward time and historical process will not surprise readers who can place this novel within Welty's

Mississippi chronicle. Again Ellen Fairchild's point of view is the most discriminating.

During the week-long preparations, Ellen is in constant touch with the remote Fairchild past, using Great-Aunt Mashula's recipes and preparing her wedding train for Dabney. Ellen also tells the comic story of Shelley's birth, one that "wouldn't wait," and, in the nearer past, recalls the death of Laura's mother in the preceding January. During the extended scene of Dabney's wedding and reception, an "old story" (p. 199) that seems to defy novelty, Ellen alone remains sensitive to "time going by." She feels "a touch, today perhaps the first touch, of fall" (p. 198) in the air, notices with some consternation that Orrin is beginning to "look like a man" (p. 208), and for the wedding picture holds "some slightly wilted" flowers "in front of her skirt" (p. 217). When news of a young girl's violent death intrudes upon the reception, as it does upon Mrs. Dalloway's party in similar circumstances, Ellen has "a vision of fate" (p. 218). Significantly, however, this is the same lost girl, discovered earlier by Ellen in the deep bayou woods, whose radiant beauty had revealed to her "a whole mystery of life" (p. 70). Ellen's memory of this encounter now enables her to discover within "fate" a timeless consolation. After Dabney and Troy return from a brief wedding trip, the family prepares for a picnic on a nearby bend of the Yazoo River. Lulled into meditation by the "rhythm" of the wagon, Ellen realizes that "one moment was enough for you to know the greatest thing." "The repeating fields, the repeating cycles of season and her own life—there was something in the monotony itself that was beautiful, rewarding— . . . They rolled on and on. It was endless. The wheels rolled, but nothing changed" (p. 240). In the course of her meditation, Ellen Fairchild has achieved the same paradoxical vision of permanence and change that Clement Musgrove, another thoughtful Virginian, discovered in the ancient forest. Her imaginative intensity not only makes Ellen an appropriate vessel for Welty's historical aesthetic but also imbues the plantation romance with a more complex attitude toward time and historical reality than it typically possessed. *Delta Wedding* will neither revere the past unduly nor lament the present because it understands that even drastic change cannot alter the essential continuity of experience. Ellen Fairchild's reconciliation of self and family is, then, an inevitable expression of a still deeper metaphysical unity which pervades *Delta Wedding.* On a ceremonial level, it is dramatized through the marriage of Dabney and Troy, whose individualism has been sealed into the Fairchilds' communal life, but this unity reaches down through strata of social and economic significance to touch an overall natural design. It is one marked with futurity, too, for as Welty subtly reminds us throughout *Delta Wedding,* Ellen Fairchild, mother of seven, is again to give birth.

Notes to Chapter 3

1. Anthony C. Hilfer, *The Revolt from the Village: 1915–1930* (Chapel Hill: University of North Carolina Press, 1969), pp. 3, 25–27. I am indebted to Hilfer's fine study both for source and background material and for his shaping of a "rubric of historical criticism" that is most pertinent to Welty's fiction.

2. George Brown Tindall, *The Ethnic Southerners* (Baton Rouge: Louisiana State University Press, 1976), p. xi.

3. "The Southern Imagination," moderator William F. Buckley (Columbia, S.C.: Firing Line, 1972), p. 7. Transcription of television broadcast, 24 December 1972.

4. Ruth M. Vande Kieft, *Eudora Welty* (New York: Twayne, 1962), pp. 19–21.

5. Linda Kuehl, "The Art of Fiction XLVII: Eudora Welty," *Paris Review* 55 (fall 1972), p. 86.

6. "The New Provincialism" (1945), in *Essays of Four Decades* (Chicago: Swallow, 1968), pp. 545–46.

7. See Edmund Wilson, "William Faulkner's Reply to the Civil Rights Program," review of *Intruder in the Dust, New Yorker,* 23 October 1948, pp. 120–22, 125–28, and Eudora Welty to the Editor, *New Yorker,* 1 January 1949, pp. 50–51.

8. See Richard Gilman, review of *The Surface of Earth* by Reynolds Price, *New York Times Book Review,* 29 June 1975, pp. 1–2, and Eudora Welty to the Editor, *New York Times Book Review,* 20 July 1975, pp. 24–25.

9. *Place in Fiction* (New York: House of Books, 1957), p. 2.

10. "How I Write," *Virginia Quarterly Review* 31 (winter 1955), p. 243.

11. Welty to the Editor, *New Yorker,* p. 51.

12. Welty to the Editor, *New York Times Book Review,* p. 24.

13. *Place in Fiction,* p. 7.

14. "How I Write," p. 251.

15. Quotation follows the text of Byrd's letter reprinted in *Southern Writing: 1585–1920,* ed. Richard Beale Davis, C. Hugh Holman, and Louis D. Rubin, Jr. (New York: Odyssey, 1970), p. 112.

16. David M. Potter, "The Enigma of the South," *Yale Review* 51 (autumn 1961), p. 142.

17. Peggy W. Prenshaw first identified the locale of *Delta Wedding* in "Cultural Patterns in Eudora Welty's *Delta Wedding* and 'The Demonstrators,'" *Notes on Mississippi Writers* 3 (fall 1970), p. 69.

18. *Jackson Daily News,* 28 November 1922, p. 8.

19. *Jackson Daily News,* 30 July 1923, p. 4.

20. *Jackson Daily News,* 13 June 1923, p. 6.

21. *Jackson Daily News,* 6 March 1923, p. 5.

22. Kuehl, pp. 85, 92.

23. David L. Cohn, *Where I Was Born and Raised* (Boston: Houghton Mifflin, 1948), p. 12.

24. Charles T. Bunting, "'The Interior World': An Interview with Eudora Welty," *Southern Review* 8 (October 1972), p. 718, and "The Dick Cavett Show," PBS, 24 May 1978.

25. *Jackson Daily News,* 18 November 1923, p. 11.

26. Cohn, pp. 26, 41–42.

27. Cohn, p. 229.

28. Cohn, p. 250.

29. William Alexander Percy, *Lanterns on the Levee: Recollections of a Planter's Son* (New York: Knopf, 1941), p. 24.

30. Bunting, p. 722.

31. Ibid.

32. Diana Trilling, "Fiction in Review,"*Nation,* 11 May 1946, p. 578.

33. John Crowe Ransom, "Delta Fiction," *Kenyon Review* 8 (summer 1946), p. 507.

34. George Tucker, *The Valley of Shenandoah; or, Memoirs of the Graysons,* ed. Donald R. Noble, Jr., Southern Literary Classics Series (1824; reprint ed., Chapel Hill: University of North Carolina Press, 1970), vol. 1, pp. 60–61. Subsequent page references are noted parenthetically in the text.

35. Quoted by Jay B. Hubbell, *The South in American Literature: 1607–1900* (Raleigh: Duke University Press, 1954), p. 248.

36. Letter of Simms to William Elliott, 7 March 1849. Quoted by Louis D. Rubin, Jr., *William Elliott Shoots a Bear: Essays on the Southern Literary Imagination* (Baton Rouge: Louisiana State University Press, 1975), p. 23.

37. *Views and Reviews in American Literature, History and Fiction,* First Series (1846). Quoted by John C. Guilds, "Simms's Use of History: Theory and Practice," *Mississippi Quarterly* 30 (fall 1977), p. 506.

38. See David Levin, *History as Romantic Art* (Stanford: Stanford University Press, 1959), p. 8.

39. William Gilmore Simms, *Woodcraft; or, Hawks about the Dovecote,* rev. ed. (Chicago: Belford, Clarke, 1888), p. 54. Subsequent page references are included parenthetically in the text.

40. My treatment of Simms is indebted primarily to Roger J. Bresnahan, "William Gilmore Simms's Revolutionary War: A Romantic View of Southern History," *Studies in Romanticism* 15 (fall 1976), pp. 573–87, John C. Guilds, "Simms's Use of History," *Mississippi Quarterly* 30 (fall 1977), pp. 505–11, and William R. Taylor, *Cavalier and Yankee* (New York: George Braziller, 1961), pp. 270–97.

41. Joseph V. Ridgely, "*Woodcraft:* Simms's First Answer to *Uncle Tom's Cabin,*" *American Literature* 31 (January 1960), p. 422.

42. Quoted in ibid., p. 423.

43. Consult Bresnahan, pp. 575–77, for an excellent discussion of Simms's elaboration of the ideal southern leader.

44. Quoted by Ridgely, p. 423.

45. Consult Taylor, p. 297.

46. Kenneth M. Stampp, *The Peculiar Institution: Slavery in the Ante-Bellum South* (New York: Vintage, 1956), p. 3.

47. Louise Cowan, "The Communal World of Southern Literature," *Georgia Review* 14 (fall 1960), pp. 248–54.

48. Kuehl, p. 85.

49. Henry F. May, *The End of American Innocence: A Study of the First Years of Our Own Time, 1912–1917* (New York: Knopf, 1959), p. 339.

50. George B. Tindall, *The Emergence of the New South: 1913–1945, A History of the South* (Baton Rouge: Louisiana State University Press, 1967), vol. 10, p. 156.

51. *Business Week,* 21 October 1944, p. 54.

52. Cohn, pp. 317–18, 327.

53. Cohn, p. 27.

54. David Bertelson, *The Lazy South* (New York: Oxford University Press, 1967), p. 40.

55. Bertelson, p. 9.

56. Bertelson, pp. 9, 38.

57. Bertelson, p. 43.

58. Bertelson, pp. 21–22, 26.

59. Bertelson, p. 20.

60. Tindall, *The Ethnic Southerners,* p. 41.

61. Stampp, pp. 3, 42, 78, and Eugene Genovese, *The World the Slaveholders Made* (New York: Vintage, 1969), pp. 28, 100–101.

62. Francis Pendleton Gaines, *The Southern Plantation,* Studies in English and Comparative Literature (New York: Columbia University Press, 1925), p. 177.

4

The South and Beyond, 1946–1972

IN *Delta Wedding* Eudora Welty's chronicle is nearly obscured by the subtlety of her method. Only by gathering and composing the scattered artifacts of Shellmound Plantation can this mute actor be made to speak its part and thus to deliver the family history whole and entire, not to the present generation of Fairchilds, for they are still too antic and self-confident to be attentive, but to the reader who has labored diligently with this extended evocation of the past. In its circling motion, Welty's lyrical method endows the relics of history with layers of significance, not only revealing the outline of the past but also probing its quintessential human dimension. In their projection of aspiration and defeat, the portrait of old Battle astride Florian, Mashula's etching on the windowpane, Marmion "hypnotized" on the surface of the Yazoo, and now George Fairchild exposed to the Yellow Dog bespeak a timeless vulnerability, each image asking in effect why life is so inexplicable. In responding to this mystery, Ellen Fairchild confronts and momentarily defeats the same prowling "beast" of change that Clement Musgrove witnessed in the forest, "softly and forever moving into profile." Her fertile imagination holds in suspension polarities which may be variously expressed as cyclic and linear time, stasis and process, community and self. That her consciousness can resist the unwanted authority of the plantation legend is firm tribute to the sureness of Welty's historicism.

When the curve of Eudora Welty's long career finds completion, the inevitable sorting and revaluing of texts will probably fix *Delta Wedding* as her superlative achievement. The most compelling evidence will be textual, for in this beautifully conceived and exquisitely executed work of art, pace, texture, structure, and point of view conspire to produce the novel's intense illusion of reality. But the prominence of *Delta Wedding* will also reflect its pivotal character in determining the shape and direction of Welty's Mississippi chronicle. In a strictly sequential way, *Delta Wedding* completes the first loop of Welty's annal, linking the present life of *A Curtain of Green* with the earlier epochs of *The Robber Bridegroom* and *The Wide Net.* Throughout, Welty's story of the individual confronting a larger external authority forms the crux of her vision, but in *Delta Wedding* the resultant tension is comprehended in distinctively southern terms. The deep ambivalence of motive which accompanies southern settlement flows into the literary plantation and is only partially diverted by the myth of a Golden Age into little pools of nostalgia. Shellmound partakes of the same bitter duality that inhabits Beechwood and Glen-Eberley. Infinitely alluring, the dense, plausible life of the Fairchilds is a direct consequence of its authentic cultural source in the prime dilemma of southern history. The books and stories which follow *Delta Wedding,* although composed in the wavering moods and circumstances of a quarter century of writing, betray in their southern phrasing the formative influence of this pivotal volume. The ensuing segment of Welty's chronicle, which moves from the 1930s into the postwar scene of casual air travel, superhighways, and racial demonstrations, continues to organize such elusive texts as *The Golden Apples* (1949), *Losing Battles* (1970), and *The Optimist's Daughter* (1972) into a substantial treatment of actual life. Paradoxically, the most direct conceptual approach to these contemporary stories lies through "The Burning," Eudora Welty's only foray into Civil War fiction. First published in the *New Yorker* in 1951 and then revised for *The Bride of the Innisfallen* (1955), "The Burning" can help to construct an adequate category of historical understanding for the last phase of Welty's chronicle.

2

In "The Burning" Welty fulfills many conventional expectations derived from the persistent genre of Civil War writing. Red-eyed

Yankee troopers turn off the Vicksburg Road, pass under a predictable canopy of mossy cedars, and neglect to dismount before confronting the sisters Myra and Theo in their finely appointed parlor. With Brother Benton off fighting and Father "mercifully" dead, unprotected southern womanhood proves vulnerable, but her aristocratic hauteur brings into high relief the coarse Yankee sensibility. As the action progresses, once-contented slaves are deterred from duty by a riotous freedom, and amid scenes of rape and plunder, the family silver is appropriated, foodstuffs greedily eaten, and Rose Hill burned in a final wrenching of republican zeal. Rather than submit to the new order, which promises to be vulgar, Miss Myra and Miss Theo hang themselves by suspending hammock cords from a pecan tree. Their slave girl Delilah lingers to ponder the ashes of a fallen culture before crossing the Big Black River to an indeterminate freedom. Perhaps it was inevitable that Welty submit to this enticing genre, especially after depicting plantation life in *Delta Wedding,* but the apparent homage paid to its more florid conventions is neither uncritical nor lacking her unique historical imprint. Welty's assimilation, selection, and treatment of the burning of Jackson and the fall of Vicksburg culminate in her identification of the most perplexing issues of southern historiography: distinctiveness and continuity.

Contemporary observers living along the Vicksburg Road in 1863 would recognize the historical accuracy of "The Burning." Like those of the fictional Myra and Theo, their "grand" fields had been burned off to prevent foraging and their tempers frayed by the oppressively hot, dry conditions that prevailed in the summer of 1863. Almost certainly, they too "were all so tired of" the acrid smoke (*CS,* p. 483) that drifted first from Vicksburg during Grant's siege and later from Jackson when Sherman's expeditionary forces burned that capital for the second time in three months. Early in 1863, Jackson had still afforded "good society"[1] for members of the Fourteenth Mississippi Infantry, who thronged such festive establishments as the Old Bowman House, but now in July, Jackson was "all chimneys, all scooped out." The dismay of Myra and Theo, who walk its ashen streets "naming and claiming ruin for ruin" (*CS,* p. 487), is reflected in the diary of a northern officer: "I never saw or heard of a city being so thoroughly sacked and burned as this place. It is indeed a great pity that so fine a city should be so destroyed."[2] Less sensitive troopers fanning out from Jackson would be recognized in the "clawed, mosquito-racked" soldiers (*CS,* p. 482) who jeer Myra and Theo and then burn Rose Hill, giving fictional substance to General Sherman's report of July 18 that "the land is devastated for 30 miles around"[3] Jackson. In her memoir Varina Howell Davis extolls the valor of Confederate troops who surrendered to Grant and Sherman only after suffering the most extreme deprivations of siege warfare. Special praise, though, is reserved for the proud women of this once-prosperous region who endured the epochal summer of 1863. They "nursed the sick and wounded," "ate mule and horse meat," and "rendered every other service that brave and tender women learn to perform in the hour of danger."[4] Perhaps they confirmed in this crucible what Miss Theo had "always suspicioned" about herself: "that I'm brave as a lion" (*CS,* p. 491).

As one critic notes, Eudora Welty's historical "facts are all in order"[5] in"The Burning," but they remain inert until we grasp the signal military significance of this phase of the War between the States. This war, Lincoln stated in 1861, "can never be brought to a close until that key [Vicksburg] is in our pocket. . . . We may take all the northern ports of the Confederacy and they can still defy us from Vicksburg."[6] Two years later, Grant massed his troops on the west bank of the Mississippi, crossed the river below Vicksburg, and on May 1, 1863, began the arduous campaign that would defeat the Confederates at Port Gibson, Raymond, Jackson, and the Big Black River, forcing the discouraged survivors to seek the illusory shelter of Vicksburg. Southern leadership was not blind to the present extremity. Jefferson Davis and Secretary of War Seddon attempted to rouse their generals, counseling "that it *were better to fail nobly daring, than, through prudence even, to be inactive,*" but after forty-seven days of siege, the metaphorical key fell into Lincoln's pocket. His southern counterpart addressed to General Johnston a bitter epistle of criticism reflecting the damaged southern cultural prospect. "Now that Vicksburg has disastrously fallen," Davis concluded with irony, the campaign's sorry record of insubordination, inactivity, and strategic blundering could be leisurely rehearsed.[7] For military historians, the events of July 1863 "mark a decided epoch in the war." Before, "the amount of success is rather in favor of the Confederates," but with the fall of Vicksburg and the burning of Jackson, control of the Mississippi Department passed to the Federals, and with it the last tie binding the two halves of the Confederacy had been severed. Slavery, the presumable catalyst of war, "received its death-blow"[8] at Vicksburg. In *So Red the Rose* (1934), it is not an accident of the novel's chronology that the illness and death of Malcolm Bedford, Stark Young's quintessential southern planter, coincides metaphorically with the protracted siege and fall of Vicksburg. It is no more an accident of chronology or propinquity that Eudora Welty has chosen the same epochal time as the historical center of "The Burning."

This process of assimilation and selection confirms again the accurate, keen nature of Welty's historical imagination, but only by studying her fictional treatment of this climactic moment in the ruin of the Old South can "The Burning" be aligned conceptually with the last phase of her chronicle. In "The Burning" Welty resists creating the same kind of mature, discerning point of view that had been granted Clement Musgrove and Ellen Fairchild. In their narrow consciousness, Myra and Theo are poignant prototypes for several generations of unreconstructed southern literary ladies, while their slave Delilah can summon only the most elementary response to the catastrophe that rocks her world. Welty also prevents the development of a dramatic point of view by obscuring scene, action, and lineage as they relate to Phinny, her Jim Bond, who perishes in the burning of

128

Rose Hill. Presumably a mulatto scion of the family, Phinny may be the son of Brother Benton and Delilah, although this misalliance is not confirmed by any reliable voice in "The Burning." His actual presence and fate are presented obliquely as well, evoked by such metonymous devices as a cup tumbling down the stairs and a bellow which signals his death in the flames of Rose Hill. At least one commentator is disturbed by this "strange, perverse-seeming narrative technique" which propounds "unnecessary ambiguity" and creates minds that are "incapable of . . . moral comprehension." But instead of resisting the "weirdly diffused, muted"[9] effect of "The Burning," the more tolerant reader will sense deliberation in Welty's fictional treatment and will adjust to her deflection of historic materials from a personal, dramatic course into a more impersonal medium. Chiefly a parable of the Old South, "The Burning" seeks to define a distinctive local culture and to address the related question of its continuity in the face of drastic historical change.

Frequently, Civil War writing has served the interests of party or section, but in "The Burning" Welty declines such poles of allegiance to project dispassionately the outer and inner shape of a unique culture. Its material reality is conveyed by images of architectural solidity, the spacious confines of Rose Hill itself; of quotidian life, the "beds, tables, candlesticks, washstands, [and] cedar buckets" carried from the doomed house; of economic productivity, the "grand," though now "worthless" (*CS*, pp. 486–487), cotton fields; and finally leisure and social privilege, Myra recumbent in the hammock or reading one of Papa's books in the summerhouse. Together, these images convey the same kind of habitual life that T. S. Eliot, a sympathetic observer of the South, designated traditional in *After Strange Gods.*[10] Its metaphysical reality, although less tangible than the material establishment of Myra and Theo's antebellum world, is also suggestively defined in the course of "The Burning." Identity, for example, is bound up with place. When the Yankees "come with orders to set the house afire," they balk at the further enormity of "burning up people's," but Theo answers with a logic borne of her rootedness: " 'I see no degree.' " Later, when Delilah is raped by the same righteous soldiers, she screamed "loudest" for herself, "who was lost now—carried out of the house, not knowing how to get back" (*CS,* p. 485). Economic factors in the form of slavery also contribute to identity and thus further reveal the inner shape of this distinctive southern culture. Upon closer examination, the apparent gaps in psychological development and character motivation that disturb Welty's critics may assume cultural significance, reflecting in part Thomas Jefferson's opinion that chattel slavery impaired the moral sense in all classes touched by its "unhappy influence." Silently, inexorably, Theo's "unremitting despotism" and Delilah's "degrading submissions"[11] coincide to permit the betrayal of Phinny, the hidden ethical center of "The Burning." His abandonment to the flames is a paradigm of the Old South's fear of racial admixture and the evil of slavery in abrogating family relationships.

In "The Burning" Eudora Welty evokes both the material and the metaphysical reality of a distinctive culture, but she recognizes as well the related question of continuity in the face of disruptive historical events. Her response may be defined by considering a very unlikely, although finally relevant, literary source. The editor of *Jackson Today,* a glossy brochure designed to promote Mississippi's capital city, depicts "The Golden 70's" as "Boom!!" and assures prospective investors that this "City of Tomorrow" stands ready "to accept the Challenge of the future." In 1970 the admission was tacit but clear enough. Jackson's long heritage of racial bitterness, culminating in the sordid spectacle of the 1960s, has been outlived, if not forgotten, by a progressive city whose self-proclaimed "history is now." Even its arch-enemy has been excused: "little did Ole General Sherman know that the flames he kindled when he burned Jackson would light the fires of its people to build a New South."[12] If Welty ever perused this brochure, she would not have been surprised by its local bragging, for this is the prerogative of booster narrative. Potentially more disturbing, though, and alien to the spirit of "The Burning" is the editorial assumption that tragic history can be easily ameliorated or, still better, made to appear discontinuous with the present and thus irrelevant to the future.

In presenting the culture of Miss Myra and Miss Theo, Welty never wavers in her conviction that it must bow to temporal necessity. This stern dictation can be inferred alone from Welty's selection of a wrenching moment in the fortunes of the Old South, but the inevitability of loss is reinforced as well by seasonally portentous imagery which marks each sister for doom. Thus the smoke from Vicksburg and Jackson carries a "prophecy of fall." The autumnal suggestion clings to Myra, combs "caught like leaves" in her "bright gold" hair; and to Theo, rustling in her abrupt movement like "clothes through winter quiet" (*CS,* pp. 483–484). Their suicide may begin as a gesture of defiance, but it is conducted in a field of butterflies, Welty's familiar signature of contingency and brief temporal forms. If the procedure were not so impertinent, it would be revealing to measure the chasm separating Welty and the collective voice of *Jackson Today* in their estimation of man's tragic potential. What can be pursued more plausibly is their respective historiographical attitude toward social change. *Jackson Today* speaks of a "Southern heritage" tempering the city's "dynamic growth," but the image of "Ole General Sherman" stripped of his thunder betrays the conception of an essentially static, unliving past. Only a melodramatic, marketable continuity of Old and New Souths can be tolerated. In "The Burning" the apocalyptic white horse which stamps in the parlor admits neither of denial nor improvement. By contrast, it enforces a tragic history which gives poignance and substance to Theo's cry of continuity: "'Remember this,'" she intoned, "as the blaze outdid them all" (*CS,* p. 487). Although her object of concern is local and immediate, Theo's admonition reverberates throughout the Welty canon, evoking the failed memorists of *A Curtain of Green,* but anticipating especially the work of historical recovery performed by Virgie Rainey in *The*

Golden Apples and most consummately by Laurel McKelva in *The Optimist's Daughter*. Memory, these later volumes will affirm, is not a storehouse of dead images but the force which discovers continuity within change.

By identifying July 1863 as another "precipitous moment," Welty further details her Mississippi chronicle. "The Burning" explores in depth a time of tragic southern history which is only suggested by the image of Mashula Hines etched on the window-pane as she awaits the return of George Fairchild from the Civil War. "The Burning" also reveals the same structural conformation that has marked each juncture in the elaboration of Welty's chronicle. Subject to vast, unyielding forces of modernity, Myra and Theo share the historic dilemma of Clement Musgrove, the reluctant pioneer, of the more intrepid Aaron Burr, and of the young girl of "A Memory," who observes a contemporary battle-ground in Livingston Park. A still more important contribution to this record can be discerned in the heightened cultural awareness which informs "The Burning." In its selection of sub-ject matter, "The Burning" reflects the primary lesson of *Delta Wedding* that the plantation was still aesthetically feasible, not-withstanding use and misuse by myriad practitioners. But the term "reflect" does not adequately describe either the close rela-tionship between novel and story or the parabolic intensity sur-rounding Welty's second venture into the manor house. Authorized by its legendary quality, "The Burning" not only confirms the southern definition of Welty's vision achieved in *Delta Wedding* but also, through its focus upon distinctiveness and continuity, provides the historical terms necessary to orga-nize her ensuing chronicle into a still more coherent southern document. Although ephemeral as the butterfly, the antebellum society of Rose Hill is pronounced in its material and spiritual development, projecting an image of rootedness and a will to preservation which are summarized in Theo's fierce injunction. The imaginative Eudora Welty is too perfectly adjusted to tem-poral necessity to be intimidated by this charge, but in the stories and novels that compose the last part of her chronicle, Welty too recognizes the passing of a distinctive southern culture and seeks through memory and imagination to preserve its essence. Later I shall examine several of Welty's nonfictional statements regarding the nature of contemporary southern society. In addition, I shall relate her concern with distinctiveness and continuity to parallel discussions conducted in the professional historical literature. But for now the most pressing need is to establish the linear progress of Welty's chronicle as it moves into the modern era. The main lines of this story can be reconstructed from *The Golden Apples* (1949), *The Optimist's Daughter* (1972), and several uncollected stories which essay racial themes.

3

A Curtain of Green is punctuated with images of modernity: the frantic bathers of "A Memory," displaced countrymen in "The Hitch-Hikers," the "Unreal City" of "Flowers for Marjorie," abrupt, violent intimacies in "Petrified Man," and the profanation of the past by smug, complacent Natchez. But while these images imply or, more accurately, invite the reader to infer a process of modernization, *The Golden Apples* dramatizes this circumstance during two generations of closely watched change in Morgana, Mississippi, Welty's "made-up Delta town."[13] Welty employs reflexive imagery, repeated characters and situations, and the nearly constant setting of Morgana to unify the seven stories which compose *The Golden Apples,* but it is finally time itself which supplies the most capacious vessel for Welty's remarkable innovation and technical daring. The action begins in "Shower of Gold" in approximately 1900, when the light-footed King MacLain leaves his hat near the Big Black River and departs for the golden West. Thereafter, "time goes like a dream" (*CS,* p. 267), encompassing the main families of Morgana as they reenact the common rituals of birth, marriage, child rearing, getting and keeping the earth's bounty, and death. In "Shower of Gold" Miss

Katie Rainey is a young wife and mother who unintentionally reveals her own attraction to King MacLain, a springtime hero, whose actual person (or perhaps only his shadow) has recently been sighted in Morgana. A dozen or so years later in "June Recital," she beams with pleasure as Virgie, her gifted, if unruly, daughter, performs the most difficult piano composition at Miss Eckhart's annual reception. Kate Rainey's exorbitant grief for her son, Victor, killed in World War I, enters the domain of public storytelling when she falls headlong upon his open grave. Purveyor of plums, peaches, and muscadines, agent of milk, butter, and eggs, "Miss Ice Cream Rainey" is a familiar presence on the MacLain Road until her death in the early 1940s. As recorded in "The Wanderers," the last chronicle of Morgana, "poor" Katie's funeral strikes still more insistently the elegiac note which has sounded throughout the half century or so of *The Golden Apples*. Time, Welty seems to affirm, is mainly "attrition" (*CS*, p. 451), a human wearing away that diminishes even the legendary King MacLain.

If time as personal fatality occupies the dramatic foreground, then it also occasions a more impersonal process whereby Morgana is transformed from a provincial hamlet into a modern community beset with all the attendant ills. As time passes, the horse and buggy give way to the motor car, pavements appear, and a telephone wire is strung through Morgan's Woods, trysting place of King MacLain and his sons, Ran and Eugene, in the fanciful sketch "Sir Rabbit." No less potent a technological symbol than Faulkner's motor car or Thomas Wolfe's locomotive, an airplane passing over Morgana is equal cause for awe and fear, leading Mr. Morrison (intrepid publisher of the *Weekly Bugle*) to brandish the family telescope like "some kind of protective weapon for what was to come" (*CS*, p. 277). What comes is the astounding suicide of his wife, Eudora Welty's Richard Cory; the loosening of sexual codes by Virgie Rainey, a modern young woman with a defiant "spit-curl"; the lonely exile of Eugene MacLain in "Music from Spain" and the corresponding anxiety of his twin, Ran, in "The Whole World Knows"; and finally the pillage of natural resources by economic interests alien to the community. By the time of "The Wanderers," Loch Morrison, Boy Scout hero of "Moon Lake," has fought in World War II and has settled down to nurture his discontent in New York City. As one might expect, these interwoven strands of personal and communal "attrition" do not lack evaluation in *The Golden Apples*. Granted insight and sensitivity by Welty, Virgie Rainey identifies the decisive alteration of a traditional society. The old MacLain Road has not changed direction, she thinks in "The Wanderers," but "now the wrong people went by on it. They were all riding trucks, very fast or heavily loaded, and carrying blades and chains, to chop and haul the big trees to mill. They were not eaters of muscadines, and did not stop to pass words on the season and what grew" (*CS,* p. 435). To their impoverishment, they will not be detained by the same kind of leisurely roadside monologue that Miss Katie delivered forty years ago in "Shower of Gold."

In its final development, the modulation of Virgie Rainey into Laurel McKelva Hand, the wronged historian of *The Optimist's Daughter,* permits Eudora Welty to relieve the tensions and discontinuities which mark the last phase of her chronicle, but this decisive achievement in the art of living can be examined only after following Welty's story into its near-contemporary period. *The Golden Apples* ends in the midst of World War II, but *The Optimist's Daughter* chooses this same troubled moment to launch the savage comedy of familial deaths which culminates in Laurel's extended meditation upon the southern past. Again, the categories of personal and communal "attrition" can help to reconstruct the linear progress of Welty's Mississippi chronicle.

It is a bitter irony that links the death of Judge Clinton McKelva and the growth in imaginative intensity of his daughter, Laurel, but this is the mordant logic which Welty pursues throughout *The Optimist's Daughter.* For much of his seventy-one years, Judge McKelva had been "a public figure" (p. 63) in

Mount Salus, another of Welty's innumerable small fictional towns in the orbit of Jackson. Perhaps with the estimable career of William Alexander Percy in mind, Welty endows Judge McKelva with a fine social conscience which prompts him to shield defenseless Negroes, to engage in flood control work after the crisis of 1927, and to inspire the young to a life of rectitude and service.[14] But "this noble Roman" (p. 72) is not entirely bland, as his surprising remarriage in approximately 1960 attests. A widower of ten years, Judge McKelva permits the underbred Fay Chisom of Madrid, Texas, to supplant the matriarchal Becky, whose domestic probity had complemented her husband's public judiciousness. Both the memory of Miss Becky's painful death in the late 1940s and the grievous chasm of class and temperament separating mother and stepmother operate powerfully upon Laurel as she escorts her father to the hospital in New Orleans, attends his fatal convalescence, and receives old Mount Salus at his funeral. During this process, the text puns avidly upon the temporal extremity of Laurel's father, granting him "plenty of time" to recover, but whatever cleverness may inform such passages is relieved by Welty's solemn, momentous treatment of Judge Mac's death. The image of his "quenched" (p. 14) face hidden with gauze reaffirms the essential irony of Welty's Mississippi chronicle: time is at once the guarantor and the destroyer of personal consciousness.

By the reach of Laurel's memory, we know both the near past of her husband Phillip Hand's death in World War II and the remote past of McKelva settlement in territorial Mississippi, but considered as a document which explores the dynamics of social change, *The Optimist's Daughter* concentrates upon the postwar years of continued modernization and technological achievement. If the "Bulldozer Revolution" which the southern historian C. Vann Woodward named and partially rued was imminent in *The Golden Apples,* then in *The Optimist's Daughter* it has entirely routed the quietude of Mount Salus and the surrounding countryside. The lone airplane which passed innocently over Morgana has been translated into a modern jet, capable of bringing Laurel from Chicago to Jackson in a twinkling, or of summoning Dr. Kunomoto, the renowned specialist from Houston, with equal rapidity. Metaphorically, the old MacLain Road which Katie Rainey guarded like Argus has also been improved and is now designated "Interstate." The "whine" of its insistent traffic, "as deafening as grief" (p. 92) itself to Laurel, attends the burial of Judge McKelva in the adjacent part of the new cemetery. Plastic flowers, artificial turf, and an obsequious mortician who speaks of "the residence" rather than "home" (p. 50) complete Welty's litany of a perverse, modern eschatology. As in *The Golden Apples,* such technological innovation is accompanied by wrenching changes in sexual mores, in patterns of settlement, and especially in the distribution of economic power. In both *The Golden Apples* and *The Optimist's Daughter,* boys and girls experiment prematurely with lovemaking, but in the 1960s, illicit sex is approved by an official teen culture and by parental attitudes born of resignation or complacency. Living somewhat unsurely in Chicago, Laurel herself responds to the same modern urge that sends Eugene MacLain to San Francisco and Loch Morrison to New York City. But the most decisive alteration in the structure of the southern community is economic. In the generation or so which separates Morgana and Mount Salus, the "wrong people" who once used the MacLain Road have not only assumed more definite shape but also occupy the traditional home of Judge McKelva and Miss Becky. As Laurel realizes in part 4 of *The Optimist's Daughter,* the intrusion of Fay Chisom McKelva into the old proprietary ways of Mount Salus is no less inevitable than "the weather." "And the weather to come," Laurel anticipates: "there'll be many a one more like you, in this life" (p. 173).

Perhaps the best way to approach "Where Is the Voice Coming From?" and "The Demonstrators" (1963 and 1966, respectively), stories which essay racial themes and thus push Welty's chronicle further into the 1960s, is to recall several critiques of her alleged racial complaisance. In reviewing *Delta Wedding,* Diana Trilling lamented the prevalence of a "narcissistic Southern fantasy" which beguiles both reader and writer, obscuring the arrogant, exploitative underside of the Fairchild myth of happiness and bounty. In reviewing *The Golden Apples,* Margaret Marshall lamented the same kind of obscurantism in the formation of Welty's "deep South" Morgana. Because "one is scarcely ever made aware of the mixed racial background" which would typify such an actual town, the reviewer is prepared to discount both the authenticity of Morgana and the aesthetic sincerity of Eudora Welty.[15] More recently, Arlin Turner has raised the question of "members of one race drawing literary characters of another race" and included "perhaps Eudora Welty" in a list of southern writers who "have introduced Negro characters without giving the problem many troublesome variables."[16] Respondents to such criticism have at least three courses. They can remind the reviewers of *Delta Wedding* and *The Golden Apples* that each book is governed internally by a socially and economically privileged white point of view which naturally accords the black retainers of Shellmound Plantation and Morgana a subsidiary status. This is a disturbing but accurate partition of significance. More positively, they can refer each critic to "The Burning," where Eudora Welty liberates the slave Delilah from the stereotypical treatment of her sisters in much Civil War writing. As we shall see, one effect of Welty's revision of "The Burning" in 1955 is to enhance Delilah's consciousness and make her personal act of memory and imagination the ethical center of this extraordinary story. But for present purposes, "Where Is the Voice Coming From?" and "The Demonstrators" offer the most appropriate form of response to these critiques of Welty's racial awareness and sensitivity. Each story has the compounded virtue of permitting racial criticism in greater harmony with the author's intention and at the same time of revealing the later stages of Welty's continuing southern story.

No public event more sorely tested Welty's poise than the murder of Medgar Evers in Jackson. Since 1961 Jackson had been the destination of many Freedom Riders, but in 1963 Medgar

Evers, field secretary of the National Association for the Advancement of Colored People, organized a strong local movement and formulated specific demands that included school desegregation and opportunities for black workers. On May 31, 600 demonstrators were arrested by a force of city policemen, sheriff's deputies, and the highway patrol. A World War II veteran, Evers compared the scene to "Nazi Germany" and castigated the "storm troopers" who yanked tiny American flags from young marchers before herding them into police wagons and garbage trucks. During the next two weeks, black leaders repeated their demands, intensified a boycott of Capitol Street merchants, and continued to lead marches, sit-ins, and prayer vigils. The *Jackson Daily News* regularly printed racial slurs and further inflamed a populace already irritated by a searing heat wave. Shortly after midnight on June 12, an assassin crouched in a thicket of honeysuckle, aimed a 1917-model Enfield rifle, and killed Medgar Evers as he returned to his home on the city's northern edge. The discarded weapon bore a "near perfect" print on its Gold Hawk sight and led to the arrest on June 22 of Byron de la Beckwith.[17] During the intervening days, Jacksonians undoubtedly assessed this event from many perspectives, but no one has given evidence of having been more deeply affected than Eudora Welty. "Where Is the Voice Coming From?" is her explicit testimony to these unholy days in Jackson, Mississippi.

An older practice whereby Welty permitted stories to "hang" in her mind "for a long time"[18] has been abandoned here, for she claims that "Where Is the Voice Coming From?" was written "overnight" and was promptly delivered to the *New Yorker*. It was so fresh a piece that the subsequent arrest and indictment of the killer necessitated strategic revision to avoid prejudicial dangers. Examination of a preliminary draft entitled "From the Unknown"[19] reveals that Welty deleted all references to Jackson and relocated the action in a nearby state, but these safeguards in no way abated the intensity with which the killer's mind had been perceived. Published on July 6, the finished story discloses the

sensibility of an unschooled marginal white who callously recounts his assassination of the black civil rights worker, Roland
Summers. His wife, to whom the deed is retold, answers with a
crude racial joke making the rounds of Thermopylae. On the next
day he wanders uptown and is exposed to the trenchant irony of
his anonymous role. In their defense, cowering townspeople de-
tect an NAACP plot intended "to get the whites in trouble."
"You can't win" (*CS,* p. 606), thinks the still unnamed assassin.
Eudora Welty's familiar style, marked by whorls of subtle imagery, is here adapted to the killer's stunted emotional perspective. Her moral indignation suffuses his rough diction and racial
epithets and resounds during the exchange of husband and wife,
whose intimacy recalls the crude relations of an earlier story,
"Petrified Man." But for all its timeliness and sustained fury,
"Where Is the Voice Coming From?" reveals temperamental
qualities not usually attributed to the tract of social protest. Its
wrath is tempered at every point by the soothing effect of Welty's
historical understanding.

Welty had tested the resources of the monologue form in
"Why I Live at the P.O.," "Shower of Gold," and *The Ponder
Heart* (1954). In each case a passing stranger is detained by a
lengthy monologue which reveals both the storyteller and the
community. "Where Is the Voice Coming From?" only slightly
modifies this format, substituting for the convention of the stranger the reader himself, who is now directly addressed. In the
speaker's crude slang and imprecise syntax, his sexual promis-
cuity and aggravated domestic relations, his pervasive hate for
the Negro, we recognize all the historical stigmata of the com-
moner sort of southern white. But whatever classifying urge this
label may stimulate is soon checked by the duration of the monologue itself. The killer's presence becomes so insistent, his voice
so continuous, that an aura of personal lyricism begins to engulf
the heinous public event. Eudora Welty imagines a weary assassin whose patience has been exhausted by the "black nigger face"
of Roland Summers on TV, by flag-waving children and "baby-

face cops" who endlessly repeat their ritual of demonstration and arrest, and finally by the intolerable heat which made "ever'thing in the world . . . hot to the touch!" (*CS*, p. 606). In revising "Where Is the Voice Coming From?" Eudora Welty attempted to understand this exasperation by assembling the escaped pieces of the killer's past. As a personal historian, she has granted him a rural heritage filled with memories of "home" and a mother who once advertised in the "county weekly": "Son: You are not being hunted for anything but to find you." Today there is no such security. "People are dead now" (*CS*, p. 607), he muses, and their simple ways have receded into a distant past. With this addition to the final text of "Where Is the Voice Coming From?" Welty characterized the anonymous killer as a displaced countryman, victim perhaps of the historic agricultural distress which forced successive waves of Mississippians to towns and cities after the First World War. His country-bred mind, prone to nostalgia and innocent of imagination, will necessarily resist any moderniza- tion of racial folkways. With no little pity, Laurel McKelva Hand would find the self-defeating monologue of "Voice" to be a prime expression of "the great, interrelated family of those who never know the meaning of what has happened to them" (p.84). Even under duress, Eudora Welty maintains her composure, as her chronicle incorporates the "wrenchingly painful and humili- ating"[20] experience of the 1960s.

"The Demonstrators" is Welty's most contemporaneous story to date, blending images of racial strife and resistance to Viet Nam in Holden, Mississippi, another "made-up Delta town." Like Morgana, its economic structure is rooted in cotton, and social prestige is narrowly distributed among several principal families, chiefly the Ducketts and Fairbrotherses, who control the mill and gin, the *Holden Sentinel,* the First Baptist church, and the mayor's office. But their hegemony is tenuous, as Welty reveals through an adroitly constructed newspaper account of two violent Negro deaths. As recorded in the *Sentinel,* the incident which forms the dramatic basis of "The Demonstators" was not fomented by "outside agitators" and therefore does not have any "racial significance." Instead, the mutual stabbing of Ruby Gaddy and her common-law husband Dove can be attributed to the immemorial enthusiasm of black Saturday night. In pursuing this interpretation, the *Sentinel* quotes Sheriff Vince Lasseter, who exults that this is one "they can't . . . blame on us," and the Rev. Alonzo Duckett, who observes piously, "And yet they expect to be seated in our churches." The reference to a "new $100,000.00 Negro school," shrine of separate-but-equal temporizing, completes the inadvertent disclosure of a nervous, guilty community contemplating the inevitability of its multiracial future. Mayor Fairbrothers's admonition to Holden that the entire episode "warrants no stir" (*CS*, pp. 619–621) possesses little inherent conviction. In composing this apt parody of southern small-town reportorial style in the 1960s, Welty again reveals an authorial tone etched with wrath and indignation, but the soothing effect of her historical understanding finally predominates in "The Demonstrators" and rescues this story as well from the domain of the blunt.

Both "The Demonstrators" and "Where Is the Voice Coming From?" are poised upon the structural contrast of public and private responses to the reorganization of a traditional society, but in choosing Dr. Strickland as the affective center of her story, Welty discovers a more sensitive medium than the bitter monologist of Thermopylae. Dr. Strickland and his father before him have served the physical and spiritual needs of Holden with the same sense of communal responsibility that motivates Judge McKelva. But the recent death of Strickland's daughter and his imminent divorce cast a pall over this public life, just as smoke from the burned-over cotton fields hangs "like anesthetic made visible" (*CS*, p. 616) in the bleak November sky. It is the existence of this intimate context which permits Welty to explore again the personal dimension of widespread social chaos.

In attending Ruby Gaddy, Dr. Strickland momentarily recalls the passing traditional life of Holden. The black woman who holds the lamp is perceived to be Lucille, a family retainer who, by her own testimony, " 'was washing for your mother when you was born.' " " 'Fixing to leave?' " asks an old woman in a "boiled white apron," and Dr. Strickland places her voice as another influence of the past. As "the sole factotum at the Holden depot," she had called out in a resonant "baritone" the itinerary that would take Strickland to medical school in New York City. A "row of dresses" hanging on the porch of Ruby's cabin enforces a still more personal definition of the past: "In an instant [Dr. Strickland] had recognized his mother's gardening dress, his sister Annie's golf dress, and his wife's favorite duster that she liked to wear to the breakfast table." This imagery of domestic and economic interdependence, of servitude and privilege, evokes the settled past of Holden so forcefully that it occasions for Strickland a "moment of vertigo" (*CS,* pp. 613–615). If the *Sentinel* account is an accurate reflector of contemporary public opinion, then this ancient time when black and white lives were interwoven has given way to mutual distrust and defensiveness. Dr. Strickland is wearied by the resultant "bitterness, intractability that divided everybody and everything" (*CS,* p. 617) in Holden, but Welty has reserved for him a still more personal application of this general social dilemma. The disruption advocated by Philip, a bearded demonstrator who visits the Stricklands earlier in June, is not restricted to socioeconomic relations. The proverbial straw which breaks the Strickland marriage is applied when Dr. Strickland cautions Philip not to falsify southern racial conditions for consumption in the North. Irene Strickland's bitter response and subsequent departure indict her husband's own form of dishonesty in personal and professional relations. Any comfortable line of demarcation that he might wish to preserve has been erased, for in "The Demonstrators" social disruption is revealed to be concurrent with personal, familial disorder. Neither "The Demonstrators" nor "Where Is the Voice Coming From?" proposes any substantial solution to the racial strife of the 1960s, but by incorporating this contemporary material into her chronicle,

Welty answers in her own time the kind of adverse criticism which accompanied *Delta Wedding* and *The Golden Apples*. Her white protagonists, both marginal and privileged, are deeply affected by a multiracial society irresistibly establishing itself in backward Mississippi.

In the most recent segment of Welty's chronicle, there are no startling, unexpected changes that would differentiate it from earlier phases. As described in *The Golden Apples, The Optimist's Daughter,* and the stories addressing racial themes, each protagonist in the postwar years must contend with the erosion of time. Indeed, their primary trouble continues to be time itself, as it was for Clement Musgrove in territorial Mississippi and for James Fairchild several generations later. Perhaps a writer whose impact upon Welty cannot be exaggerated best expresses this universal predicament. As Lily Briscoe observes a seascape of Virginia Woolf's composing, she is momentarily daunted by the knowledge that "distant views seem to outlast by a million years . . . the gazer and to be communing already with a sky which beholds an earth entirely at rest." Personal and cosmological time compare only unfavorably in the tense universe that Virginia Woolf projects in *To the Lighthouse* and which Eudora Welty shares. In the last part of Welty's chronicle, this essential tenseness is heightened again by her placement of protagonists at decisive points in the evolution of Mississippi society. Both Virgie Rainey and Laurel McKelva Hand must respond to a modern world of jet travel and social experimentation which has been drawn abruptly from a provincial culture rich in simple folkways. Framed in meditation, their imaginative reply to bristling social change reaffirms the timeless "spiritual element" which has marked each epoch of Welty's chronicle. But while the troubled years of Morgana and Mount Salus do not alter the metaphysical, structural, or spiritual definition of Welty's historicism, they do represent a further shift in emphasis which was adumbrated in *Delta Wedding.* The southern tone achieved in that pivotal volume is both sustained and developed as Welty continues to observe her contemporary world. The last phase of Welty's chronicle is not invaded by any special kind of southern dogma or polemic, but it does betray a firmer, more fully articulated sense of a distinctive southern tradition as it passes from actuality into the realm of memory and imagination. As reported in personal essays and numerous interviews, Eudora Welty's reflections upon her homeplace and the state of contemporary southern society provide a useful first step in defining this tradition. These observations must then be understood within the larger context of the professional historical literature before the reader turns critical attention to *The Golden Apples* and *The Optimist's Daughter,* primary bearers of "the immoderate past."

4

As befits her enigmatic homeplace, Eudora Welty has displayed different moods and stances when commenting upon the South. When she was heralded in New York City, the thirty-two-year-old author of *A Curtain of Green* expressed wry amusement at the lingering image of the belle and at her admirers in the North. "Every Southern girl can play one Chopin waltz,"[21] Welty facetiously told *Publishers Weekly* on December 6, 1941. Much later, however, when the focus of national concern had shifted from global demagoguery and had settled briefly upon Jackson, Mississippi, cynosure of racial conflict in the early 1960s, Welty became less tolerant of the outsider's ignorance and reluctantly assumed the role of a southern apologist. With exasperation she describes the call of an inquiring reporter from New York City shortly after publication of "Where Is the Voice Coming From?" "Had anybody burned a cross on my lawn, he wanted to know. I told him, No, of course not. . . . The people who burn crosses on lawns don't read me in *The New Yorker.* Really, don't people know the first thing about the South?"[22] It was a combination of similar unknowing calls demanding that Welty the novelist become a dissenting pamphleteer and her own awareness of "synthetic" writing about the South being "done in other parts of the country"[23] which inspired Welty's most concentrated reflection upon the southerner as writer and citizen. Published in 1965, "Must the Novelist Crusade?" reaffirms that even in these "relentless" days, the imaginative writer "stands outside time." But Welty is also aware of the unique dilemma and potential borne by the contemporary southern novelist. As a southerner the writer belongs to "a hated people," object of "vast unparticularized" national disdain, and is thus prone to "hate back." Redeemed from this "devastating emotion" by an access of love, the same writer can undertake a delicate mission of reconciliation, being "locally blessed with an understanding and intimate knowledge" of the region not available to the outsider. The southern writer alone can portray the South with passionate objectivity. Although Welty does not "presume" to represent her "fellow Southern writers,"[24] she speaks with a wisdom and authority which advance the reluctant pronouncer of "Must the Novelist Crusade?" to just such a role.

By a judicious selection of these and many other passages, it is relatively easy to establish the frequency and variety of Welty's reflections upon the South. But as one veteran interviewer learned in 1972, it is a more difficult task to discover what, if anything, she considers to be distinctively southern. Joined by Walker Percy on a segment of William Buckley's "Firing Line," Welty proved wary and uncooperative when asked to address the topic of this symposium: "The Southern Imagination." To myriad restatements of the prototypical question, "What exactly is the Southern Imagination?" Welty answered variously: "Well, I don't know," that she took the South "for granted," was not "a bit interested in preserving the home of Jefferson Davis," could not *"say"* if New England people were more "taciturn" than southerners and, when baited by Buckley, would not even vouch for the existence of "Spanish moss" in lower Mississippi. As his more lengthy replies suggest, Walker Percy was a willing or at least more adept contributor to this perennial topic of southern symposia. In searching for the springs of the southern imagination, he invoked Allen Tate's well-known account of the origins of the Southern Literary Renascence and approved C. Vann Woodward's definition of southern history as essentially tragic. Equipped with "his peculiar tradition," Percy's hypothetical southern writer might somehow "humanize the new American culture" which is a product of postmodern economic forces. His more tailored performance on "Firing Line" undoubtedly won for Percy the laurel of a good panelist, but judged substantially, Welty's more halting remarks actually take the lead in exposing and identifying the elusive core of southern distinctiveness. Contained within her repeated emphasis upon the prevalence of talking in the South is the germ of a full, rich southern tradition.

The explication of this tradition begins inconspicuously enough when Welty permits herself to respond more fully to William Buckley's query, "What is it in the South that grabs people and causes them to want to write about it?" Welty explains that "the Southerner is a talker by nature, but not only a talker—we are used to an audience . . . and that does something to our narrative style." Still probing for a southern essence, Buckley agrees that "the social contract" may be "more vivid" in the South than in New York City, but he doubts that this cohesion "transfers automatically on through the disembodied intermediary of a book." Because of its illuminating effect, Welty's answer will be quoted in full.

> Well, I can tell you something that I think would apply; that is, if you grew up in the South when things were relatively stable, when there was a lot of talk and so on, you got a great sense of a person's whole life. This is because you know all of the families. You know several generations because they all live together. You know what happened to So-and-so clear through his life. You get a narrative sense of your next door neighbor instead of someone you just meet in the supermarket, which you do today, or you just see people in flashes. You had a sense of what happened to them and probably why, because look what happened to her grandmother—[brief inter-

jection by Buckley]—and you watch life and it is happening. Well,
that is a novel. I don't mean you would take somebody's life and
make a novel, but your turn of mind would be a dramatic one.[25]

Welty's expansiveness on the southern quality is not the fruit of
any forced discursive flowering. It emerges instead from "the
workmanship point of view of the novelist" which she had maintained throughout this interview. But Welty's emphasis upon
the peculiar communion of talker and audience in the South
invites at the same time a more theoretic formulation of the
implied social value and dynamic processes operating within her
memory of a distinctive culture. Although Allen Tate was wont
to apologize (with no little immodesty) for the alleged inferiority
of his scholarship, his remarks in "A Southern Mode of the
Imagination" can provide the historical and intellectual framework needed to bring out the unique significance of Welty's
loquacious Southerner.

Published in 1959, Tate's brilliant assemblage of "surmises
and guesses" both extends and refines an earlier essay, "The Pro-
fession of Letters in the South" (1935), in which he likened "on
an infinitesimal scale" the sudden prominence of southern literature after 1920 to "the outburst of poetic genius" in late
Elizabethan England. In each historical instance, the "curious
burst" of literary intelligence reflects the special complexity of
the age: "a crossing of the ways" marked by the dwindling of a
feudal order and the concurrent rise of commerce. In "A Southern
Mode of the Imagination," Tate does not repudiate his earlier
conception of the "perfect literary situation" (a phrase borrowed
from his equally perceptive essay "Emily Dickinson"), nor does
he alter his earlier calendar of southern watershed dates. The time
of antebellum simplicity, the relative cultural isolation of the
South from 1865 to 1920, and its first-rate literary production
after World War I continue to serve Tate as the dial of southern
fortunes in progressive America. His amplification of 1959 simply offers new, more precise terms to distinguish these phases of
the southern mind. It is not at all coincidental that he too invests

storytelling and talking in the South with considerable social significance.

Located at "a crossing of the ways," the modern literary sensibility which emerged in the South after 1920 possessed detachment and could thus portray ironically the most intimate regional experience. In "A Southern Mode of the Imagination," Tate designates this new intensity as "the dialectical mode" and not surprisingly traces its source to "Plato, the dialectician," who "reaches first principles" by means of the abstruse "give and take between two minds." In its most subjective form, this inductive method becomes "the mind talking to itself." By contrast, the "traditional Southern mode of discourse" is "rhetorical." Formative in the Old South and still notable until the "long moment" of southern innocence ends in 1914, this method "presupposes somebody at the other end silently listening." Instead of talking to himself,

> the southerner always talks to somebody else, and this somebody else, after varying intervals, is given his turn; but the conversation is always among rhetoricians; that is to say, the typical Southern conversation is not going anywhere; it is not about anything. *It is about the people who are talking,* even if they never refer to themselves, which they usually don't, since conversation is only an expression of manners, the purpose of which is to make everybody happy.

Tate concludes that "this may be the reason why Northerners and other uninitiated persons find the alternating, or contrapuntal, conversation of Southerners fatiguing."[26] If the modern dialectician is detached, ironic, and thus capable of "the arts of literature" which begin in "self-examination," then "the old Southern *rhetor,*" descendant of Aristotle, Cicero, and Castiglione, is more simple, less self-conscious, an easy practitioner of the political, social, and domestic arts. As Tate affirms, the rhetor's mode of discourse is the mirror of a unified culture whose center "was the family."[27] "A Southern Mode of the Imagination" will prove extremely useful in chapter 5 in comprehending the alternate style of *Losing Battles* and *The Optimist's Daughter,* consecutive

149

novels which formally recapitulate Tate's historical schema, but his remarks are more immediately useful in giving historical and intellectual substance to Welty's quintessential Southerner who (as she assured William Buckley) has been talking "from the cradle."

In the most general sense, Tate helps the reader to see that Welty herself, in her sustained contrast of a past and present South, has claimed the ironic ground of the modern dialectician. More particularly, though, his analysis in "A Southern Mode" illuminates the sense of a distinctive tradition which she evoked on "Firing Line" and in other statements as well. Eudora Welty's memory of growing up in the South "when things were relatively stable, when there was a lot of talk and so on," restates in more homely, experiential terms Allen Tate's definition of southern rhetoric as "the manners of men talking in society." Just as Tate characterizes this society as stable, placed, and familial in accent, so Welty gravitates toward exempla of geographic and generational unity. Because families once stayed put and the generations lived together, you as a neighbor "got a great sense of a person's whole life" and thus were seldom surprised by novel developments. After all, Welty stresses on "Firing Line," "look what happened to her grandmother." Today, however, people are met casually in "the supermarket" or are seen only "in flashes," betraying a haste in social relations which comports ill with "the alternating, or contrapuntal, conversation" of Tate's leisurely rhetorical mode. "Porch-sitting,"[28] Tate and Welty would agree, is time-consuming, but in a traditional society this is not a reproach. Finally, Tate's emphasis upon the self-disclosure of the *"rhetor,"* his conversation "not [being] about anything" save *the people who are talking,"* helps to accentuate the individualistic core of Welty's southern tradition. This quality is evident on "Firing Line," especially when Welty the novelist defends her interest only "in human beings who are alive," but was stated more explicitly during an earlier interview in 1972. "Chekhov," she told Linda Kuehl, is "very close to the South." "You know, in

Uncle Vanya and *The Cherry Orchard,* how people are always gathered together and talking and talking." Although "no one's really listening," Welty detects their underlying "love and understanding," a "knowledge and acceptance of each other's idiosyncracies" [*sic*]. "That kind of responsiveness to the world, to whatever happens, out of their own deeps of character seems very southern to me,"[29] Welty affirms. She and Allen Tate may operate upon different levels of intellectual formality, but their image of the Southerner talking "from the cradle" identifies the components of a distinctive culture: a placed, homogeneous, stationary family of individuals living in close proximity and possessing a reasonable allowance of leisure.

There is strong presumptive evidence that Welty's sense of a distinctive southern tradition may derive in part from her own closely guarded family life. Looking back, she remembers a much younger self climbing into the front seat of the car and instructing her parents to " 'start talking, please.' "[30] Transposed into fictional terms, this plea of the ten-year-old out for a family drive may be the ultimate source of Laurel McKelva's more somber remembrance in *The Optimist's Daughter.* "For every book" in the family library, she "had heard their voices, father's and mother's. And perhaps it didn't matter to them . . . what they read aloud; it was the breath of life flowing between them, and the words of the moment riding on it that held them in delight" (p. 118). It would not be surprising if the source of Welty's tradition is familial in nature, but her identification of a unique heritage also draws her inadvertently into the middle of an often unruly academic debate regarding southern distinctiveness and its twin, continuity. Briefly reconstructing the terms of this debate conducted in the professional historical literature will permit both testing of the bases (or criteria) of Welty's distinctiveness and framing more cogently the related questions of its outer limits and continuity. Still more importantly, reconstructing this debate will prepare for concluding discussion of *The Golden Apples* and *The Optimist's Daughter,* which offer the kind of resolution that novelists of the ironic type invariably prefer.

As Carl Degler reveals in *Place Over Time* (1977), few southern historians of the last quarter century have resisted the call to pronounce upon the distinctiveness of the South. Although none may deny the historic fact of distinctiveness, Degler observes that there is considerable disagreement over "the degree and the persistence of that difference." In assessing degree, Charles Sellers, Jr., and Grady McWhiney occupy one end of the scale, citing evidence which indicates that in 1861 "differences between races and sections were no more pronounced than similarities." Historians, McWhiney concludes, "have tended to magnify the differences between Northerners and Southerners out of all proportion." Degler explains that "quite the opposite emphasis is seen in the work of Eugene Genovese, who considers the culture of the antebellum South so different from the North's that he talks of a divergence in world views." C. Vann Woodward also marvels that such a "great slave society" as the Old South possessed could exist "in the heart of a thoroughly bourgeois and partly puritanical republic."[31] In assessing persistence, historians again align themselves at opposite poles. In *The Everlasting South* (1963), Francis B. Simkins claims that "the region, despite many changes, is as much different from the rest of the United States today as it was in 1860." Both Harry Ashmore and John Egerton deny this conservation of southern identity, the latter arguing that the modern South "is no longer simply a colony of the nation, an inferior region, a stepchild; it is now rushing to rejoin the Union, and in the process it is becoming indistinguishable from the North and East and West."[32] The special success of *Place Over Time* is that Carl Degler can avoid these extremes of degree and persistence and yet take a decisive stance on the most trying issues of southern history.

For Degler "the undoubted reality of *The* South" rests upon certain aspects of the region which are "objectively discernible." Key statistical indexes of distinctiveness include a near-tropical climate "favorable to tobacco, cotton, sugar, and rice," an "ancient" rurality, "paucity of cities," and dearth of manufacturing conferred upon the South by the dominant plantation system, a relatively homogeneous population reflecting the South's "disproportionately small" share of European immigration, and finally "the human warmth and security of its commitment to family and kin."[33] In establishing the persistence or continuity of this unique southern identity, Carl Degler does not underestimate the reciprocal nature of his argument. For example, in evaluating Eugene Genovese's contention that the Old South possessed "a ruling class with economic interests, political ideals, and moral sentiments" radically different from the nation, Degler correctly infers that the defeat in 1865 of such a unified planter class would align Genovese with historians who see southern history beset primarily by grave discontinuities. Thus Degler argues closely to restrict the uniqueness of Genovese's South, concluding that while the region "was and is" distinctive, "its system of values" has always been "quite congruent" with that of "the rest of the country."[34] Having established a logical base for continuity, Degler can recognize the reality of a changing South, especially after 1945, but emphasize one which remains essentially the same. One example will suffice to reveal Degler's continuing dependence upon "objectively discernible" data. In 1860 some 84 percent of southern laborers were engaged in agriculture, in contrast with only 40 percent of laborers in the rest of the United States. As Degler notes, the "deep" commitment to agriculture "implied by these figures flowed naturally from the South's unique commitment to slavery." But even with the passing of this institution, the modern South retains its agricultural character, although by a narrower margin of rural preference. In the 1940 census, 40 percent of white southerners were counted as farm residents, as contrasted with 16 percent living outside the South. Twenty years later, the white southern percentage had dropped to 11 percent, while the non-South figure fell to 6.4 percent.

Although Degler recognizes the proportional decrease in these figures, his evocation of the "ancient and persistent rurality of the South"[35] stands at least for the present.

Because Eudora Welty is an imaginative writer, she does not measure southern distinctiveness, change, or continuity as deliberately or contentiously as Carl Degler, but she is not without authoritative attitudes and opinions on these closely interrelated issues. For example, Welty projects the fact of southern distinctiveness in both fiction and essay form. With no little self-irony, Aunt Tempe laments the marriage of her daughter, Mary Denis, to Mr. Buchanan, the sexually importuning "Yankee that wants his windows washed three times a week." Although the immediate context is humorous, the complaint of Aunt Tempe for her absent daughter in the North deepens the aura of a distinctive southern life which pervades *Delta Wedding*. When Welty becomes an essayist, the same contrast of regions becomes more insistent and invidious. If the modern South still retains vestiges of its cohesive "porch-sitting" days, then New York City is "a no man's land," a place where "you may have the . . . most congenial friends, but it's extraordinary if you ever know anything about them except that little wedge of their life that you meet with the little wedge of your life. You don't get that sense of a continuous narrative line,"[36] Welty explained in 1972. More recently, this sectional awareness, and with it the lingering fact of southern distinctiveness, has been confirmed by a literary application which followed publication of *The Eye of the Story* in 1978. When asked by Reynolds Price to characterize the "different problems" of writing stories and essays, Welty answered, "I think of writing stories as *going south* and writing essays as *going north*."[37]

Eudora Welty and Carl Degler not only accede to "the undoubted reality of *The* South" but they also share essentially the same distinguishing criteria. Each defines a region which is unique in the nation because its people is relatively cohesive and unified, more nearly settled than geographically mobile, and less rushed than other Americans by the bustle of urban living. By inference,

Welty's criteria of a distinctive southern tradition possess the inherent capacity to withstand analytical testing. Perhaps the most prudent way to summarize the formal relationship between Welty's more experiential and Degler's factual data is that they are mutually enhancing bodies of knowledge. Although caught in their lyric and tabular moods, the fiction writer and historian continue to betray a hereditary attraction to each other. Much the same congruency can be observed in Welty's and Degler's recognition of profound changes affecting southern culture after 1945. In "The Abode of Summer" Welty can recall with some plausibility the "ribbony afternoons" of an idyllic southern childhood. "From the beginning of our lives," she murmurs in 1952, "we knew . . . the swimming of ice in china pitchers of tea or lemonade, ceiling fans wheeling on porches, [and] punkas in the oldest houses in stately back-and-forth above the long table." But in less than two decades, Welty's southern reflections would be purged of such nostalgia, the "dreamlike" summers of youth interrupted by racial demonstration in Jackson, which fought inevitable change more resolutely than Little Rock or Birmingham. The ensuing corruption of values, epitomized by the slaying of Medgar Evers, would prompt Welty to observe caustically that Snopes and Compson "isn't a very lasting distinction any more"[39] in Mississippi, but the most overt measure of Welty's vanishing South is her awareness of the gradual merging of distinctive American cultures. Echoing Carl Degler's marshaled data on rurality, Welty affirmed in 1972 that regions "are not as different from one another as they used to be. In the South or in New England or the Southwest, small towns still have a living identity, but I think you're certainly aware of the life of the country as a whole flowing through everywhere."[40]

As his title indicates, Carl Degler's intention in *Place Over Time* is to demonstrate the continuity of southern history within a changing social structure. Rhetorically, he writes with a sense of contributing to an extended academic debate, seeking in particular to dismantle the exaggerated hypotheses of Eugene Genovese.

Steeped in the social, political, and economic history of the region, Degler employs a quantitative method of analysis to advance his own more moderate conception of "the nature of southern difference from the rest of the nation, yesterday and today." If Welty and Degler were to be examined conceptually, the evidence derived from her fiction, essays, and interviews and from the portrait of a notable historian reflected in *Place Over Time* would indicate a theoretic consensus regarding the perennial questions of southern historiography. Both the fact and nature of southern distinctiveness and its susceptibility to modification in time are perceived by Welty and Degler to operate within essentially the same limits of definition. They also possess the kind of temper or instinct which directs each to discover continuity within a fluid system of change. This impulse was tested more fully in Degler's earlier work. Published in 1974, *The Other South* explores patterns of intellectual dissent in the nineteenth century, but Degler concludes rightly that even the most intrepid southern minds invariably bowed to racial orthodoxy. Time is abridged, as antislavery proponents, Unionists, southern Republicans, and Populists reveal a quintessential southern identity. There is no need to emphasize again Welty's pursuit of a similar constancy in history, but the present intersection of novelist and historian is finally more revealing as evidence of their subtle differentiation. The surge of Carl Degler's data on rurality, for example, provides the ingredients for a unified view of southern history, but as a statistical projection of continuity it does everything except live. In the last phase of Eudora Welty's chronicle, the missing elements of personal memory and imagination will be supplied by Virgie Rainey and Laurel McKelva Hand. Neither they nor Welty will defy the dominion of fact, but the medium in which each operates as a historian of southern continuity is not finally statistical in nature but meditative. As a final caveat, Welty will achieve her vision of an essential continuity underlying southern history without any capitulation to the plantation legend or its doctrinaire thesis of decline and fall.

In "Henry Green: A Novelist of the Imagination," Eudora Welty makes an apparently surprising comparison between the English novelist and William Faulkner. At a glance, no two writers are more dissimilar. The author of *Party Going* (1939), *Loving* (1945), and *Concluding* (1948) writes in the astute, austere tradition of English social comedy, while Faulkner is often bardic, expansive, and tolerant of the American fustian. Welty discerns, however, their underlying "kinship" of cultural perception, which identifies at the same time her own formative view of contemporary southern society. Henry Green and William Faulkner "are not too far apart," she thinks: possessing deep, intuitive knowledge of "the complicated social structure" they inherit, "each reflects on the fate of individual man set down very much alive in a dying society."[41] In Henry Green, dramatic rendering of this quandary often occasions a savage social comedy centered upon the loneliness and frustration of "people who have lost their active functions."[42] In Faulkner, the same "fate" can have more dire epistemological consequences, ushering Quentin Compson, for example, into a sealed chamber of abstract, subjective potentiality which "cannot determine development."[43] Welty most nearly approximates the tone of Henry Green in sections of *Delta Wedding* which recreate the trivial, meandering flow of everyday life. She can also raise her modernist voice to summon R.J. Bowman, Eugene and Ran MacLain, and Harris of "The Hitch-Hikers," anguished characters who have despaired of any redeeming social experience. But Welty's more characteristic response to the shared image of "individual man set down very much alive in a dying society" is not governed by the canons of social comedy or the dictates of philosophic pessimism. Rather this cultural demise, whose death blow was struck in "The Burning," becomes a positive condition of growth for Welty's two main protagonists of the modern and contemporary South. It is the unremitting spiritual effort of Virgie Rainey and Laurel

McKelva which gives dramatic import to the last phase of Welty's Mississippi chronicle. In earlier sections of chapter 4, its linear extension was traced, and the waning of a distinctive southern tradition received conceptual and historiographical consideration. It remains now to locate within the fiction itself evidence of this same historic process, so that it can be absorbed and evaluated by Virgie Rainey and Laurel McKelva Hand. Their exertions to understand the complex relation of past, present, and future experience have been phrased with bittersweet clarity by Amantha Starr, the displaced heroine of Robert Penn Warren's *Band of Angels* (1955): "We have to try to make sense of what we have lived, or what has lived us."

In the latter parts of Welty's chronicle, the imperial aspect of time which "has lived us" generates a more profuse imagery of illness and death. If "The Burning" may be considered the ultimate historical point of departure for this last phase, then the funereal catalogue begins with Myra and Theo and the mysterious Phinny, includes next the vulnerable citizens of Morgana, touches with "the rumour of mortality" such innocents as Uncle Daniel Ponder of *The Ponder Heart* and such enduring figures as Granny Vaughn of *Losing Battles,* and culminates in *The Optimist's Daughter,* Eudora Welty's memento mori. Together these volumes produce a rate of morbidity which is higher and more concentrated than earlier segments of Welty's chronicle, but this enhanced fatality is not merely a gratuitous study in pessimism. Ultimately, it is a consequence of Eudora Welty's attempt to dramatize the decline of a distinctive southern heritage by investing illness and death with metaphoric, cultural significance. "Kin," an excellent although neglected story, confirms the heuristic importance of this poetic process in the last phase of Welty's chronicle. It is also worth remarking that in date of publication, "Kin" stands between Virgie Rainey and Laurel McKelva and can thus possibly provide a window on the past and future development of Welty's most discerning protagonists.

First published in 1952 and then reprinted in *The Bride of the*

Innisfallen, "Kin" is a tale of relentless "attrition" set in small-town and rural Mississippi during the 1930s. Briefly described, the present action begins when Dicey Hastings, a young "engaged" woman living in New York City, returns to her native Mississippi for a long-delayed visit. She discovers that the southern spring is well advanced, but this is a cruel, calamitous April which only accentuates the illness of Aunt Ethel and the sexual frustration of her daughter Kate. "Propped up" inside her "tester bed," Aunt Ethel surveys the world of her sickroom as if "she were riding in some old-fashioned carriage" sent to relieve the present discomfiture of a lady. But it is Kate and Dicey who are dispatched to Mingo, "the home place," in response to a "gilt-edged card" containing somber news of their Great-Uncle Felix. "Must *watch* him—day and night" (*CS*, p. 539), Sister Anne has written, to prompt a visit from the new arrival. During the nine-mile trip to Mingo, Dicey's urban eye is gradually readjusted to the once familiar landscape but is confounded anew by a spectacle of Sister Anne's composing. This is picture-taking day in the country. In concert with an itinerant photographer, she has transformed the *"primitive"* home of her cousin Felix into a studio glaring with "multiplied lights" (*CS*, p. 560). To accommodate the country folk, Felix has been moved to a small storage room in the back of the house, adjacent to the bathroom. "A heavy bulk, motionless, in a night-shirt," Great-Uncle Felix gazes at his visitors without focus or, Dicey thinks, "conviction" (*CS*, pp. 553–554). The velvety western pasture which commands his subsequent attention is not a field of rebirth or renewal, but the locus of Felix's defeat. " 'Hide' " (*CS*, p. 555), he counsels Dicey and Kate, in anticipation of tardy Yankee troopers whose approach to Mingo has been intimated by Sister Anne.

"Kin" is a relentless tale of "attrition" which ends by predicting the death of Aunt Ethel and Great-Uncle Felix and the spiritual nullity of Kate. Projected into an ever-narrowing future, she may soon explain "Why I Live at the Bank!" in still another rendition of the old maid's lament. In "Kin" Eudora

Welty treats this level of personal fatality with uninterrupted poignance and respect, but it also points metaphorically to the condition of "a dying society." In happier days, the "courtly" (*CS*, p. 543) Uncle Felix was not only the undoubted arbiter of ethical behavior but also the warm, loving center when the entire "connection" descended upon Mingo for traditional Sunday dinners. As Dicey remembers, "it was eating against talking" (*CS*, p. 557) for an extended family which included even such remote cousins as Sister Anne. Built when Mississippi was a wilderness, the home of Uncle Felix provides a local habitation for Welty's sense of a distinctive southern tradition: a placed, homogeneous, stationary family of individuals living in close proximity and possessing a reasonable allowance of leisure. This tradition, however, proves vulnerable in time, as the metaphoric structure of "Kin" reveals.

If Flannery O'Connor were writing this story, the *"itinerant"* photographer would be a more demonstrable devil. As it is, this "spook" (*CS*, p. 552) from Yankeedom tempts Sister Anne to vanity and installs in the parlor his infernal apparatus. Accordingly, Sister Anne becomes an incarnation of the divided modern sensibility. In alternating bursts, she addresses Kate and Dicey with a conversational and conspiratorial air. In a parody of rootedness and leisure, she veers back and forth between the sickroom and the parlor, where this efficient businesswoman assists the photographer, Mr. Alf J. Puryear. His literary and sociological antecedence never doubtful, this model of hustling, peripatetic individualism finds little resistance in Mingo to his entrepreneurial ways. He easily corrupts Sister Anne with the promise of a complimentary photograph and then defeats the local peasantry, which is made vulnerable by curiosity and boredom, prime defects of an agrarian society suffering economic depression. It is, however, the sequestering of Uncle Felix which verifies Welty's intention to assimilate his personal tragedy to the level of southern cultural fate. In the tiny storage room, his "motionless" form merges with other dusty, "useless objects" of a once vital past. Peering into the gloom, Sister Anne Fry surveys this scene of ruin with the surprise of "a prospector" (*CS*, pp. 553–554) who has stumbled upon the memorial artifacts of a traditional society. As her name implies, she will probably suffer the eternal agonies reserved for the ahistorical.

Although it "improves" upon the story, this description of "Kin" is not entirely misleading. By maintaining a fairly strict correspondence of image and idea. Welty approaches "the limit of·allegory"[44] and thus projects in near-ideological form her complex of attitudes regarding southern distinctiveness and its apparent decline. Uncle Felix *is* the stricken body of the South. But at the same time, this story reveals that it is not entirely comfortable with its elevation and thus attributes to Dicey Hastings a role which insinuates personal dramatic qualities into Welty's parable of southern loss. By returning to Mingo, Dicey has momentarily interrupted her hasty life in New York City and allowed a realm of memory and imagination to assert itself. In this susceptibility she receives from Felix a scrawled note of assignation: " 'River—Daisy—Midnight—Please.' " To the inflexible Kate, this is merely an old man's mistake, for Aunt Beck was the long and honored wife of Uncle Felix. But to the "engaged," more intrepid Dicey, the confused revelation of hidden passion strikes an aesthetic rather than ethical note. By entering her own passion, Dicey can remember "the moment" of Felix's ancient meeting in the woods and confess that "I even saw Daisy" (*CS*, p. 561). Felix's fall from rectitude is fortunate, because it provokes the modern Daisy to rediscover the essential humanity of her "courtly" progenitor and to savor the fresh, living character of the past. Hers is a moving vision of continuity embracing past, present, and future, but it is Virgie Rainey and Laurel McKelva, also living in "a dying society," who fulfill more boldly the challenge of this circumstance. Although valuable in its own right, "Kin" is finally more important to the present study as preparation for *The Golden Apples* and *The Optimist's Daughter*. In each book, Welty continues to employ a metaphorical technique of characterization to evaluate time passing in distinctively southern terms. The personal and cultural forms of "attrition" that emerge momentarily isolate Miss Katie Rainey and Judge McKelva as imperiled exemplars of tradition before permitting them to recede into a rich texture of change and contingency.

In "Shower of Gold" Miss Katie Rainey served unknowingly as a gauge or measure of the relative wholeness of Morgana in approximately 1900. This cultural role is validated mainly by the easy, colloquial tone of her voice, as she detains a willing passer-by on the old MacLain Road. In its duration and leisureliness, its close affinity with the rhetorical mode that Tate and Welty designate "Southern," Miss Kate's dramatic monologue becomes the formal literary embodiment of a still vital, still harmonic culture suspended in the last moment of innocence. In "Shower of Gold" literary form recapitulates culture, as it continues to do throughout *The Golden Apples*. Ran and Eugene MacLain, for example, give personal and cultural definition to the ensuing chronicle of Morgana, a disturbing record of modernization that has already been described in sufficient detail. Their gravitation toward soliloquy and interior monologue, subjective forms of the dialectical mode, attests implicitly to the erosion of communal consensus and the defeat of a public basis of identity. It remains, however, for Kate Rainey to represent still more poignantly in "The Wanderers" this modern instance of a dwindling traditional society.

In old age Miss Kate is all restraint and diminution. Made careful by "a light stroke," she no longer tempts the descent to the MacLain Road but moves "with effort" back and forth across her narrow yard. From "the autocracy of her stroke," Miss Kate directs the life of her daughter Virgie, "past forty now," but she herself is a model of vulnerability. During the hurried days of her "last summer," she is assaulted by "the trafficking" of the MacLain Road. "Clear up where she was, she felt the world tremble; day and night the loggers went by, to and from Morgan's Woods," their passage unrelieved by any compensatory song of commerce. Should "you" pass by and see her there on the ridge, on her hill "in the creeping shade," Welty assures the hasty that Kate Rainey will permit voyage and not detain with conversation. Indeed, "she looked ready to ward you off . . . in case of pity, there in her gathered old-lady dress." In its new dispensation of speed, efficiency, and economic exploitation, the MacLain Road makes solitary and inaccessible to the community a figure who inadvertently expressed its collective life: "like the lady on the Old Dutch Cleanser can," Morgana "took . . . for granted" Miss Katie Rainey, who had watched "the turn of the road" (*CS,* pp. 428–429) for nearly forty years. Welty's subsequent treatment of her death and funeral continues to invoke metaphor as a vivid means of identifying a transforming historical moment, but her evaluation of this process can be illuminated by digressing briefly into a recent study of the historical imagination.

In *Metahistory* Hayden White devises a multilayered schema consisting of literary, ideological, and linguistic categories to describe the variety of nineteenth-century European historiography. White begins by identifying Romance, Tragedy, Comedy, and Satire as the four essential plots of history, associating each with a characteristic "Mode of Argument" and with a dominant poetic trope. The tragic explanation of history, presently relevant to "The Wanderers," views the world as resistant to man's dream of transcendence. His "unremitting enemy" death introduces into life, not only an antagonistic relation between mind and abstract "forces at play in the social and natural worlds," but also a more terrible strife reflected in "states of division among men" which typify their unhappy history.[45] The reconciliation marking the end of tragedy is actually *"a revelation"* of "inalterable and eternal" laws governing human existence. According to Hayden White, mechanism is the usual form of "nomological-deductive" argument whereby the tragic historian "seek[s] to explicate the point of it all." His search is for the laws "that are presumed to govern history in the same way that the laws of physics are presumed to govern nature." As a consequence of this pursuit of "universal and invariant causal relationships," both "the variety and color" of actual historical circumstance are diminished by its typification of social process.[46] Plotted as tragedy, rationalized through mechanism, this distinctive world view is grasped figuratively by metonymy, a trope which is congenial with the vision and form of the tragic historian. By virtue of its substitution of a part for the whole, metonymy as a form of metaphoric transference is reductive and divisive in character rather than selective and integrative. As White explains, "in Metonymy, phenomena are implicitly apprehended as bearing relationships to one another in the modality of part-part relationships, on the basis of which one can effect a *reduction* of one of the parts to the status of an aspect or function of the other."[47] Logically, the extrinsic relation of phenomena which results can be expressed as causal pattern, but when transposed into moral and social terms, a metonymical characterization of history apprehends man living in division with himself, his natural and spiritual faculties at war; and men existing "*contiguously* with one another, as separate and as separated beings,"[48] in a divided social state. This suspenseful array of Hayden White's erudition bears no efficient relation to *The Golden Apples* or to the more particular instance of "The Wanderers," but it does provide an orderly approach to Kate Rainey's death and funeral and promises to instruct us further in the definition of Welty's southern historiography.

Announced "with a thrust of pain from somewhere unexpected," Kate Rainey's final stroke draws "a simple line" of causality through her body, "dividing it in half" (*CS,* p. 430) with indisputable evidence of mortality. It is this same feared mystery which composes Morgana into a group of mourners who gather to acknowledge reluctantly the tragic attenuation of time. "'I'd come and I'd go again,'" an aged King MacLain muses within Virgie Rainey's hearing, "'only I ended up at the wrong end'" (*CS,* p. 443). Stealthy and surprising, man's "unremitting enemy" continues to supply the later stages of Welty's chronicle with tragic plots and the tacit governance of mechanical causality. It is, however, Welty's use of metonymy which constitutes the most precise description and evaluation of the spiritual state of Morgana as it reenacts the traditional funerary rites. As Virgie realizes, this procedure may begin in charity, but the effect is always self-revelation of the community. "Always in a house of death, Virgie was thinking, all the stories come evident, show forth from the person, become a part of the public domain. Not the dead's story, but the living's" (*CS*, p. 433). Told with innocence and self-irony, this communal story of "attrition" is a somber reflection upon the condition of southern culture in the early 1940s.

Once the "callers and helpers" have restored the ill-kept home of Kate Rainey to domestic order, they can participate in an extended scene of metonymical drama. Wrapped in perpetual mourning, Cassie Morrison's "black-stockinged legs" wade cautiously "among the impeding legs of the other women" who occupy Virgie's parlor. Their "murmur" forms not a web of actual conversation, but an emanation of sound through which Virgie moves dreamily, "head, breasts, and hips in their helpless agitation." Instructed by "Mr. Bitts" (the exploitative lumber magnate Mr. Nesbitt) to " 'cheer up,' " Virgie watches the "fat, hurt back" of her retreating employer as he approaches a more obedient object of kindness. In the meanwhile, "Food—two banana cakes and a baked ham, a platter of darkly deviled eggs, new rolls—and flowers kept arriving at the back," without any syntactical inference of human agency. Miss Snowdie, however, is busy preparing the body, and when the work of this gentle mortician has been completed, the metonymical drama of evaluation can proceed to its climax. "The door opened. Miss Snowdie stood against it, sideways, looking neither in nor out," but from the adjacent parlor filled with "waiting talk," only "the end of the bed and Miss Katie's feet could be seen" by the mourners. As a trope of personal characterization, metonymy reveals body without inwardness in the populace of Morgana, a reduction of whole to part which is manifest by their sentimental, curious response

to the stern mystery of Kate Rainey's death. " 'She looks beautiful!' " the ladies exclaim, "bending over the bed as they would
bend over the crib of a little kicking baby." As a trope of communal characterization, metonymy builds upon this severed human condition by deploying mere shells of sensation in a parody
of mutual concern. The isolation and violence which result are
experienced most acutely by Virgie Rainey. " 'Come see your
mother,' " demand the "bright" voices and the pulling "hands" of
"people who had never touched her before." But because "their
faces hurt," Virgie recoils in self-defense and claims the space
which now separates all the citizens of Morgana: " 'Don't touch
me' " (*CS,* pp. 432–435). Ironically, in "The Wanderers" the
"living's" story records the dissolution of a traditional southern
society. If the whole "lady on the old Dutch Cleanser can" once
expressed its order and coherence, her "feet" seen from afar now
evaluate the present condition of personal and communal schism.

In *The Optimist's Daughter* the process of investing Judge
McKelva with a representative identity depends upon his possession of the personal history and temperament of a traditional
southern gentleman. The McKelva library is a carefully furnished
museum which rivals Shellmound for its power of evoking the
Mississippi past. Portraits of Clint McKelva's father and grandfather, "the Confederate general and missionary to China," as
well as a "massive, concentrated" desk imported from Edinburgh
by the earliest generation of arrivers reconstruct a family history
that is coterminous with the settlement of territorial Mississippi.
Strategic references to the old "McKelva place on the river"
(pp. 118–121), ruined by the flood of 1927, not only complete
the assimilation of this town-dwelling family to the plantation
heritage of the Fairchilds, but also create a broad historical perspective for understanding the temperament of Judge Mac. Eulogized as a "noble Roman" (p. 72) by the platitudinous mayor of
Mount Salus, Clint McKelva nonetheless summarizes the virtues
implied by this familiar mythological characterization of antebel-

lum culture. This is not a tradition of intense metaphysical inquiry, as the collection of Dickens, Tennyson, and *Sherlock Holmes*
crowding his library attests, but an ideal of civic and familial
responsibility executed with decorum and noblesse oblige. A
patriarchal figure in Mount Salus, Judge McKelva practices the
daily political and judicial arts necessary to the maintenance of
public order, unselfishly commits himself to the *"drudgery"*
(p. 120) of flood control work, and assumes an enlightened,
protective attitude in racial matters. Through the presence of
Major Bullock, a bumbling, sentimental, self-indulgent aristocrat, Welty provides a satiric counterweight to Clint McKelva's
mythological advantage, but her reservations only qualify moder-
ately the humane, compassionate tradition which he represents.
If Katie Rainey resembles the durable "lady on the Old Dutch
Cleanser can," then Judge McKelva finds his metaphoric
identification as a figure of tradition with Miss Becky's staunch
climber: "utterly strong," its root "may be a hundred years old!"
(p. 114).

Because death keeps its own time in *The Golden Apples* and *The
Optimist's Daughter,* each book is governed by the same "invariant" natural law. The "simple line" of causality "dividing"
Kate Rainey's body is redrawn by Miss Verna Longmeier, the
addled busybody seamstress of Mount Salus. When Judge
McKelva's casket is taken from the house, she foretells his disin-
tegration. " 'He'll touch down where He took off from. . . . Split
it right down the middle.' Her hands ripped a seam for them"
(p. 89). Neither the cosmetology of Mr. Pitts, the obsequious
mortician, nor the sentiment of the community, which again
views the corpse as if it were a "new baby" (p. 64), can diminish
the essential hardship of Welty's tragic plotting and mechanistic argument in *The Optimist's Daughter.* But again the urgency
of her social concern leads Welty to imbue this kind of private,
personal event with communal significance. The poetic process
begins in earnest when the sprawling family of Wanda Fay

Chisom arrives from Madrid, Texas, to help with the mourning.

Mother Chisom is a storehouse of untimely memories regarding her cancer-stricken husband, who could digest only "tap water" (p. 71) at the end, and her eldest son Roscoe, a suicide, who "was pretty as a girl" in his coffin. Despondent, he just " 'stuffed up the windows, stuffed up the door, turned on all four eyes of the stove and oven,' said Mrs. Chisom indulgently" (p. 75). The insensitivity implied by these and other ill-timed anecdotes is expressed more bluntly by the legend on Bubba Chisom's pickup truck, "Do Unto Others Before They Do Unto You" (p. 90), and by his omnipresent son Wendell, a towheaded outlaw "wearing a cowboy suit" and "double pistol holders" (p. 69). Such intimations of violence not only attend ironically Mother Chisom's sanguine depiction of her "clustering," "snuggled in" (p. 70), trailer-dwelling family but also help to define the peculiar intensity of her most successful child, the erstwhile typist Fay Chisom McKelva. Insensitive, grasping, willful, she betrays the narrow resources of her heritage by her violent entry into the scene of mourning. "Fay at that moment burst from the hall into the parlor. She glistened in black satin. Eyes straight ahead, she came running a path through all of them toward the coffin." In his dotage, Major Bullock trusts that she will "be a little soldier," but Fay throws herself "across the coffin onto the pillow, driving her lips without aim against the face under hers." When Mrs. Chisom observes " 'like mother, like daughter' " (pp. 84–86), readers can savor her unsuspected irony, but our attention is better directed to the metonymical evaluation of Fay's falsifying embrace. As a climax to the collision of class and temperament which has marked this near-allegorical scene of mourning, the insatiable lips of modernity consume the last vestiges of an altruistic southern conscience. By burying Judge McKelva in the new part of the cemetery, far removed from the grave of his first wife, Fay both literally and figuratively completes the severing of Becky's ancient climber from its roots.

In its fading day, the community of Mount Salus possesses neither the material nor spiritual resources needed to resist this appealing although deadly woman.

6

To borrow a phrase from the novel *Flood* (1964), Robert Penn Warren's study of decline in the contemporary South, the traditional society of Morgana and Mount Salus is "falling to pieces." The corrupting agent is not specifically the man-made reservoir that will drown Fiddlersburg, Tennessee, but similar forces of encroaching modernity traveling the old MacLain Road or passing by Mount Salus on Interstate 55. What Penn Warren and Welty both realize is that the kind of pleasant small-town southern life celebrated by Willie Morris in *North Toward Home*[49] has lost its social, economic, and moral authority with the passage of time. In the last segment of Eudora Welty's chronicle, this somber fact is projected by an enhanced fatality which threatens to assimilate her to the vision and form of a tragic historian. As Welty observed in 1980, "you can't live in the South and not be conscious" of its history of defeat. "There's a general memory of death and devastation on the premises,"[50] she added with some resignation. But although Welty's evolving regional identity may have shown her more clearly the appalling vulnerability of man in society, the reader who has followed the development of her chronicle will not be unduly alarmed by the wistful tone of this last formulation. Eudora Welty's fiction has always courted trouble and disruption, but at the same time her profoundly intuitive mind seeks to regain stability by discovering the spiritual order behind history. As the inheritors of Eudora Welty's vanishing South, Virgie Rainey and Laurel McKelva assume this burden of the spirit as they reenact the familiar drama of the individual resisting "a dying society." In their pursuit of the underlying continuity of southern history, each character marks a different point on the continuum of spiritual effort, but together Virgie Rainey and Laurel McKelva represent the most difficult, impressive victory for Eudora Welty's historicism. To ease analysis, their meditation can be divided into the phases of memory and imagination, complementary parts of an aesthetic process designed to identify and preserve the core of southern history.

Not surprisingly, the death room of Kate Rainey evokes for her daughter the cloying, suffocating quality of life in Morgana. "Behind the bed the window was full of cloudy, pressing flowers and leaves in heavy light, like a jar of figs in syrup held up. . . . The clock jangled faintly as cymbals struck under water, but did not strike; it couldn't" (*CS,* pp. 431–432). Further intensified for Virgie during the watch and burial, this aura of the "over-sweet," of life harshly restricted in "a dying society," is relieved only when she retreats to the Big Black or to the old country home of MacLain. There the closed society of Morgana opens upon a vista of personal freedom which encourages meditation and renewal. It is worth remarking here that although Welty's nonconforming individual is disloyal to the lingering southern community, his dissent is neither inherently nor absolutely valuable and thus always anticipates a further stage of development.

After the first round of mourning has been completed in "The Wanderers," Virgie makes her way "through the old MacLain place and the pasture and down to the river." Adrift in the Big Black, Virgie feels a brief cessation of movement and regresses to the most primitive realm of experience.

> She felt . . . the many dark ribbons of grass and mud touch her and leave her, like suggestions and withdrawals of some bondage. . . . She moved but like a cloud in skies, aware but only of the nebulous edges of her feeling and the vanishing opacity of her will. . . . In the middle of the river, whose downstream or upstream could not be told by a current, she lay on her stretched arm, not breathing, floating.

Her prose no less portentous than the situation, Welty affirms that "Virgie had reached the point where in the next moment she might turn into something without feeling it shock her" (*CS*, pp. 439–440). With such visionary antecedents as Lawrence's Ursula Brangwen and Katherine Anne Porter's Miranda, Virgie has descended beneath the level of personal feeling, will, and social attention to experience the freedom of a pristine awareness. Her transparency to this universe of possibility will prepare her not only to resist further threats and blandishment of the community but also to follow memory and imagination to a point of stability in the welter of experience.

After the interment of her mother, Virgie travels "the seven winding miles" to MacLain, a tiny, nearly extinct hamlet, whose uncrowded environs confirm her liberation in the Big Black. "Virgie Rainey on a stile, bereaved, hatless, unhidden now, in the rain," surveys in memory the history of her region. Its duration is recorded by "the old iron bell in the churchyard" resembling "a fallen meteor," and by the iron treads of the stile, "worn not by feet so much as by their history of warm, spreading seats." A more particular historical ambiance is evoked by funerary images of trouble and travail. Looming against a bleak October sky, "the Confederate soldier on the shaft looked like a chewed-on candle, as if old gnashing teeth had made him." The nearby cemetery is a compendium of aspiration and defeat, containing four generations of MacLains, Miss Snowdie's people, and the Confederate dead in a section of their own hallowing. Through Virgie's memory, we learn of both the immediate and remote past as it is conveyed by the solemn monuments of Cedar Hill. "Here lay Eugene," Virgie thinks, "the only MacLain man gone since her memory." The substantial portion of his life lived in exile in San Francisco remains unknown to Virgie, but she recalls the bitterness which attends his return to Morgana and governs subsequent behavior. Still more remote to memory is a tale of frontier violence loosely attached to Eugene's great-grandfather. "Didn't he kill a man, or have to," Virgie recalls, struggling to tell "the long story behind it, the vaunting and wandering from it" (*CS*, pp. 457–458). As memorist, Virgie Rainey succeeds in

171

recreating at least the outlines of the past; the time of founding, personal and corporate violence, alienation and death, compose an orderly, if dark, text of Mississippi history. But while Virgie's outline may satisfy the limited demands of chronology, it can assume power and depth only when memory is aided by imagination in seeking the inner meaning of history. The definition of this more personal realm begins with Virgie's discovery of old Miss Eckhart's marker on Cedar Hill.

It is a happy inspiration which directs Virgie's eye to "the dark, squat stone" (*CS,* p. 459) of her piano teacher in "June Recital." There Miss Eckhart's tyrannous instruction in musical passion and Virgie's youthful defection had created an impasse which is presented in terms commensurate with their sense of lofty mission. Relentless voyagers, "they were deliberately terrible. They looked at each other and neither wished to speak. They did not even horrify each other" (*CS,* p. 330) when Miss Eckhart and Virgie met briefly near the end of "June Recital." But in "The Wanderers" majesty fades under the force of memory and is replaced by Virgie's new sympathy for the dilemma of her outcast tutor. In this moment of imaginative extension, Virgie perceives the lesson of the once "threatening" illustration of "Perseus with the head of the Medusa" which adorned Miss Eckhart's "studio." "She had absorbed the hero and the victim and then, stoutly, could sit down to the piano with all Beethoven ahead of her. With her hate, with her love," Miss Eckhart "offered Virgie her Beethoven. . . . That was the gift she had touched with her fingers that had drifted and left her" (*CS,* p. 460). Reconciled to the past, Virgie is now joined on the stile by an "old wrapped-up Negro woman" who in turn accepts her abundant gift of love. For them the physical universe is transfigured and time momentarily relieved of its progression. "The world beating in their ears," Virgie and the dolorous black woman "heard through falling rain the running of the horse and bear, the stroke of the leopard, the dragon's crusty slither, and the glimmer and the trumpet of the swan" (*CS*, pp. 460–461). Renewed in meditation, Virgie is now prepared to leave Morgana and perhaps "go far."

In its transcendence, Virgie Rainey's "precipitous moment" of vision does not abrogate the facts of local southern history. Instead, it is her remembrance of this distinct heritage which discloses through the "falling rain" of Cedar Hill the essence of time itself. As "the running of the horse and bear" and "the trumpet of the swan" coalesce in Virgie's hearing, history and myth abandon their presumed mutual hostility and become indistinguishable avenues of perception. Freed from the collective mind of the community, Virgie Rainey emerges as a recognizable historicist whose act of memory and imagination assimilates her to Clement Musgrove and Ellen Fairchild. Their intense scrutiny of the Mississippi past and present, invariably marked by change, declension, or the insincerity of the community, subdues chaos by extracting a timeless human story. But although the last phase of Welty's chronicle repeats this familiar drama of change and adaptation to a new environment, it also provides a sterner test for Virgie Rainey and especially for Laurel McKelva Hand. By 1940 the failure of tradition not only enhances the normal fatality of Welty's chronicle but also threatens to overwhelm the individual with the enormity of his or her loss and the succeeding vacuum of cultural value. The fact that Virgie Rainey's middle years are spent in thrall to "a dying society" validates the influence of a distinctive southern heritage even as it is dispersed by a plural age. But a still more trying problem confronts both Eudora Welty and her searching characters of the modern and contemporary South: what kind and degree of historical continuity can be anticipated when traditional values no longer possess an actual geographic locale? In reaching toward Miss Eckhart, Virgie Rainey begins to answer this question, but in the last phase of Welty's chronicle, it remains for Laurel McKelva to build more deliberately and intensively upon Virgie's foundation work of memory and imagination. Laurel's deeper experience and more complex human relations inform her meditation and permit resumption of a distinctive southern tradition. Because she intervenes chronologically, Dicey Hastings can serve as a useful figure of transition.

In her relation to Virgie Rainey and Laurel McKelva, Dicey Hastings is a character who both summarizes the past and indicates the future. Looking back to Virgie's prophecy of departure, she has indeed gone "far," practicing absence as the most effective means of resistance to the community. Virgie Rainey has not yet been touched deeply by physical love, but the "engaged" Dicey Hastings has been urged forward by Welty into a more complex commitment. Accordingly, her return to Mississippi is not entirely voluntary but dictated by the illness and aging of those left behind. It is here that the dramatic circumstance of Dicey Hastings and Laurel McKelva converge, "Kin" anticipating in person, situation, and imagery the later novel, but subtle factors of differentiation are finally more important in framing an approach to *The Optimist's Daughter.* Dicey's nascent love inspires memory and imagination, makes the illicit passion of old Uncle Felix tolerable, and plucks the blushing Daisy from the reticent past. By comparison, the wary Kate can summon only a judgment and disbelief. The conclusion of "Kin" does not, however, allow this invidious contrast to stand without some fairly weighty qualification. As Kate and Dicey leave Mingo, they revert unexpectedly to a schoolgirl's idiom. "Excruciated" by the passionate datum of the past, they "leaned against each other" and "gasped and choked," until eyes "streaming" (*CS,* p. 564) with laughter had been excused from further vision. Although her advanced emotional state may permit Dicey to penetrate the past, her experiential limitations as one who has not yet savored and perhaps lost love diminish the authority of her vision. It remains for Laurel McKelva to bring this kind of emotional complexity to bear upon the traditional values of the past. Her meditation too may be divided into phases of preparation, memory, and imagination, as Laurel reflects upon the necessary changes of Mount Salus.

In his provocative essay entitled "What Survivors Do," Lewis P. Simpson turns to his own family history to illustrate the memorial aspect of southern culture. His fancy primed by Thomas Nelson Page's *Two Little Confederates,* Simpson was ready "as a kid in the 1920's" to glorify aged veterans of the Lost Cause who still inhabited the small Texas town of his raising. Simpson's self-confessed attraction to antebellum romance was implicitly sanctioned by a father who as lawyer and litterateur respected the canons of genteel writing, firmly segregating the realm of male-ironic-profane expression from that of formal literary endeavor. The result, Simpson recalls, was "one book of verse of stultifying sentimentality" and several southern tales marked as well by "an excess of piety and a deficiency of irony." The larger relevance of "What Survivors Do" will be explored in chapter 5, for Simpson can shed needed light upon the allusive texture of the last phase of Welty's chronicle, but his remarks invite more immediate application to the present situation of Mount Salus and to its observer, Laurel McKelva Hand. Deployed around the casket like so many spokes of a wheel, the mourners can no more safely venture beyond conventional "pieties associated with remembrance"[51] than can the elder Simpson or the son who once consulted Thomas Nelson Page for his southern history. To prepare for meditation, Laurel must resist this piety of the community, not by advancing a narrow accuracy of remembrance, but by recognizing that the past is finally immune to actual "help or hurt" (p. 179).

The Chisoms of Madrid, Texas, are ill bred and indelicate, but old Mount Salus realizes that their assault upon decorum is only the rind of a pervasive social process. "So powerful is the strain toward a democratic uniformity in our society that the emerging lower and middle classes have tended to replace the old aristocratic upper class in social significance,"[52] John Dollard observed after studying a small Mississippi Delta town in the 1930s. In a fury of denial, the community of Mount Salus responds to such "rivalry" (p. 82) by composing an enlarged memorial portrait of Judge McKelva. The rhetoric of apotheosis attributes to this "noble Roman" fairness of judgment, high spirits, sweetness of temper, and the kind of invincible courage which permits high ethical action. " 'Remember the day,' " Major Bullock prompts, " 'when Clint McKelva stood up and faced the White Caps?' " Presumably, these spiritual forebears of the Chisoms were disarmed and dismissed by McKelva grandiloquence: " 'Back to your holes, rats!' " (pp. 79–80), he ordered those who would storm the jail to execute mob justice. Considered in its own right, this wall of pious myth which the community builds is a form of self-protection, but it represents at the same time a grave threat to the historical imagination. In contesting the memorial portrait of Judge McKelva, Laurel is tempted to rest her case as a wronged historian upon mere accuracy of remembering.

At first Laurel attempts to correct the communal remembrance by disengaging the actual from the apocryphal. To the statement that "underneath it all," Clint McKelva "had a wonderful sense of humor," Laurel answers politely that "underneath it all, Father knew it *wasn't* funny." To the impertinent speculation that Clint McKelva's constitution "really must have been kind of delicate," Laurel answers still more curtly, "Father *was* delicate" (pp. 72–74). But she reserves her deepest disapproval for the communal assimilation of Judge McKelva to the florid code of the southern gentleman. Whether Major Bullock wavers in response to his own rhetoric or to morning toddies is a question which does not long detain Laurel. She emphasizes instead the inherent improbability of the White Caps episode. " 'I don't think that was Father,' " Laurel whispers to a friend, as Major Bullock "was going irrepressibly on." " 'He had no patience for show' " or " 'use for what he called theatrics.' " Major Bullock, Laurel concludes, is " 'trying to make Father into something he wanted to be himself' " (pp. 79–80). To the extent that Laurel dwells upon the unfairness of this appropriation, she reveals ironically the lingering influence of "a dying society" upon her own exceptional sensibility. Marked by "an excess of piety," the historical template of Mount Salus at first molds Laurel into a defensive historian who is preoccupied with validating the past. Her preparation to remember and to imagine a more profound kind of historiography will be achieved only when Laurel recognizes that the past is inviolable because it is over and complete.

Laurel's protectiveness appears first when she pleads that the coffin remain closed, extends next through her correction of Mount Salus's remembering, and reaches a blur of urgency when Fay Chisom strides headlong into the scene of mourning. " 'Stop her,' Laurel said to the room," before Fay fastens upon the body of Judge McKelva with the harsh lips of her resentful code. Amid the ensuing action of Fay's theatrics, Mother Chisom's doting approval, and the wavering concern of Major Bullock for the distraught widow, Laurel achieves an enabling view of the sacred, inviolable character of the past. The profane cosmetology of Mr. Pitts had created the illusion that "danger" to the "lived life" of Clinton McKelva "was still alive," but his indifference to the corrosive kiss transfixes Laurel and reveals that "now there was no longer that." Accordingly, she can "give up bearing the weight of that lid" (pp. 85–87) which had exposed Judge McKelva to the vying of old Mount Salus and the intruders from Madrid, Texas. The crux of metaphysical wisdom upon which Laurel will expand in parts 3 and 4 of *The Optimist's Daughter* is that "the living's" story, whether framed in piety or irony, operates upon an aesthetic plane and thus does not imperil the actual existence of a beloved father. Once this ontological distinction has been made by Laurel, her defensive historicity falls away and she can begin to compose her own portrait of the past. Judge Mac's life is over and complete, perfect, except as it will be recalled in memory and evaluated through imagination.

In the sequence of Laurel's meditation, the funeral of Friday is followed by periods of increasing solitude until on Sunday eve-

177

ning she reaches the stillest moment in Eudora Welty's Mississippi chronicle. Escorted "in gallant fashion" by Major Bullock,
Laurel arrives home after an evening of reminiscence with her
"bridesmaids." Their "grieving" and evocation of Laurel's brief
marriage to Philip Hand sound a controlling elegiac note in part
3 of *The Optimist's Daughter,* but it is their juxtaposition of Fay
Chisom and Miss Becky Thurston McKelva which defines the
antithetical poles of Laurel's meditation. Upon entering the
house, she is assaulted by a "never resting" bird, a frantic chimney swift, whose "shuttling through the dark rooms" (pp. 127–
130) recapitulates Fay's audacious career in Mount Salus. Locked
for protection in a tiny sewing room, Laurel discovers in her
mother's cherry secretary and brass-bound trunk the remnants of
a life lived with dignity and control. If the chasm separating
these two vivid women marks the outset of Laurel's meditation,
then their gradual reconciliation under the force of memory and
imagination signals the final, mature phase of Laurel's historiography.

Evidence of Judge Mac's domestic nature and of Becky's keen
devotion are discovered by Laurel in the tiny sewing room, "all
dark," where her mother's secretary and trunk reveal a cache of
feminine memorabilia. A copy of *McGuffey's Fifth Reader,* saved
letters from Clinton to Becky, innumerable romantic snapshots,
a carved stone boat with the initials C.C.M.McK., and letters
from mother to daughter contribute to the emerging portrait of
the past. But this development will not be achieved by mere
identification or even collocation of relics pertinent to the old life
of the McKelvas. In reflecting upon the poetic structure of *A
Curtain of Green,* Kurt Opitz employed the image of "fine
threads" running to "a hidden center, suggesting by their trace
. . . a secret core in life."[53] It was the signal failure of Albert and
Ellie Morgan, Clytie Farr, and Sara Morton to follow this tracery
which occasioned the pathos of Welty's first volume. A more
resourceful and determined quester, Laurel not only succeeds in
identifying the documentary evidence of the past but also returns

in memory to the "hidden center" of its vitality. By reattaching object to original emotion, Laurel will approach the inner meaning of history. Throughout the night, the imperative nature of this task is suggested both by the turbulence of the elements and by the near-presence of Fay's hovering self, frantic harbinger of her imminent return to Mount Salus.

Prompted by Laurel's memory, the contents of Miss Becky's sewing room disclose a common referent in her early life and subsequent visits "up home" in West Virginia. As a young, unmarried schoolteacher, Becky would recite the academic verses of McGuffey's *"quivering and shivering"* poetry while riding to school in Beechy Creek. " 'I memorized with no great effort, dear,' " Becky once assured her disbelieving daughter. Letters "tied in ribbons," "grayed and stippled" photographs of Becky and Clinton posing in "a leafy glade," and the carved "bit of slatey stone" form the record of a courtship conducted atop "the highest roof in the world." Becky's round of marital responsibility in Mount Salus is interrupted each summer so that she may savor anew the misty river "where it rounded the foot of the mountain," the "sweet long grass that swept" upland, and the boisterous society of her six brothers, who told "so many stories" that "she cried." Undertaken in joyful anticipation, ended with something approaching distress, these annual visits of Becky Thurston McKelva and Laurel are freshly evoked by the poignant trunk, "—*this* trunk," Laurel thinks, filled "with all the dresses made in this room" (pp. 135–141). As the mute, forgotten impedimenta of the past are made to bear again their lost emotion, the filaments of memory transport Laurel to the "hidden center" of her mother's extraordinary intensity and will. Once Dr. Bolt had warned the dying Becky not to presume to know the mind of his Presbyterian God. " 'Young man,' " she replied, " 'there's a white strawberry that grows completely in the wild' " on Nine Mile Mountain. Should the outlander find them " 'by mistake,' " he might pick and cradle the berries in a hat lined with leaves, but his hesitation would " 'finish 'em.' " Only the person who can act like a mountain would "'stand and eat them on the spot'" (p. 149). For Miss Becky Thurston, Nine Mile Mountain was not a chimerical time enhanced by the torment of her fatal cancer but a religious experience which initiated her into the breathtaking, although precarious, way of human existence.

As a determined, resourceful memorist, Laurel redeems the past from obscurity by reattaching object to emotion. Miss Becky's sewing room and Uncle Felix's gloomy ell may begin as museums of a remote, untouchable past, but through the agency of memory the former is restored to activity, containing once again the "pedalling and whirring" of the machine and Laurel piecing together "fallen scraps of cloth" (p. 133) which await her design. The mature pattern, though, still eludes Laurel, not because memory lacks power or direction, but because an element of reservation inhibits her partaking of the emotion of the past. By inference, she too might cradle the berries, but this lingering defensiveness cannot resist the contents of "the last pigeonhole" of Becky's desk. The last of twenty-six pigeonholes contains letters from Laurel's grandmother to Becky, "her young, venturesome, defiant, happily married daughter" now installed in Mount Salus. "Widowed, her health failing, lonely and sometimes bedridden," Grandmother Thurston writes nevertheless with a "bravery and serenity" which "Laurel could hardly believe." Something more intense than belief, however, is inspired when Laurel encounters her own name in these hastily scrawled notes. "I will try to send Laurel a cup of sugar for her birthday. Though if I can find a way to do it, I would like to send her one of my pigeons. It would eat from her hand, if she would let it." The pigeons that had affrighted Laurel during visits "up home," grossly "eating out of each other's craws," now release "a flood of feeling" which permits Laurel to enter imaginatively "a secret core in life." It is the immemorial hunger of all humans, whether expressed in joy or humiliation, belonging or exile, which Laurel now shares on an intimate, dramatic level. Liberated from "the old perfection" (pp. 153–154) of her remembrance, Grandmother Thurston, Miss Becky, Judge Mac, and especially the lost husband Philip Hand begin to dance "up and down"—the language is Virginia Woolf's—in the "invisible elastic net" of Laurel's imagination. The major work of part 4 of *The Optimist's Daughter* will both test and expand the limits of this historical imagination by exposing Laurel to Fay Chisom McKelva, whose return to Mount Salus on Monday morning coincides briefly with Laurel's preparations for departure. In their engagement, Fay's distrust proves unalterable, but Laurel wins a new tolerance which is not without cultural import.

Throughout *The Optimist's Daughter,* Eudora Welty has pressed into symbolic service the most quotidian objects of local culture. It is not surprising, then, that a satiny breadboard should direct the last stage of Laurel's meditation. Built by the "perfectionist" Philip Hand, "desecrated" by Fay Chisom McKelva, the forgotten breadboard is discovered by Laurel in the same instant as Fay's return from Texas. " 'You mean to tell me you're still here?' Fay said," as Laurel surveys the "scored and grimy" record of Philip's exacting industry. " 'Look. Look where the surface is splintered—look at those gouges. You might have gone at it with an icepick.' " To Laurel, who would astonish the saints with her piety, Fay replies, " 'Who wants an everlasting breadboard? It's the last thing on earth anybody needs!' " (p. 172). In her pragmatism and complacency, Fay proves impervious to Laurel's plea that she respect the intention and artistry of the maker. " 'Do you know what a labor of love is? My husband made it for my mother, so she'd have a good one. . . . it's made on the true, look and see, it's still as straight as his T-square. . . . My mother blessed him when she saw this' " (pp. 175–176). When Fay responds with harsh literalness that Philip Hand is " 'dead, isn't he?' " Laurel raises the old board in anger: "She had been ready to hurt Fay. She had wanted to hurt her, and had known herself capable of doing it" (pp. 177–178). The historian who has progressed through stages of defensiveness to evoke in memory and imagination the timeless core of human motivation is here tempted to reenact the harsh law of Fay's nature. The force which stays her hand permits Laurel to place both Fay Chisom and the emblematic breadboard within the full perspective of history. With this last delicate adjustment of the historical imagination, Welty prepares Laurel to resume her life in Chicago and directs the reader to a resolution of the ancient battle over continuity and discontinuity in southern history.

Waiting in memory like "Lazarus" (p. 154), Philip returns from "a death made of water and fire" (p. 160) to support Laurel during her confrontation with Fay. In courtship and marriage, Philip Hand emboldened Laurel, so that her view "of love as shelter . . . fell away from her like all one garment" (p. 161). Philip also released Laurel from an artistic shyness or reserve. An architect and inveterate maker of useful things, Philip "taught her to draw, to work toward and into her pattern, not to sketch peripheries" (p. 161). But for all the radiance of their work and love, Philip "was not an optimist—she knew that." A house built "to stand, to last, to be lived in," he realized, might entail "the same devotion and tireless effort" as one made "of cards" (p. 162). Accordingly, even the most conscientious builder of houses, families, or cultures cannot insure them against the dive of a kamikaze in World War II or a pert little typist encountered at the Southern Bar Association in New Orleans. Renewed in memory, Philip's harshest gift to Laurel is his recognition of this imponderable element in human history. It is her insight into the same ironic process which now reconciles Laurel to the appearance of Fay, who always "was coming" (p. 174), and to the violence of her will, which resists humane conception. Isolated, "without any powers of passion or imagination," Fay "could only strike out those little fists at random, or spit from her little mouth" (p. 178), with scarcely more control than the impulsive chimney swift. But for all his guarded cynicism, Philip Hand was also a resolute maker who once confessed to his wife that he got "a moral satisfaction out of putting things together" (p. 161). Although gouged and begrimed, the breadboard remains intact, "a labor of love" which expresses both relationship and deliberate resistance to the undifferentiated flow of life. No longer a weapon, the old board is slowly lowered in charity, its palpable form assimilated by Laurel and now reprojected as ethical resolve. Her assertion that the desecrated board contains "the whole solid past" (p. 178) of love and understanding may be lost upon Fay, but the reader understands that it signals the conclusion of Laurel's prolonged meditation upon the perpetual fight of history. Having found a place even for Fay Chisom in the McKelva family history, Laurel can depart with confidence for a new life in Chicago.[54]

7

Earlier in chapter 4, "The Burning" provided the conceptual terms needed to study the last phase of Welty's Mississippi story. Here it can function with still greater effect to confirm the unity of her chronicle in the span of years marked by "The Burning" and *The Optimist's Daughter*. First published in 1951, "The Burning" was revised for inclusion in *The Bride of the Innisfallen* (1955). Generally, the effect of Welty's revision was to remove elements of explication and transition, concealing in fuller darkness the mournful origins of Phinny and underscoring the darting, surrealistic logic of association which supplants more traditional plotting. These alterations do tighten and improve the reading text, but they were dictated as well by a deeper intent regarding Delilah's characterization. As "The Burning" becomes more opaque, more reluctant to entertain questions of mere verisimilitude, it makes room at the center for Delilah's enhanced consciousness and greater receptivity to the stirring events of 1863. This focusing in the second version necessitated the cutting of a long declamatory passage which had cast Delilah's antecedent, Florabel, in a role hardly to be differentiated from the mute nature that her name connotes. "As a slave," Florabel "was earth's most detached visitor." Her temperament formed by an accretion of commands, she could only wait and witness, indiscriminately serving "the creation and the destruction." In short, "the world had not touched her."[55] What sets Florabel and Delilah apart is the latter's increased vulnerability to time, especially as it draws the individual into the moral drama of relationships. This development reflects in part the pressure of collection, for *The Bride of the Innisfallen and Other Stories* is dedicated to the mysteries of the inner life, but it also points to the underlying shape of Eudora Welty's Mississippi chronicle. Delilah's dawning awareness contributes significantly to Welty's familiar pursuit of historical continuity.

For Miss Myra and Miss Theo, reality has lapsed insubstantial. Their dim parlor glimmers with "precious, breakable things" of which gentlewomen never seem to tire. Carved flowers dance chastely around the ceiling, and the "pretty chair" upon which Myra rests evokes by way of comparison the "red, rubbed" confines of her ring box. A more profound distortion lies concealed within the illusory depths of an elaborate mirror which overhangs the mantel. Its Venetian frame modestly fills with "dusted pictures" when Myra and Theo are pushed to the floor. It reflects not the "grimacing, uneasy" horse that also violates their sanctuary but "a white silhouette, like something cut out of the room's dark" (*CS,* pp. 482–483). The only reality it returns with any degree of authority is the features of these delicate ladies who have symbolically embraced the mirror when "The Burning" commences. Thereafter the isolation, the excessive refinement of sensibility, and the narcissistic penchant of both Miss Myra and Miss Theo ensure their alienation from historical currents which sweep away the economic foundations of antebellum culture. Their suicide may not lack a certain measure of heroic resistance, but it testifies more conclusively to the failure of the historical imagination. Ironically, this power is assumed by Delilah, erstwhile slave, who emerges as a more complex figure than either of her mistresses. In "The Burning" she alone suffers the full drama of time, as her mind still charged with the nullity of slavery strains to accept freedom and moral responsibility. Although beyond the confines of the present study, a full examination of both texts of "The Burning" would reveal that even the most modest alteration contributes to the centering and heightening of this dramatic crux.

After Delilah has helped Miss Myra and Theo to commit suicide, instinct leads her back to Rose Hill and dictates that such familiar, work-a-day objects as "an iron pot" will evoke the old security of the slave's appointed duty. But it is finally the elegant Venetian mirror, lodged in "the chimney's craw," which leads Delilah beyond instinct into the more creative realms of memory and imagination. Adjusted horizontally, the same mirror had readily conspired with Myra and Theo to censor a harsh reality. Lying "face-up in the cinders," it now catches the full "July blaze" and provokes a vision of social chaos which "felled" Delilah flat. Paradoxically, the intense heat which consumes Phinny gives new life to the mirror's once placid surface. Images of martial strife appear, meld with remembered scenes of Venetian life which adorned the mirror's gilded frame, and then spiral "down to bottomless ash." Delilah "dreaded the fury of all the butterflies and dragonflies in the world riding, blades unconcealed and at point—descending," but her meditation upon catastrophe veers suddenly to encompass "one whale made of his own grave, opening his mouth to swallow Jonah one more time." The memory of his "homely face," peering "from the red lane he'd gone down," is restored to vividness, for "he was her Jonah, her Phinny, her black monkey," although "it was long ago he was taken from her the first time." Rising "stiffly" from the ashes, Delilah "cocked her head, looked sharp into the mirror, and caught the motherly image" of a fierce protectress. "Then she looked in the feathery ashes and found Phinny's bones" (*CS*, pp. 492–493). For several commentators, the elusive, elliptical course of Delilah's meditation signals only hallucination, primary evidence of Welty's failure in "The Burning" to create a mind capable of "moral comprehension."[56] But just as other presumed gaps in narrative structure have revealed the silent operation of cultural factors, so Delilah's vision becomes more intelligible and revealing of moral perspective when examined as a timely social document. In particular, this approach not only illuminates the underlying logic of Phinny's association with Jonah, surely the most abrupt, puzzling juncture in Delilah's meditation, but also prepares the reader to grasp the nature of her victory in "the feathery ashes" of Rose Hill.

Welty's biblical allusion is apt, for the story of Jonah swallowed by the whale has historically appealed to the Negro's imagination. In the 1920s an old black man told his distinguished interviewer, Howard Odum, that this legendary fish represented "the terror of the sea." While being transported from Africa, the Negro "saw de whales and fishes" and "de race hain't nebber got over it yet."[57] Perhaps the dismay which "felled her flat" over the mirror's cracked, swollen surface bespeaks this fearful heritage, but for Delilah the apparition of Jonah has more positive ramifications as well. "Rising again from the waters below," the triumphant whale both contradicts a pattern of chaotic descent and conveys the same sense of eternally recurring hope with which the Negro invested this parable. "Slap!" goes the old spiritual when Jonah "struck the water," but if his delivery after three days prefigured Christ's Resurrection, then it prophesied still more acutely the slave's own release from bondage. Historically, the events of 1863 ensured the slave's ultimate release from physical bondage, but as Delilah's amended name implies, Welty is more concerned with restoring the inner freedom and moral responsibility denied by a system which "recognized no permanent human relationship other than master and slave."[58] In "The Burning" the inevitable corruption of the slave's moral nature is implied when Delilah, shorn of mercy and courage, silently consents to the betrayal of Phinny. But in her subsequent vision, Delilah is redeemed, both from her race's historic fall into degradation and from the immediate sacrifice of

Phinny. Resurrected in memory, Delilah's "black monkey" is imaginatively linked with Jonah, familiar symbol of physical and spiritual regeneration in the Old South. Those who claim that the catastrophic events of "The Burning" have "no meaning, no moral implication"[59] for Delilah, have not only missed the social and cultural vibrations of her meditation but have also dismissed the subtle inflection of her conscience, the renewed affinities which bind Delilah and her probable son. With the "treasure" of Phinny's bones carefully "tied up" in "a square" torn from her skirt (*CS*, p. 494), Delilah is last seen crossing the Big Black River, her head exposed to the light from a newly "opened sky."

Considered in relation to much Civil War writing, "The Burning" represents a bold experiment in treating the character of the slave. As Robert Lively notes, Civil War fiction has historically failed "to understand individual slave characters or to wake in readers any real sense of identification with them."[60] Novels illustrating abolitionist themes have preferred such caricatures as the noble child of nature or his less wholesome counterpart brutalized by the whip. With no less fervor, southern partisans embellish the legend of the trusted servant, devoted to his master and so perfectly assimilated to antebellum life that emancipation has only a hollow ring. Led by Faulkner, Eudora Welty and a host of other moderns have succeeded in freeing Civil War writing from the grip of racial or sectional ideology. The imperfect encounter of Phinny and Delilah, for example, is not an occasion for indictment or defense; instead, it allows Welty to fulfill the highest aspiration which Robert Lively accords the historical novelist: "if bold, he seeks to define the content of hope, the anatomy of torment, the nature of man."[61] But while "The Burning" can be studied fruitfully from a generic point of view, it is more imperative to place Welty's single reenactment of Civil War history in firmer alignment with the last phase of her chronicle. Delilah's moment of self-contemplation not only gives moral definition to the past but also anticipates the future development of Virgie Rainey and Laurel McKelva Hand. Ironically, it is Delilah, the least of Welty's characters, who ensures the final continuity of her Mississippi chronicle.

Eudora Welty and Carl Degler define essentially the same distinctive southern tradition. For Degler, the persistence of this unique heritage is still a verifiable truth, resting in the lucidity of statistical analysis. Eudora Welty's evidence of historical continuity is more personal and dramatic, residing instead in a structure of meditation which is governed by regional values. In commenting upon Chekhov, whom Welty considers to be "very close to the South," she stressed the "love and understanding" which animate his characters, their "knowledge and acceptance of each other's idiosyncracies" [*sic*], and a capacity to respond to the fortuitous from inexhaustible "deeps of character." Because these qualities touch so intimately the individualistic core of Welty's tradition, they seem "very Southern"[62] to her. By cherishing Phinny's bones, Delilah fulfills Miss Theo's fierce injunction to "Remember" the destruction of Rose Hill. But what Delilah preserves through a halting act of memory and imagination is not the idyll of leisure and privilege which Myra and Theo indicate but a cluster of humane values that has for Welty distinctive regional significance. In their subsequent recognition of Miss Eckhart and Fay Chisom as members of the human family, Virgie Rainey and Laurel McKelva continue to define through progressively richer acts of memory and imagination a permanent locus for the usable southern past. At first glance, no two characters are more dissimilar than Delilah, who possesses only the germ of a sensitive moral nature, and Laurel, whose equable temperament represents the achievement of full humanity. But although their seasons of maturity may differ radically in degree, Delilah and Laurel are unified in their timeless motive of love. Located at the outset of a dire historical process, Delilah symbolically expresses faith in the future by redeeming a child from oblivion. Placed at the melancholy conclusion of the same process, Laurel reaffirms this instant of maternal resolution when the raised board is stayed from violence by "the memory of the child Wendell" (p. 178). Through recurring imagery of situation, Eudora Welty signals unmistakably the persistence in time of a distinctive "Southern character." Perhaps this continuity of moral value is what she identified in her most recent interview. After testifying that "there's a general memory of death and devastation on the premises," she concluded on a more confident note: "I still feel there is a Southern character—a view, an outlook, a leaning toward certain forms of life—that will persist for a time anyway."[63]

Notes to Chapter 4

1. William D. McCain, *The Story of Jackson: A History of the Capital of Mississippi, 1821–1951* (Jackson: J. F. Hyer, 1953), p. 194.

2. McCain, p. 201.

3. Ibid.

4. Varina Howell Davis, *Jefferson Davis: A Memoir* (New York: Belford, 1890), vol. 2, pp. 420–21.

5. Elmo Howell, "Eudora Welty's Civil War Story," *Notes on Mississippi Writers* 2 (spring 1969), p. 9.

6. Quoted by A. A. Hoehling, *Vicksburg: 47 Days of Siege* (Englewood Cliffs, N.J.: Prentice-Hall, 1969), p. 1.

7. Quoted by Varina Howell Davis, *Jefferson Davis*, vol. 2, pp. 423, 437.

8. The Comte De Paris, *History of the Civil War in America*, ed. John P. Nicholson (Philadelphia: Porter and Coates, 1883), vol. 3, pp. 400–401.

9. Ruth M. Vande Kieft, *Eudora Welty* (New York: Twayne, 1962), pp. 155–56.

10. T. S. Eliot, *After Strange Gods: A Primer of Modern Heresy* (New York: Harcourt, Brace, 1934), pp. 15–21.

11. These familiar excerpts from Jefferson's *Notes on the State of Virginia* are quoted by Winthrop D. Jordan, *White over Black: American Attitudes toward the Negro, 1550–1812* (Chapel Hill: University of North Carolina Press, 1968), p. 432.

12. *Jackson Today: A City of Change/Challenge* (Jackson: Chamber of Commerce, n.d.), unpaginated.

13. Linda Kuehl, "The Art of Fiction XLVII: Eudora Welty," *Paris Review* 55 (fall 1972) p. 93.

14. See chapters 15, 20, and 24 of William Alexander Percy's *Lanterns on the Levee: Recollections of a Planter's Son* (New York: Knopf, 1941).

15. Diana Trilling, "Fiction in Review," *Nation,* 11 May 1946, p. 578, and Margaret Marshall, "Notes by the Way," *Nation,* 10 September 1949, p. 256.

16. Arlin Turner, "Dim Pages in Literary History: The South since the Civil War," in *Southern Literary Study: Problems and Possibilities,* ed. Louis D. Rubin, Jr., and C. Hugh Holman (Chapel Hill: University of North Carolina Press, 1974), p. 42.

17. *Jackson Daily News,* 1 June 1963, p. 8, and *New York Times,* 14 June 1963, pp. 1, 15.

18. Robert Van Gelder, "An Interview with Eudora Welty," *Writers and Writing* (New York: Scribner's, 1946), p. 288.

19. Printed in *Write and Rewrite: A Study of the Creative Process,* ed. John Kuehl (New York: Meredith, 1967), pp. 4–18.

20. Eudora Welty, "The Demonstrators," *New Yorker,* 26 November 1966, pp. 62–63. Subsequent page references are included parenthetically in the text.

21. "New Writers: Eudora Welty," *Publishers Weekly,* 6 December 1941, p. 2100.

22. Walter Clemons, "Meeting Miss Welty," *New York Times Book Review,* 12 April 1970, p. 2.

23. Kuehl, "Art of Fiction," p. 86.

24. "Must the Novelist Crusade?" (1965), in *The Eye of the Story,* p. 155.

25. "The Southern Imagination," moderator William F. Buckley (Columbia, S.C.: Firing Line, 1972), pp. 1–3. Transcription of television broadcast, 24 December 1972.

26. "A Southern Mode of Imagination" (1959), in *Essays of Four Decades,* p. 584.

27. "A Southern Mode of Imagination," pp. 588–89.

28. Buckley, "The Southern Imagination," p. 2.

29. Kuehl, "Art of Fiction," pp. 74–75.

30. Michiko Kakutani, "South Is Wherever Eudora Welty Is," *New York Times,* 27 June 1980, p. C8.

31. Quoted by Carl N. Degler, *Place Over Time: The Continuity of Southern Distinctiveness* (Baton Rouge: Louisiana State University Press, 1977), pp. 4–5.

32. Degler, pp. 2–3.

33. Degler, pp. 7–18, 131.

34. Degler, pp. 67–68.

35. Degler, pp. 14, 43.

36. Kuehl, "Art of Fiction," pp. 80, 93.

37. Reynolds Price, "Eudora Welty in Type and Person," *New York Times Book Review,* 7 May 1978, p. 7.

38. "The Abode of Summer," *Harper's Bazaar,* June 1952, p. 51.

39. Kuehl, p. 87.

40. Charles T. Bunting, " 'The Interior World' An Interview with Eudora Welty," *Southern Review* 8 (October 1972), pp. 727–728.

41. "Henry Green: A Novelist of the Imagination," *Texas Quarterly* 4 (autumn 1961), p. 255.

42. Frederick R. Karl, *The Contemporary English Novel* (New York: Noonday, 1962), p. 184.

43. George Lukács, "The Ideology of Modernism" (1956), in *Issues in Contemporary Literary Criticism,* ed. Gregory T. Polletta (Boston: Little, Brown, 1973), p. 716.

44. The phrase is employed with reference to *The Wide Net* by Robert Penn Warren in "The Love and the Separateness in Miss Welty," *Kenyon Review* 6 (spring 1944), p. 257.

45. Hayden White, *Metahistory: The Historical Imagination in Nineteenth-Century Europe* (Baltimore: Johns Hopkins University Press, 1973), p. 9.

46. Ibid., pp. 11–17.

47. Ibid., p. 35.

48. Ibid., p. 301.

49. In *North Toward Home* (Boston: Houghton Mifflin, 1967), Willie Morris evokes the special ambiance of Southern small-town life just before World War II. In Yazoo City, Mississippi, he remembers "something spooked-up and romantic, which did extravagant things to the imagination of its bright and resourceful boys" (p. 29).

50. Kakutani, p. C8.

51. Lewis P. Simpson, "What Survivors Do," in *The Brazen Face of History: Studies in the Literary Consciousness in America* (Baton Rouge: Louisiana State University Press, 1980), pp. 233–35.

52. John Dollard, *Caste and Class in a Southern Town* (New Haven: Yale University Press, 1937), p. 79.

53. "Eudora Welty: The Ordeal of a Captive Soul," *Critique* 7 (winter 1964–65), p. 82.

54. My conclusions regarding Laurel differ significantly from those of Thomas D. Young in his very useful study *The Past in the Present: A Thematic Study of Modern Southern Fiction* (Baton Rouge: Louisiana State University Press, 1981), pp. 87–115. Specifically, Young's conclusion that Laurel is finally "bound by traditional values little more than Fay is" (p. 114) seems to underestimate the force of memory and imagination in securing the values of the past, although they no longer possess an actual communal frame of reference.

55. "The Burning," *Harper's Bazaar,* March 1951, p. 247.

56. Vande Kieft, *Eudora Welty,* p. 156.

57. Howard W. Odum and Guy B. Johnson, *The Negro and His Songs: A Study of Typical Negro Songs in the South* (Chapel Hill: University of North Carolina Press, 1925), p. 141.

58. Jordan, *White Over Black,* p. 160.

59. Howell, "Eudora Welty's Civil War Story," p. 4.

60. Robert A. Lively, *Fiction Fights the Civil War: An Unfinished Chapter in*

the Literary History of the American People (Chapel Hill: University of North Carolina Press, 1957), p. 49.

61. Lively, p. 78.
62. Kuehl, "Art of Fiction," pp. 74–75.
63. Kakutani, p. C8.

5

Conclusion

"And You're Left with History"

T HE problem of history in *The Optimist's Daughter* may be reviewed by quoting a remarkable passage from *The Velvet Horn* (1957). In Andrew Lytle's superlative novel, Jack Cropleigh thinks "about history" as he and his nephew Lucius return from "the peaks of Laurel" to mourn the young boy's father:

> History, the backward-stepping rocks of a dry stream bed, that tells you where you've been, if you can backtrack yourself. The young can't see; the old looking back to see forward: all bewildered, caught up by feeling or revery. Who's to show the way? Joe Cree, dead in the house, resurrected now in Lucius. Jesus, what a brief mortality. Lucius will weep, sleep, afterwards wake to eat a hearty breakfast: the drought will break, the rains come, the season turn, and you're left with history. History, the delayed surprise. [1]

Parts of this passage apply cogently to the person and discipline of Laurel McKelva Hand. Neither "young" nor "old," not hobbled at the last by "feeling or revery," Laurel does indeed discover where she has "been," meeting the implied challenge of Jack Cropleigh's meditation. "Resurrected" in Laurel, the sensitivity of Judge Mac and the fortitude of Miss Becky will be practiced hereafter in "a postsouthern America." [2]

In a very real sense, it is Welty herself, not Laurel, who has been "left" in the last phase of her chronicle with the bare, irreversible facts of historical change. Welty's "surprise" was perhaps "delayed" but certainly not complete nor incapacitating, for she has always been adjusted to the passage of time and to the vicissitudes of history. But the disappearance of the actual southern community did leave a distinct mark upon nearly all of

Welty's writing after *Delta Wedding*. The legendary, parabolic quality of "The Burning," "Kin," and "The Whole World Knows," the frequency of type names such as Holden, Mississippi, Uncle Felix, and Sister Anne Fry, and Welty's unaccustomed attraction to the topical in "Voice" and "The Demonstrators" testify to the stress of modern history upon the writer's imagination. The culmination of this stress in *The Optimist's Daughter* forms the subject of chapter 5. Ultimately, such gifted protagonists as Virgie Rainey and Laurel McKelva Hand confirm Welty's artistic control, but her witness to the acceleration of southern history after World War II also presents an occasion for defining more sharply the postulates of intellectual and literary history which may be said to attend her practice of the literary vocation. Lewis P. Simpson's conception and articulation of the modern "Republic of Letters" will be influential in giving final shape to Welty's southern chronicle. A brief summation and enlargement of Laurel McKelva's privileged position in Welty's chronicle, further study of the special relationship between *Losing Battles* and *The Optimist's Daughter,* and identification of a habit of literary allusion which becomes pronounced in *Delta Wedding* and persists thereafter will supply the stages of this concluding discussion.

2

For the purpose of summation, it is both convenient and revealing that Walter Sullivan selects *The Optimist's Daughter* to illustrate his well-known thesis of cultural and literary decline in the contemporary South. In *Death by Melancholy* (1972) and *A Requiem for the Renascence* (1976), he accumulates an extensive list of corrupting agents: the hydrogen bomb, Bennett Cerf and the *New York Times,* scientism, feminism, and sociology, the civil rights movement, mechanized farming, urban concentrations of power, and finance capitalism. Acting in concert after World War II, these "inversions" of modern life disrupted the traditional southern community, eroding both its material and metaphysical wealth, and thus deprived the writer of the assuring center of his vision. Because the imaginative southern writer draws his or her strength from the local community, he will reveal unerringly the pernicious effect of this "Breaking of Nations."[3] For Walter Sullivan, comparison of *The Golden Apples* and *The Optimist's Daughter* illustrates the sorrowful nexus of cultural and literary decline which marks the end of the Southern Literary Renascence.

Sullivan recognizes that the force of society acts throughout *The Golden Apples* to adjudicate ethical violations (Virgie's sexual license) and to provide a basis for personal identity, but he is more impressed by the community of Morgana during the funeral of Kate Rainey. Fulfilling unconsciously their roles in an integral society, "old men talk quietly; women move from dining room to kitchen; young wives complain; preachers proselyte; [and] children play in the yard without ever quite breaching the general decorum." Compare this dignified office of burial, Sullivan challenges, with "our own funerary practices—the mortuary, the mausoleum, the crematoreum." Even Virgie Rainey in her final solitude and imminent departure from Morgana is only a distant "harbinger of the . . . dissolution of community and of the chaos that ultimately will ensue."[4] This social development is complete by the time of *The Optimist's Daughter.* As a consequence, Sullivan argues, Welty's moral vision undergoes an analogous weakening or deterioration. Deprived of community by "the social and philosophical alterations which afflicted southern society after World War II," an uncertain Welty cannot provide Laurel McKelva with a plausible identity or a constant direction in life. "It is here," Sullivan concludes, "in the development of Laurel, that we miss the rich comprehensiveness which enhances Miss Welty's earlier work." Virgie Rainey, for example, "can still find the meaning of the past by her reconciliation with Miss Eckhart," but Laurel "achieves no more than an uneasy peace with life and time before she leaves Mount Salus forever . . . and goes back to

Chicago." Walter Sullivan affirms that "the postmodern world with its loss of community and myth will no longer support her"⁵—or Eudora Welty, for that matter.

The most immediate, apparent critique of Sullivan's thesis is that it will tolerate misreading. During the obsequies of Kate Rainey, Morgana is not the conclave of dignified, integral folk that he claims. But the application of Sullivan's thesis to Welty finally reveals a more serious problem than local misinterpretation of the text. By reading *The Optimist's Daughter* as a document of resignation, Sullivan fails to understand that Welty's last novel is grounded structurally and spiritually in her Mississippi chronicle. Structurally, the modern and contemporary phases of Welty's larger story generate the same kind of conflict that has attended her long procession of Mississippi history. In their respective ages, Clement Musgrove and Laurel McKelva encounter the same avatars of will, the same exponents of what Leon Howard has termed "the Baconian impulse," who periodically erupt in the historical field. They signal in turn the inevitability of a new age, a perennial modernity which at first advances the cause of chaos, but which soon settles into a predictable life. Spiritually, this drama of cultural transformation is always observed and evaluated by a figure of pronounced sensitivity. Through memory and imagination, these well-burnished reflectors of spiritual value affirm a timeless human essence *within* the ceaseless flux of history. The continuity which emerges is at once a cause and a symptom of Welty's long-standing confidence in human nature. If Sullivan had examined *The Optimist's Daughter* from the structural and spiritual vantage point of Welty's chronicle, perhaps he would have recognized Laurel both as a participant in typical history and as its most profound evaluator. In the past, this failure to discern the cultural unity of Welty's work could be attributed to several causes, including her lyrical method, the sway of formal and mythological criticism, and fear that a "local" Welty would delimit the range of moral implication. Sullivan, however, is not inhibited by any of these factors. Instead, he fails

196

to recognize the underlying shape of Welty's chronicle because of his undue allegiance to the antebellum myth of an organic southern community. There is, as Lewis Simpson observes, a "lingering glow of the Confederacy in Sullivan's heart."[6] By considering the special relationship of *Losing Battles* and *The Optimist's Daughter,* we can place in more telling perspective both his and Welty's final alignment with this myth of a lost order and thus evaluate Welty's own practice of the literary vocation in the South.

3

Published in 1970, *Losing Battles* appears to have been written with Thomas Wolfe's formula for books that "boil and pour" firmly in mind. Although the Renfros and the Beechams are impoverished by Fairchild standards of affluence, *Losing Battles* is more richly furnished than even the bounteous world of *Delta Wedding.* As Robert Heilman notes, Welty is not a reluctant namer of "flowers, fruits, vegetables, weeds, trees, animals, soils, terrains, articles of clothing [and] household objects,"[7] paraphernalia that naturally accompany the celebration of Granny Vaughn's ninetieth birthday. During the thirty or so hours of reunion, her assembled family, including three generations of lineal descendants, is reinforced by members of the Banner, Ludlow, Medley, and Alliance communities to provide Welty with a multitude of dull, memorable, striving, defeated, cooperative personalities, who compose inadvertently a faithful record of family life in northeast Mississippi, the cherished mountain home of Troy Flavin. Almost to a fault, reviewers and later commentators have been generous in praising a book whose incessant dialogue courts tedium, but oddly enough only Walter Sullivan has noted its apparently equivocal location in Welty's Mississippi chronicle. Placed between *The Golden Apples* and *The Optimist's Daughter,* books which trace the decline of southern community from 1900 to 1960, *Losing Battles* is deemed "a long look backward"[8] into the relative tranquillity of the 1930s. By implying that Welty has indulged herself in a retrospective glance, Sullivan merely dismisses what appears to be an anomalous development in the last phase of her chronicle. But if one looks without prejudice at *Losing Battles,* it not only assumes a rightful place in Welty's work but also through its special relationship with *The Optimist's Daughter* implies her superb control of potent southern mythologies that would otherwise compel belief.

In *Losing Battles* numerous sensory images, loquacious visitors, and outlandish episodes compose the reunion, a "preeminent symbol of family feeling,"[9] whose outward sign is the act of talking itself. Persevering through gibes and jokes at their expense, innumerable interruptions and diversions, and the family's propensity for correction, the tireless talkers of *Losing Battles* create through a profusion of tale, anecdote, reminiscence, and confession what Robert Heilman has aptly termed "group consciousness."[10] Whether the speaker is Aunt Beck, Uncle Noah Webster, or Miss Beulah Beecham Renfro herself; whether the tales are intended to bring young Jack home from prison, to probe the cloudy parentage of his wife Gloria, or to lament the zeal of Julia Mortimer, indomitable teacher of generations of Banner children, the accent in *Losing Battles* invariably falls upon familial possession of the past, endurance in the present, and resolute hope for the future. As recorded in *A Guide to the Magnolia State* (1938), the region of the northeast hills remained in the 1930s "Mississippi's chief stronghold" of a "sturdy and self-sufficient" folk, "slow to accept changes," for whom "the home and the church" were "the centers of all social life."[11] Perhaps at some time this fertile volume either stimulated or confirmed Welty's interest in the provincialism of Banner and surrounding Boone County, but the ultimate source of *Losing Battles* is buried more deeply in the seasonal logic of her Mississippi chronicle. Diametrically opposed to *Losing Battles* in texture, structure, and point of view, *The Optimist's Daughter* can bring into fuller light both the imaginative rationale of Welty's penultimate novel and the special terms upon which she has preserved a unique "Southern character."[12]

In the sequence of *The Golden Apples,* literary form restates the social history of Morgana. Delivered in approximately 1900, Kate Rainey's dramatic roadside monologue expresses the corporate life of the community before it declines into anguished self-consciousness. This is the quality of aggravated personalism which dominates the next generation of Ran and Eugene Mac-Lain, whose characteristic expression is soliloquy and interior monologue. Published respectively in 1970 and 1972, *Losing Battles* and *The Optimist's Daughter* demonstrate the same cultural progression, although with greater profundity and an enhanced sense of resolution. Where *Losing Battles* is a densely textured encyclopedia, boisterous with event and episode, *The Optimist's Daughter* is a more sparsely furnished work whose element of fable has been pared back to allow meditation. Where *Losing Battles* orchestrates contending voices until they embody "group consciousness," *The Optimist's Daughter* is relentlessly personal and introspective, the segments of conversation which attend the official mourning of Judge McKelva merely preludes to the solitary, self-conscious work of meditation. If by some magical act Laurel could be transported into the vivid world of Banner, she would find brief tonal agreement only with Vaughn Renfro, Jack's twelve-year-old brother, who is granted the sole lyrical passage in *Losing Battles.* "Riding through the world, the little boy, moonlit, wondered" (p. 363), distantly echoing in his solitary ramble and pensive mood the isolation of Laurel and the metaphysical structure of her meditation. By juxtaposing "a pure talk story"[13] with one that is studiously contemplative, Welty has created pervasive, unspoken metaphors for the spiritual condition of Banner and Mount Salus. The succession of *Losing Battles* and *The Optimist's Daughter* confirms the drastic changes in southern culture which regulate the last phase of Welty's chronicle. Paradoxically, by taking "a long look backward" in *Losing Battles*, Welty anticipated the postmodern world of *The Optimist's Daughter*.

As noted in chapter 4, the special relationship between *Losing Battles* and *The Optimist's Daughter* can be organized more formally by reference to Allen Tate's "A Southern Mode of the Imagination." In Tate's terminology, the reunion talk is like Judge Moody's stranded Buick: perched high on Banner Top, it continues to hum smoothly without "going anywhere" or being "about anything." Instead, the talk of *Losing Battles* "is about the people who are talking." Implicit in "the alternating, or contrapuntal, conversation" of Welty's assembled fictioneers is a rhetorical mode of address which affirms "the whole solid" Beecham enterprise. The language of *The Optimist's Daughter* intrudes naturally here, for Laurel is also a staunch affirmer of the past, but her characteristic expression is not dramatic or rhetorical. As a practitioner of Tate's dialectical mode, Laurel employs a tragic experience of love and its loss, detachment gained through long absence from Mount Salus, and most importantly her ironic eye which is produced by the decline of southern community. Both in "A Southern Mode of the Imagination" and in relation to Welty, Tate's categories function primarily on a descriptive level, identifying successive stages of the southern mind. Although Welty does not question the integrity or utility of these intellectual categories, her typical artistry seeks instead to represent their underlying continuity of human motive. In this subtle working of Welty's historical imagination, she poses a challenge to understanding that Walter Sullivan's analysis fails to comprehend. His reluctance to be encouraged by the paradoxical shape of Welty's thought brings into clear focus their respective attitudes toward the vicissitudes of southern history.

While it is true that Sullivan's stern theology precludes a sentimental or idealized image of the southern community—even during its alleged time of antebellum splendor, the South exemplified for Sullivan the usual "angularities of good and bad"[14]—it is also true that his critique of Laurel portrays an essential stasis in the assumed definition of a traditional society. *The Optimist's Daughter,* Sullivan concedes, "is filled with life, as Miss Welty's work always is, but at crucial moments, at turns in the story where we look for revelations, we find not so much ambiguity as uncertainty." The most equivocal moment in *The Optimist's Daughter* is occasioned by the emblematic breadboard. "The imagery," Sullivan notes, "is organic and clear":

> the disparate elements of Laurel's past join in this work of her husband's hands, and for a moment Laurel is almost ready to fight Fay for possession of it. But it is the dream, the memory, not the board which count. Content to leave behind physical reminders of what might have been, Laurel relinquishes the board and except for her departure the story is finished.[15]

Only by the actual, geographic possession of her heritage could Laurel fully satisfy the terms of Walter Sullivan's romantic southern conscience. Because he has not adjusted to the perennial reality of a changing South, he feels only the pull of melancholy in *The Optimist's Daughter* and thus does not recognize the creative role that Laurel McKelva plays in preserving a distinctive "Southern character." By resigning the emblematic breadboard rather than fighting Fay for its ownership, Laurel plumbs her own "deeps of character" to summon the "love and understanding"[16] which define her heritage. Her departure from Mount Salus is not necessarily an exile but may be comprehended in the terms of *I'll Take My Stand.* "Provincialism," Stark Young explained, "does not at all imply living in the place on which you base your beliefs and choices. It is a state of mind or persuasion. It is a source."[17] Without ever announcing himself as such, Walter Sullivan emerges as a historian of southern discontinuity, while Welty preserves through memory and imagination the unbroken succession of humane values, if not their more palpable southern institutional forms.

Examining the special relationship between *Losing Battles* and

Conclusion

The Optimist's Daughter not only reconfirms the mutual attraction of Welty's texts and the coherence of her chronicle, but also helps to pose more insistently the related questions of her control of the myth of a distinctive southern community and the consequent terms in which she has preserved a unique "Southern character." Undoubtedly, a part of Eudora Welty's imagination could not avoid hearing the "long, withdrawing roar" of a lost tradition of order and stability, one that was made especially acute in Jackson, where the paucity of antebellum homes and astonishing industrial growth after World War II confront the artist with extremes of loss and progress. The element of melancholy implicit in the sterner fatality of *The Golden Apples* and each succeeding text conveys the magnitude of Welty's perceived loss. But before this sadness becomes a reigning, numbing influence upon the artistic spirit, it is lifted and redeemed by Welty's gifted protagonists who discover order and coherence within the midst of change. If it is not too fanciful to assemble these fictional creatures—the superior "I" of "A Memory," Clement Musgrove, Ellen Fairchild, Virgie Rainey, and especially Laurel—then perhaps we can hear their silent approval when Welty explained on "Firing Line" that she was not "a bit interested in preserving the home of Jefferson Davis."[18] They would know, as do we, that in naming Myra and Theo's home Rose Hill, Welty remembered Rosemont, the boyhood home of Jefferson Davis, without transforming it into a shrine of the Lost Cause. As Delilah issues from the ruin of the past, she strikes the note of freedom and renewal which summarizes Welty's control of potentially coercive southern materials. It remains, however, for Laurel to draw out all the implications of this liberation from an actual southern community. Her subsequent life in "a postsouthern America" raises intriguing, relatively unaddressed questions regarding Eudora Welty's practice of the literary vocation. The postulates of intellectual and literary history implied by this practice can be approached by considering all too briefly and superficially the

202

element of literary allusion which becomes pronounced in *Delta Wedding* and persists thereafter.

4

Considered in terms of plot and historical vision, *The Robber Bridegroom* reveals the formative influence of such diverse sources as the Brothers Grimm and the western historian Frederick Jackson Turner. Even the language and imagery of Turner's frontier thesis have been adopted by Welty with little if any compensatory disguise. But *The Robber Bridegroom* still remains as fresh and self-insistent as Jamie Lockhart's bold motto: "Take first and ask afterward." Indeed, any apologetic asking is made unnecessary by Welty's complete assimilation of sources which otherwise might earn *The Robber Bridegroom* the dismal fame of being derivative. At least on the surface, the kind of literary allusion which can be identified in the last phase of Welty's chronicle warrants more serious questions of influence and intention. With some plausibility, reviewers and later critics have reported Faulknerian echoes in *The Golden Apples* and "The Burning,"[19] but these native soundings are finally less pronounced and implicative than literary allusions which point unabashedly to modern European sources, chiefly Yeats, Joyce, and Virginia Woolf.

In *The Golden Apples* Welty makes allusion to selected lyrics of William Butler Yeats. As Thomas L. McHaney explains in his fine study, the rape of Mattie Will Sojourner in "Sir Rabbit" is cast "in the language" of Yeats's "Leda and the Swan" (1924), while fragments of "No Second Troy," published in *The Green Helmet and Other Poems* (1910), contribute ironic resonance to Ran MacLain's bitter lament in "The Whole World Knows."[20] Still more substantive reference to Yeats occurs in the earlier story, "June Recital." Lines from "The Song of Wandering Aengus" (1897) flare into memory as Cassie Morrison recalls her "opposite," Virgie Rainey, a quester on more intimate terms with

203

Yeats's visionary god who pursues "the golden apples of the sun." A Joycean presence can be felt in "Music from Spain" and "The Wanderers." The structure of Eugene MacLain's personal dilemma closely parallels that of Leopold Bloom. Each is a middle-aged exile emotionally separated from his wife who mourns a dead child during a day of urban wandering. Perhaps the sharpest impression of Bloom's fluid consciousness is conveyed by Eugene's response to the "dark full-face" of *"Miss Dimdummie Dumwiddie."* Culled from the paper which Eugene carries, the alluring "newsprint face" (*CS*, pp. 395–396) momentarily becomes a cynosure of his romantic longing. More discrete fragments of *Ulysses* may be detected in *The Optimist's Daughter* when Mr. Tom Farris, the blind piano tuner of Mount Salus, taps his way into the funeral of Judge McKelva (pp. 78–79), but it is "The Wanderers" which reveals a more continuous, profound Joycean presence. The language of Gabriel Conroy's final meditation in "The Dead" clearly influences Welty's description of Virgie Rainey's "precipitous moment." "October rain on Mississippi fields. The rain of fall, maybe on the whole South, for all she knew on the everywhere. She stared into its magnitude" (*CS*, p. 460). The practice of Virginia Woolf both revealed to Welty the import of such moments of transparency and helped her to give poignance and structure to their unique Mississippi expression. As Welty herself testified, Virginia Woolf "was the one who opened the door."[21] Michael Kreyling's comparative study of the imagery, structure, and theme in *To The Lighthouse* and *The Optimist's Daughter* warrants his conclusion that the affinity of these novelists "is too intimate for the term 'influence.'"[22] As a belated note of agreement, it can be added that the distance from Mrs. Dalloway's London to Shellmound is traveled with equal confidence by Welty's discerning literary intelligence. When the Memphis photographer intrudes upon Dabney's wedding party with news of a young girl's violent death, we marvel first at Welty's daring appropriation of Dr. Bradshaw's news and then at its perfect accord with the distinctive world of *Delta Wedding*.

If the ideal critic possesses a wary nature, then his deepest misgivings may at first be engaged by Welty's allusive turn of mind. Not only do several allusions point with extraordinary directness to their sources, but also the entire allusive enterprise coincides with the regional identity that emerges in *Delta Wedding* and thereafter deepens the southern quality of Welty's chronicle. Perhaps through some curious displacement of literary logic, the enhanced allusiveness which marks the last phase of Welty's Mississippi story betrays a growing dependency, an erosion of self-confidence engendered by the constant gaze of what David Potter has termed the southern "Sphinx." This is not a frivolous hypothesis produced merely to be displaced by a more congenial one, for the overlay of Welty's allusiveness (summarized above only briefly and by no means completely) and her engagement with the most perplexing issues of southern historiography is potentially ominous and warrants scrupulous attention. At the very least, it is true that Welty's delayed or, perhaps, simply intensified southern awareness raises the ideological quotient of her work, occasioning near-formulaic plots which betray an incipient rigidity of ethical design. Perhaps this first hypothesis has sufficient authority to be pursued by a different investigator. But at the same time, reference to Lewis P. Simpson may provide a second, more credible way of understanding Welty's allusion to the corps of modern masters. His influential conception and articulation of a "Republic of Letters" bears importantly upon Welty's final control of potentially unruly southern materials and her orientation to the postulates of literary modernism.

In several remarkable essays, including the seminal "What Survivors Do," Lewis Simpson has identified a "Republic of Letters" whose founding and historic development have determined the modern literary vocation. Simpson marks the beginning of modern history with "the exodus of the medieval 'clerks' . . . from the *res publica Christiana* to an emergent, secular *res publica litteraria*." The resultant separation of the realms of state, church, and letters inspired "a great critique of man and society, nature and God, and finally of mind itself." But in "the rising realm of secular letters," rational mind was not merely an instrument of analysis; instead, it became the willful model of history and society, "transferring all that the human consciousness comprehends as existence into itself." As Lewis Simpson notes, Sir Francis Bacon, "the eminent contemporary representative of mind," sealed this reversal by confirming that "Knowledge is power."[23]

Simpson is adept at tracing the course of this knowledge within the "Republic of Letters." Liberated from piety and doctrine, the Renaissance literary mind enlarged its domain, but in such troubled creations as Hamlet, Macbeth, and Don Quixote revealed the burden of its new subjectivity. "Shakespeare," Simpson observes, "experienced in his imagination of Hamlet and Macbeth the imposition of the burden of history that the consciousness had to assume with the depletion of the life of the consciousness incorporated in myth and traditionalism."[24] Finally, Simpson concludes, "both Shakespeare and Cervantes are motivated by a tension toward the dread knowledge that the displacement of society by mind is irreversible."[25] But from the Renaissance until the late eighteenth century, the internalized dialectic of mind and history, self and society, will and nature, is relatively stable, providing the imaginative writer with a secure home in the "Republic of Letters." Indeed, at this point, with "the invention of the American Republic," the "great critique" of modernity is fulfilled by an actual society "modeled on a rational, secular mind."[26] "Knowledge is [still] power," even if Poor Richard becomes its homely voice.

What one commentator has called "the high truculence of modern literature" derives from the sense of crisis which next enters the "Republic of Letters" in the nineteenth century. "This crisis," Simpson explains, "has been evident since it became clear in the last century that another realm, that of science, had erupted into history out of the realm of letters."[27] "No longer synonymous with the terms *letters* or *literature,* mind in the aspect of science" had "set up in business for itself" and had sought to become the sole "interpretant of history."[28] At this critical point, literary mind is confronted by the dire, if delayed, consequences of its original separation from the realms of church and state: "loss of transcendent reference for being and a tendency . . . toward the closure of history in the self of the writer."[29] The nineteenth-century writer, including Carlyle, Dickens, Arnold, and Hardy, registered this sense of crisis, perhaps most acutely in the errant idealism of *Jude the Obscure,* but it remained for the next generation of writers located precisely "at the deep core of modern literature" to exploit fully the irony of their historical dilemma. The "struggle" of Eliot, Yeats, Joyce, and other moderns "to redeem the symbolic literary order"[30] from the hegemony of science is shared by the modern writers of the American South, who contribute with peculiar intensity to what Lewis Simpson calls "the modern cultural dialectic." Establishing their affiliation depends, however, upon a brief statement of the literary situation of the antebellum southern writer.

Lewis Simpson offers a fresh perspective upon the oft-discussed political responsibilities of the nineteenth-century southern man of letters. In large part, his responsibility to defend slavery determined the literary function, but this unenviable duty involved Simms, Timrod, and others in a sharp, although unrecognized, historical irony. As citizens of the Enlightenment American Republic, they quite predictably employed mind to defend the culture of slavery; however, their choice of tools and their object of defense were profoundly ill suited. Ironically, the southern intellectual employed rational discourse to defeat politically its historic origin and ultimate source of epistemological authority: "the principle of self-determination."[31] The effect of this identification of mind and slavery, Simpson concludes, was "a subtle alienation" of the antebellum South from the "Republic of Letters" and its autonomous critique of human motives. Accordingly, at the end of the Civil War, "the South was left to serve as the symbol of the defeat of mind in America."[32] Perhaps the only factor that separates the antebellum southern writer and his twentieth-century counterpart is the latter's self-awareness of the irony of his historical situation. This understanding is treated brilliantly by Lewis Simpson in "What Survivors Do," an essay that probes the affiliation of modern European and southern writers within the "Republic of Letters," the true "homeland" of the modern literary mind.

"What Survivors Do" is marked by Simpson's deep personal and formal knowledge of southern life and letters and by a scholarly and critical method which identifies undetected or scarcely noted circuits of literary and intellectual history. Simpson begins with an acute distinction between "a modern flowering of southern literature" and "a flowering of modern literature in the South."[33] The latter modification is preferred by Simpson; it both draws a sharper line between the literature of the Southern Renascence and its nineteenth-century antecedent and also stresses the incursion of a modernist ideology into southern letters after World War I. Affrighted by "the intellectual disorders" of the nineteenth century, appalled by their culmination in the vault of World War I, the modern literary mind realized that history was not "a story" but "an ineluctable process or series of processes" whose net effect was "the disappearance of the community of kinship, custom, and tradition."[34] In resisting this flow, Proust, Mann, James, Eliot, Yeats, and other moderns discovered both their subject matter and what Lewis Simpson calls the "ironic historicity" of their citizenship in the "Republic of Letters." Undoubtedly, their general intellectual freedom and specific dissent from post-Reformation Christianity were conditioned by the "great critique" which coincides with the rise of the secular state. But at the same time, the alarming advancement of scientific knowledge in the nineteenth century prompted the modern to restore control to the humanistic realm of letters by seeking "a reversal" of mind and society. In this struggle with history, memory would make accessible again the mysteries of being. There would, however, be no aesthetic release from the self-perceived irony of this unique literary situation. This tension is put cogently by Simpson: the modern writer "was a participant in a struggle to redeem the symbolic literary order, the Republic of Letters, as the model of history; and yet was acutely aware of an impulse to reject it, even to destroy it . . . to return to the service of a society of myth and tradition."[35]

As noted above, Simpson portrays an antebellum South isolated from "ironic historicity" by the imperative to defend slavery. The effects of this charge, Simpson continues in "What Survivors Do," also marked the next generation of writers, who employed a "rhetoric of pious remembrance" to oppose their grievous historical fate. Only after World World I would this long-standing evasion of history be relieved by the assimilation of Faulkner, Tate, John Crowe Ransom, and Robert Penn Warren to "the ironic mode of the modern literary mind." Rejecting "the memorial high tone" of postbellum southern writing, these "gifted" Southerners probed "the whole intricate irony of the South living the long aftermath of its confused and disastrous attempt to establish itself in history as a nation."[36] The flowering of this endeavor is too well known to be rehearsed here. It is more important to stress that the major texts of the Southern Renascence—*The Sound and the Fury, Absalom, Absalom!, The Fathers,* and particularly *I'll Take My Stand*—ascribe to the local writer the same ironic place in the "Republic of Letters" possessed by his European tutor in modernity. After World War I, the southern writer was absolved of "pious remembrance" by his restoration to an international order predicated upon the efficacy of literary mind. At the same time, however, he was led to reject mind as a model of history and society that had failed in the chaos of World War I. In resisting this modern "culture of rationality," the writer summoned to consciousness an element that was (in Simpson's terms) "tantalizingly present in the southern memory." Accordingly, "when the Proustian-Joycean literary mind began to take over in the South," the antebellum image of an integral society was stripped of its defensive, romantic trappings and was assimilated to "the subtle, complicated, and pervasive structure—or aesthetic—of memory that came into full flowering in Western literature after World War I."[37] In conclusion, it only remains to be shown that Eudora Welty has adopted the same "aesthetic" of memory and thus claimed her place in the modern "Republic of Letters."

5

It is not surprising that Simpson quotes Eudora Welty in "What Survivors Do" to illustrate both the efficacy of the modern literary vocation and its cosmopolitan character. "Remembering," Welty affirms in "Some Notes on Time in Fiction" (1973), "is so basic and vital a part of staying alive that it takes on the strength of an instinct of survival, and acquires the power of an art." This "life's work," Welty concludes, was achieved with no greater intensity than by Proust, who "left masterpieces that are like clocks themselves, giant clocks . . . sounding for us the high hours of our literature."[38] The "sounding" of Welty's fiction is neither so commanding nor prolonged, but her "life's work" has been shaped as well by the modern drama of history and memory, self and community. Understood in this light, the allusive design which marks the last phase of Welty's chronicle is not capitulation to the burden of southern mythology. Instead, it is a recognition that local memory is at once unique and a species of world history. But by claiming kinship with Yeats, Joyce, and Woolf, Welty has achieved considerably more than a "southern appropriation of the twentieth-century literary mind."[39] Through her final disposition of Laurel McKelva Hand, Welty exerted control over the myth of an integral community, the richest and potentially the most coercive material that any artist could desire.

It is only necessary now to heighten the postulates of intellectual and literary history implied by Welty's attribution to Laurel of memory, imagination, and a "postsouthern" existence in Chicago. Laurel possesses an inner complexity which, "on an infinitesimal scale" (Tate would say), resembles the subjectivity of Hamlet and Macbeth. They share the effects of their creators' "exodus . . . from the *res publica Christiana*": the isolation or closure of history in the self and a resultant "tension toward the dread knowledge" that this process is "irreversible." In *The Optimist's Daughter,* the secularization of the organic Western community is projected onto a southern landscape whose final locus is the solitary, isolated consciousness of Laurel McKelva Hand. Her "struggle" brings to a definitive, climactic stage the stress of modern history which marks the last phase of Welty's chronicle. Through the resources of mind—specifically, through memory and imagination—Laurel conducts an encounter with modernity designed to recover and preserve the humanistic essence of her heritage. In resigning the emblematic breadboard, Laurel achieves her own "precipitous moment" of vision, but this striking development is measured by an austere irony of situation that propels her into the mainstream of "postsouthern America."[40] This final disposition of Welty's most gifted protagonist betrays the author's own ironic place in the modern "Republic of Letters." For Welty and Laurel, there will be no release from the internal dialectic of self and community, in part because the actual traditional society has been swept away in the long process of secularization, but more importantly because "no writer could really imagine returning home from the exodus"[41] to embrace again piety and belief. In short, Welty's resistance to modernity, her shared attempt with Yeats, Joyce, Woolf, Faulkner, Tate, and Penn Warren "to redeem the symbolic literary order," was conducted wholly within the realm of subjectivity and was achieved by its own mindful tools. In deploring this eventuality, Walter Sullivan would seem to demand either that Welty alter history or reject her necessary orientation to the postulates of literary modernism.

Conclusion

Placing Welty within the "Republic of Letters" is important in itself, but it has the greater advantage of focusing her final control of southern materials. Because of its vivid frontier settlement, its complicated plantation ethic entailing slavery, civil war, and the gradual decline of hereditary values, the South in general and Mississippi in particular present the modern literary imagination with unusually clamorous circumstances. As her fiction, essays, and interviews reveal, Welty's sense of a regional identity was deepened appreciably by the civil rights movement of the 1950s and 1960s and by the merging of distinctive American cultures which was accomplished in the following decade. Living continuously in Jackson, Welty observed closely this process of modernization, the small provincial capital of her birth transformed in the next seven decades into a metropolitan center with a diverse, highly mobile population approaching 300,000. But Welty's historicism has behaved admirably throughout. This ability to reconcile process and stasis, time and eternity, self and community, is, it seems clear, a reflection of Welty's citizenship in the modern "Republic of Letters." Relieved of the extremes of belief and rationalism, Welty discovered in this realm a suppleness of mind which is essential to the reconciler's art. More specifically, she discovered the means of forming an *image* of the South, one stripped of its historic defensiveness, romance, and ready applicability. There is finally a coolness at the core of Welty's work, a reserve or restraint that Walter Sullivan quite accurately notes, but it does not preclude her fulfilling the role of the modern vocation of letters. "The man of letters is primary in keeping open the possibility of man's apprehension of the truth of his destiny beyond time."[42] Although etched in irony and pictured in displacement, Welty's preserved "Southern character" testifies to the strength of this moral "possibility." Her Mississippi chronicle is finally the outward shape of a passionate interior drama that has preoccupied all serious writers of the modern South and, before that, all chroniclers of Western culture.

Notes to Chapter 5

1. Andrew Lytle, *The Velvet Horn* (New York: McDowell, Obolensky, 1957), p. 101.

2. Lewis P. Simpson, "The Closure of History in a Postsouthern America," in *The Brazen Face of History: Studies in the Literary Consciousness in America* (Baton Rouge: Louisiana State University Press, 1980), p. 269.

3. Walter Sullivan, "In Time of the Breaking of Nations: The Decline of Southern Fiction," in *Death by Melancholy: Essays on Modern Southern Fiction* (Baton Rouge: Louisiana State University Press, 1972), pp. 87–96.

4. Walter Sullivan, "Community," in *A Requiem for the Renascence: The State of Fiction in the Modern South* (Athens: University of Georgia Press, 1976), pp. 47–49.

5. Sullivan, "Rainbow's End," in *A Requiem for the Renascence,* pp. 51–57.

6. Simpson, "The Closure of History," p. 257.

7. Robert B. Heilman, "*Losing Battles* and Winning the War," in *Eudora Welty: Critical Essays,* ed. Peggy W. Prenshaw (Jackson: University Press of Mississippi, 1979), p. 273.

8. Sullivan, "Rainbow's End," in *A Requiem for the Renascence,* p. 52.

9. Heilman, "*Losing Battles* and Winning the War," p. 293.

10. Ibid., p. 291.

11. *Mississippi: A Guide to the Magnolia State* (New York: Viking, 1938), pp. 500–503.

12. Michiko Kakutani, "South Is Wherever Eudora Welty Is," *New York Times,* 27 June 1980, p. C8.

13. Charles T. Bunting, "'The Interior World': An Interview with Eudora Welty," *Southern Review* 8 (October 1972), p. 717.

14. Sullivan, "Myth," in *A Requiem for the Renascence,* p. 10.

15. Sullivan, "Rainbow's End," in *A Requiem for the Renascence,* pp. 53–56.

16. Linda Kuehl, "The Art of Fiction XLVII: Eudora Welty," *Paris Review* 55 (fall 1972), p. 75.

17. Stark Young, "Not in Memoriam But in Defense," in *I'll Take My Stand,* ed. Louis D. Rubin, Jr. (1930; reprinted, New York: Harper and Row, 1962), p. 344.

18. "The Southern Imagination," moderator William F. Buckley (Columbia, S.C.: Firing Line, 1972), p. 7. Transcription of a television broadcast, 24 December 1972.

19. See Hamilton Basso's review of *The Golden Apples, New Yorker,* 3 September 1949, pp. 63–64, and Alfred Appel's discussion of "The Burning" in *A Season of Dreams: The Fiction of Eudora Welty* (Baton Rouge: Louisiana State University Press, 1965), pp. 139–40.

20. Thomas L. McHaney, "Eudora Welty and the Multitudinous Golden Apples," *Mississippi Quarterly* 26 (fall 1973), pp. 591–93, 605–606.

21. Kuehl, "Art of Fiction," p. 75.

22. Michael Kreyling, "Life with People: Virginia Woolf, Eudora Welty and *The Optimist's Daughter*," *Southern Review* 13 (spring 1977), p. 250.

23. Lewis P. Simpson, "The Southern Republic of Letters and *I'll Take My Stand*," in *A Band of Prophets: The Vanderbilt Agrarians After Fifty Years*, ed. William C. Havard and Walter Sullivan (Baton Rouge: Louisiana State University Press, 1982), pp. 71–73.

24. Simpson, "The Legend of the Artist," in *The Brazen Face of History*, p. 207.

25. Simpson, "The Southern Republic of Letters," p. 73.

26. Ibid., p. 74.

27. Simpson, "The Bard and the Clerk," in *The Brazen Face of History*, p. 167.

28. Simpson, "The Southern Republic of Letters," p. 85.

29. Simpson, Preface, *The Brazen Face of History*, p. xiii.

30. Simpson, "The Southern Republic of Letters," p. 85.

31. Ibid., p. 77.

32. Ibid., p. 81.

33. Simpson, "What Survivors Do," in *The Brazen Face of History*, p. 238.

34. Ibid., p. 241.

35. Simpson, "The Southern Republic of Letters," p. 85.

36. Simpson, "What Survivors Do," pp. 236–38.

37. Ibid., p. 238.

38. Quoted in ibid., pp. 240–42.

39. Ibid., p. 239.

40. Simpson, "The Closure of History," p. 269.

41. Simpson, "The Southern Republic of Letters," p. 85.

42. Simpson, "The Bard and the Clerk," p. 178.

Index

215

Index

Livvie, 44, 66, 67, 71, 72

"Livvie," 44, 66, 67, 71

Lockhart, Jamie, 22, 23, 24, 28, 68

Lockhart, Jenny, 44, 66, 67, 70–71, 72

Lockhart, Rosamond Musgrove: 22, 23, 24; compares with girl of "A Memory," 28

"Looking Back at the First Story," 15–16

Losing Battles: 125, 158; equivocal position in Welty's chronicle, 197–202; related to *The Optimist's Daughter,* 197, 198–202; significance of talk in, 198, 200; sources for, 198–99

Loving, 157

Lytle, Andrew, 14, 193

Macbeth, 211

Man-Son, 109

McCord, Cash, 44, 66, 71

McHaney, Thomas L., 203

McInnis, Don, 44, 67

McInnis, Sabina, 44, 66, 67, 71

McKelva, Becky Thurston, 136, 178–80

McKelva, Clinton (Judge): characterized, 136, 166–67; compared with Dr. Strickland, 142; as exemplar of tradition, 162, 166–67; eulogized, 176

McKelva, Fay Chisom: 136, 137, 177; metonymically evaluated, 168; confrontation with Laurel, 181–83

McKelva, Laurel. *See* Hand, Laurel McKelva

MacLain, Eugene, 157, 162, 204

MacLain, King, 134

MacLain, Randall (Ran), 157, 162

McMickle, Clinton, 91

McWhiney, Grady, 152

Mansfield, Katherine, 42

Marblehall, Mr.: 64; historical imagination characterized, 18; as most enigmatic figure in *A Curtain of Green,* 18–19; dual life of, 18–19; cultural significance of, 30

Marian, 17

Marie, Miss Baby, 66

Marshall, Margaret, 138

Mayes, Joel, 45, 48, 58–59, 65

McRaven, Laura, 90

Meinecke, Friedrich, 74–75, 76

"Memory, A": 132, 133, 202; significance of in *A Curtain of Green,* 20; as most personal of Welty's stories, 26; plot summarized, 26–27; influence of Jackson, Mississippi, in, 27–28; girl compared with Clement Musgrove, 27, 75–76; girl as artist, 28; structure of dual perspective in, 28–29; unique position in *A Curtain of Green,* 29; cultural significance of, 30–31; girl's historical dilemma in, 36. *See also* Chapter 1, 26–31

Mencken, H. L., 6, 35, 106

Metahistory, 163–64

M'Hook, Root, 109

Miller, Perry, 113, 114

Mississippi: A Guide to the Magnolia State, 10, 21, 62, 198

Mississippi River: 44–45; historical significance of, 69–70; as symbol in *The Wide Net,* 72

Mississippi, state of: 3, 8, 14, 155; poverty of, 9–10; formative of a distinctive literary intelligence, 37–38; historical development of, 63–64; BAWI program, 70; artistic poverty of, 83–84; physical geography of, 88–89; mechanization of agriculture, 109–10; migration to the Delta, 110–11; dislocation of Mississippians after World War I, 141; racial conflict in, 145; folk culture in the northeast hills, 198; aesthetic character of, 212

"Moon Lake," 135

Morgan, Albert, 17, 18, 178

Morgan, Ellie, 17, 18, 178

Morgana, Mississippi (town in *The Golden Apples*): 133, 136, 137, 138, 141, 144, 165–66, 195, 196, 199; advance to modernity of, 134–35; as traditional society in decline, 169

Index

Morris, Willie, 169

Morton, Jason, 10–11, 30

Morton, Sara: 10–11, 178; goal of, 15–16; cultural significance of, 30

Mount Salus (town in *The Optimist's Daughter*): 136–37, 144, 175–76, 177, 199; traditional society in decline, 169

Murrell, James: 45, 64, 65; historicity of, 49, 55; reaction to heron, 57; interpretation of Natchez Trace, 60

Murrell, John (c. 1804–1844), 49, 53–54, 55, 63, 64

Musgrove, Clement: 30, 94, 128, 144, 202; reaction to Jamie Lockhart, 22; foresees a new era, 23; significance of speculative temper, 24; meditation, 24–26; modern counterpart in *A Curtain of Green*, 26; compared with the girl in "A Memory," 27, 28–30, 75–76; contrasted with Rosamond and Jamie, 34; his historical dilemma, 36; as philosophic center of *The Robber Bridegroom*, 68; compared with Burr, Dow, Murrell, and Audubon, 68; with Ellen Fairchild, 120, 124; with Miss Myra and Miss Theo, 132; with Virgie Rainey, 173; with Laurel McKelva Hand, 196

Musgrove, Rosamond. *See* Lockhart, Rosamond Musgrove

Musgrove, Salome, 23, 25

"Music from Spain," 135, 204

"Must the Novelist Crusade?" 29, 146

Myra, 128, 132, 184, 188

Natchez Indians, 25

Natchez, Mississippi, 18, 19

Natchez Trace: 44–45; significance in "A Still Moment," 60–61; historical significance of, 69–70; as symbol in *The Wide Net*, 72

New England Mind, The, 113, 114

New Yorker, The 145

New York Times, 194

North Toward Home, 169

O'Connor, Flannery, 160

Odum, Howard, 9, 10, 11, 37, 186

"Old Mr. Marblehall": 81–82; time in, 18; sources for, 19; cultural significance of, 30–31; influenced by plantation legend, 34

Opitz, Kurt, 15, 178

Optimist's Daughter, The: 144, 145, 151, 166–69, 178; anticipated by "The Burning," 132; personal and communal "attrition" in, 135–37; time in, 136–37; as document exploring social change, 136–37; related to *The Golden Apples*, 137, 195–96; metaphorical technique of characterization in, 161–62; death in, 167–68; significance of sewing room in, 178–80; symbolism of breadboard in, 181–82, 200; problem of history in, 193; traces decline of southern community, 197; located in Welty's chronicle, 196–97; related to *Losing Battles*, 197, 198–202; language of, 200; compared with *To The Lighthouse*, 204; references to *Ulysses* in, 204

Other South, The, 156

Page, Thomas Nelson, 32, 175

Parkman, Francis, 100

Partheny, 108

Party Going, 157

Peculiar Institution, The, 116, 117

Percy, Walker, 27, 146, 147

Percy, William Alexander, 92, 110, 136

Petrie, Mr., 6

"Petrified Man," 6, 140

Phinny, 128–29, 130, 186, 187

"Piece of News, A," 16

Place Over Time, 152–56

Plantation legend, 31–32, 35, 86–88

Plantation fiction, 31–32, 86–88, 96–106, 117, 119–120

Ponder Heart, The, 140, 158

Porter, Katherine Anne, 171

Potter, David, 88, 205

"Powerhouse," 3, 6

Index

value of her chronicle, 73; her historicism, 73–76, 144, 212; as contemplative historian, 74; examines communal myth of small-town living, 80–81; localism in her fiction, 81; regional identity, 81, 83–84; interview on "Firing Line," 82, 146–48, 150, 202; attitude toward regional writing, 84; her southern character, 85, 115–16; contribution to plantation novel, 117–18, 119–21; irony of her chronicle, 136; concept of southern distinctiveness, 144–45, 150–51, 154–56, 188–89; as southern apologist, 145; comments on South, 145–48; as modern dialectician, 150; comments on Chekhov, 150–51, 188; recognition of vanishing South, 155, 193–94; as historian of southern continuity, 156, 201; compares Green and Faulkner, 157; enhanced fatality in last phase of chronicle, 158; as tragic historian, 169; effort to discover spiritual order behind history, 169; literary allusions in her fiction, 203–205, 210; influenced by Virginia Woolf, 204; comments on Proust, 210; place in "Republic of Letters," 210–12; identified with Laurel McKelva Hand, 211

"What Survivors Do," 175, 205–209, 210

"Where Is the Voice Coming From?": 142, 145, 194; contribution to Welty's chronicle, 137, 143–44; as evidence of Welty's racial awareness and sensitivity, 138–41; as revision of "From the Unknown," 139, 141; plot summarized, 140; use of monologue in, 140

Where I was Born and Raised, 91–92

"Whistle, The": 9; historical background, 10; as challenge to scientific optimism, 10; as critique of regional planning, 11–12; compared to *God Without Thunder*, 11–12; patterns of imagery, 16; contribution to unity of *A Curtain of Green*, 15–16; cultural significance of, 30–31

White, Hayden, 163–64

"Whole World Knows, The," 134–35, 194, 203

"Why I Live at the P.O.," 16, 17, 140

Wide Net and Other Stories, The: 31, 44, 66, 74, 125; reviewed, 41–43; unity, 43, 44, 45, 62, 63; myth criticism in, 44; related to *A Curtain of Green* and *The Robber Bridegroom*, 46, 72–73; imagery in, 65–67; principle of selection observed in, 67; critics' attitudes toward characters, 67–68; epical structure, 69; significance of river and Trace in, 69–72; unity of questers in, 71–72; influence of historical figures, 75–76; lyricism as source of continuity, 77. *See also* Chapter 2, 41–79

Wilson, Edmund, 83–84, 85

"Winds, The," 44, 65–66, 71

Wolfe, Thomas, 80, 81, 134, 197

Woodcraft, 100–106

Woodward, C. Vann, 136, 147, 152

Woolf, Virginia, 144, 181, 204, 210, 211

"Worn Path, A," 3, 14

World the Slaveholders Made, The, 116–17

Yazoo Delta, 109–11

Yeats, William Butler, 203–204, 207, 208, 210, 211

Young, Stark, 128, 201